I0112598

THE TRANSFORMATION ECONOMY

THE TRANSFORMATION ECONOMY

GUIDING CUSTOMERS TO ACHIEVE THEIR ASPIRATIONS

B. JOSEPH PINE II

HARVARD BUSINESS REVIEW PRESS
BOSTON, MASSACHUSETTS

Printed in the United States of America

10 9 8 7 6 5 4 3 2 1

The web addresses referenced in this book were live and correct at the time of the book's publication but may be subject to change.

Cataloging-in-Publication data is forthcoming.

ISBN: 979-8-89279-137-3
eISBN: 979-8-89279-138-0

The paper used in this publication meets the requirements of the American National Standard for Permanence of Paper for Publications and Documents in Libraries and Archives Z39.48-1992.

To He who truly transforms people
now and forever and guides
who we are meant to be

CONTENTS

PREPARATION

You're leaving value on the table.

Whatever you sell to your customers today, I guarantee you they want *more.* I'm not talking about being better, faster, and cheaper, or delivering higher quality or greater convenience. It's not about having more features and benefits, more engagement and sensory delights.

All those things, and everything else you do for customers, are not enough. People don't buy what you sell because they value your offerings in and of themselves. The offerings are *means,* when what customers truly want are *ends.*

The ends they desire are to have a better life or a better business. To be healthier, wealthier, wiser. To have meaning and purpose. To not just buy, but to *become* who they want to become. To not just have, but to *be* who they are meant to be. To not just go through life, but to *flourish.*

If you do not offer such ends, then you're on your way to becoming a commodity supplier to some other company, one that understands that what customers seek today is the achievement of their aspirations.

What people want, in short, is to be transformed.

The good news is that you don't have to completely overhaul everything about your business. You can begin with what you have today, reflect on what you already do for the aspirations of your customers—the *why* of what they buy from you—and then innovate, add, or purchase everything else you need to guide them to achieve those aspirations. It starts with figuring out what business you are really in.

Understanding Economic Offerings

There are five and only five genres of economic output:

- Commodities (fungible stuff)
- Goods (tangible things)
- Services (intangible activities)
- Experiences (memorable events)
- Transformations (effectual outcomes)

These five offerings form the Progression of Economic Value, from least valuable (commodities) to most valuable (transformations). While most economists recognize only the first three, in early 1994 I realized that experiences were also a distinct economic offering. They had always been around but were lumped economically into services. There's great distinction, however, between such uneventful activities as having mail or packages delivered, visiting a gas station, repairing an appliance, eating at a fast-food outlet, or signing up for internet service, and such memorable events as going to a concert or a movie, learning to play the piano, immersing yourself in a video game, or sitting down to a five-course meal at a fine-dining establishment.

I shared that insight with my biggest client at the time, Jim Gilmore, and after joining forces to create Strategic Horizons LLP, a thinking studio that helps companies create greater economic value, in 1997 we published our first article on the concept, "Beyond Goods and Services."[1] Then in 1999 we wrote the first edition of our book *The Experience Economy: Work Is Theatre & Every Business a Stage.*[2]

Back in the 1990s and early 2000s, in speeches, workshops, and consulting with clients I had to argue that experiences were truly a distinct economic offering, and that we would soon shift from the Service Economy to the Experience Economy.

No longer. For many years now I've been able to just state the idea and everyone gets it. No one objects, for the reality is all around us. We're deep into the Experience Economy. We've read umpteen articles on how people prefer experiences over things, how the former make us happier than the latter, and we know it in our bones. But the Experience Economy is not the end.

The Next Shift

Now the economy is shifting from experiences to that final offering, transformations. From creating memories to achieving aspirations. From ephemeral events to lasting change. From time well spent to time well invested.

Transformations, too, have always been around and treated economically as mere services, but there's an even greater distinction between the two. There is simply too much disparity between eating a salad at McDonald's and building muscle at a fitness center, between managing someone's books and partnering in their success, between providing information and imparting wisdom, and between advice from an app and guidance from a spiritual counselor.

Funny thing is, transformations were there from the very beginning of my 1994 discovery, in the "Beyond Goods and Services" article, and even in the last two chapters of *The Experience Economy*. In some ways, the first eight chapters of that book were a Trojan horse to get readers to understand that the greatest economic value lies in helping customers become who they want to become.

People have been asking me for twenty-five years when I was going to write a full book on the Transformation Economy. My response was always twofold: I don't know enough about transformations, and the world isn't ready for it.

Those statements are no longer true.

All along I've paid attention to the possibility that the economy based on transformations would supersede the one based on experiences, and I've studied and worked with companies that were in fact guiding their customers to transform. My knowledge has increased greatly, particularly over the past five years. One result: the 2022 *Harvard Business Review* article "The 'New You' Business," which I wrote with Lance Bettencourt, professor at Texas Christian University; Jim Gilmore; and Dave Norton, founder of the insights consultancy Stone Mantel.

Dave has been particularly helpful in this thinking thanks to the Collaboratives, yearlong multiclient studies I've worked on with him and colleagues for a number of years. We gather people together from many different companies to research various topics around experience innovations (Stone Mantel's specialty), with each participating business walking away with a new experience strategy. For the past few years the Transformation Economy has been one of the key objects of study, with qualitative and quantitative insights emerging.

So, I definitely knew enough about the Transformation Economy to start this book, and as with all my books, I learned so much more in the writing.

And, man, is the world ready now! This is true of both customers, who increasingly recognize they need help in achieving their aspirations, and companies, which increasingly understand the economic value they can create by getting into the transformation business. As we concluded that 2022 HBR article:

> Competing on transformations makes a company responsible for working with customers to define the transformation each one seeks, identify the barriers to success, and orchestrate all the goods, services, and experiences needed to

> support them during their journeys. Such business models will be much harder to imitate than those that offer only goods, services, or experiences. And they promise to generate handsome rewards—not only profits but also the knowledge that the company has truly made a profound difference in its customers' lives.[3]

And, I would add, in their own businesses.

Embracing the Transformation Economy

In working with clients on going beyond goods and services, I've often taken a team on a learning excursion to see some of the best (and a few of the worst) experience companies as consumers. On such expeditions they don't just see but viscerally feel the increasing desire for experiences over things, enabling them to comprehend and empathize with their own customers (even B2B customers) and see the greater value that could be created by staging experiences for them. So in this book, I want you to better comprehend and sympathize with customers and see the greater value that can be created by guiding transformations for them.

My intention is for you to not just understand but viscerally feel the shift into the Transformation Economy and the great opportunity that it entails for you and your business. To that end:

In chapter 1 you will read about the Progression of Economic Value and learn that the economic function of the fifth and final offering is *guiding*. Just as you extract commodities, make goods, deliver services, and stage experiences, you guide transformations. You will also learn that the key reason transformations create more economic value than any other offering is that they generate *time well invested*. Customers—properly called *aspirants*—invest their time in your transformations, under your guidance, which pays them dividends far into the future as they become a "new you." Moreover, you are what you charge for, and so being in the transformation business economically means charging for the demonstrated outcomes your customers achieve.

In chapter 2 you will learn the end purpose of guiding transformations: helping your aspirants flourish. For any and all businesses, fostering human flourishing is the reason for being; consciously or unconsciously, that's why customers buy from you, because they want to better their lives. By guiding people across one or more spheres of transformation—health & well-being, wealth & prosperity, knowledge & wisdom, and purpose & meaning—you take them to higher and higher levels of flourishing, with profit the measure of how well they benefit from your offerings.

Chapter 3 begins by making the point that all transformation is identity change—that aspirants desire to go from X to Y. You'll discover the categories of aspirants—whether people, organizations, businesses, or communities—and what catalyzes their need for transformation. You will also learn about the types of aspiration—that sometimes it is for wholesale metamorphosis, while at other times it's to cultivate some new aspect of identity, refine an existing aspect, or realize a large-scale ambition.

In chapter 4, recognizing that transformations build atop experiences, you will learn how to go beyond merely memorable experiences to highly meaningful, deeply transporting, and, finally, truly transformative ones. You can turn any experience into a transformative one through what I call *encapsulation*—the crux of guiding—by surrounding it with three activities: preparation beforehand, reflection afterward, and integration on an ongoing basis.

Chapter 5 will broaden your thinking on transformative experiences, showing how you can become a transformation guider by successfully staging experiences that are cohesive, robust, personal, and dramatic. Each one of these elements represents a set of ideas, principles, and frameworks—including a framework for creating the transformation journey for each aspirant—that enable you to heighten the level of your transformative experiences.

In chapter 6 you will delve deeper to learn how to turn transformative experiences into full-on transformation offerings via what I call the Delta Model. This chapter extends the lessons of the previous three to show you how to guide aspirants depending on the type of transformation required to achieve their aspirations. You will further understand the four roles of transformation guides and each one's best use: expert, coach, counselor, and alchemist.

Finally, chapter 7 brings it all together and includes key lessons that will enable you to turn your enterprise into a premier transformation guider, beginning with the three essential phases of guiding: diagnosis, encapsulated experiences, and follow-through. These phases are encapsulation writ large, enabling you to discover each individual's aspiration and then design the set of experiences that helps them achieve it—and sustain it through time. You will further learn different ways of charging for change. Doing so will put you economically in the business of this fifth and final economic offering, completing your shift into becoming a transformation guider.

Each chapter deepens your understanding of transformations and how to create and guide them in your business, enabling you to not only compete but thrive in the emerging Transformation Economy.

Seizing the Opportunity

No matter where you are on the progression or what you offer, there's opportunity in this new economy. Manufacturers and service providers will (and must) continue to exist, even if on a commoditized basis, to offer what customers—both people and businesses—value. And they can still take advantage of the new economy by *transformationalizing* their offerings—making them transformation*al,* if not full transformations—as well as by being valued suppliers to those enterprises that do offer the highest value of economic offering. But no matter what, goods and services will continue to employ fewer people, lessen their contribution to GDP, create less economic value by comparison, and largely become commoditized.

We're undergoing a radical shift from increasingly commoditized goods & services to more highly valued experiences & transformations. And while the Experience Economy has made great strides, we have yet to see its full flowering, and companies have not yet completely embraced the ideas, principles, and frameworks that will enable them to create the Transformation Economy.

As these happen more and more over time, experience stagers will undergo some diminishing, but not nearly as much as with previous economic offerings. Why? Because of the simple fact that transformations are built atop experiences, so therefore all experiences are potentially transformative. Almost everyone has had a proverbial life-changing experience that just happened out of the blue. In chapter 4 you'll learn the trick for turning any experience into a transformation. (Well, it's not really a trick—it's been known and discussed for decades and is well supported with research.) Again, it's about encapsulation: preparing people for the experience they are about to have, helping them reflect on it afterward, and then integrating the changes they desire to make into their lives.

Preparing to Read This Book

You are now reading a preparation rather than a preface. It's my goal for you to be transformed by reading this book. I trust that what you have read thus far will prepare you to absorb the ideas, principles, and frameworks ahead and enable you to develop ideas for what you can do—personally and corporately—to shift into the Transformation Economy and thereby create greater economic value with your offerings.

To that end, before you continue to the first chapter, ask yourself these questions, taking the time to answer them thoughtfully, honestly, and thoroughly:

- What business am I in today?
- What genres of economic offering(s) do I have?
- Do I see the forces of commoditization operating in my industry?
- What are the ends to which my current offerings are the means?
- Can I imagine being in the business of guiding transformations?

Let these questions open your mind to the possibilities of the Transformation Economy. You can even start to work on your business along the way.

At the end of each chapter you will encounter several questions that ask you to reflect on what you learned. Taking a few minutes with them will greatly increase the chance that this book will have an impact on you and make a difference for your business. You'll also find questions to prepare you for the lessons of the next chapter, which will further get you ready to absorb what you read.

Further, this preparation is bookended by a reflection after chapter 7 to help you embrace everything you've learned across the entire book.

Of course, I can only invite you to read, consider, and use the questions within. The choice is up to you. But I guarantee you will gain much greater rewards from this book if you choose to do so.

At the end of your reading journey, you will then need to integrate what you learned into your life and your business. Many of you will have enough understanding and be in the right position to make this happen on your own, and I look forward to someday learning what you did to become a premier transformation guider. There are also many companies, coaches, and consultants available to help you.

Strategic Horizons and I are also available to guide you down this path. Go to www.StrategicHorizons.com/integration to learn how.

—B. Joseph Pine II
Stillwater, MN
June 2025

Strategic Horizons LLP
105 Woodland Trace
Aurora, OH 44202 U.S.A
+1 (330) 995-4680
Explore@StrategicHorizons.com

THE TRANSFORMATION ECONOMY

1

GETTING INTO THE TRANSFORMATION BUSINESS

Transformation. It's a big word, one filled with hopes, dreams, and especially aspirations. But so often it comes with trepidation, hesitation, and doubt. We tend to need help for our efforts to have any chance of yielding significant change.

For enterprises the world over, this is an opportunity: to get into the business of transforming customers, whether people or organizations, by helping them achieve their aspirations. As my colleagues and I discussed in the pages of *Harvard Business Review*:

> Even though we're all filled with hopes, aims, and ambitions, significant change is incredibly hard to accomplish on our own. Enterprises should recognize the economic opportunity offered by the *transformation* business, in which they partner with consumers to improve some fundamental aspect of their lives—to achieve a "new you."[1]

Offering transformations means understanding the *why* behind what customers buy from you—their aspirations for improving aspects of their lives—and then bringing together the resources to make that outcome happen. Taking this approach doesn't mean you have to stop what you're doing now. You may be doing well by making goods or providing services. But it does mean you need to realize that whatever you sell today is a means to an end. So focus on going beyond the benefits customers currently receive and do whatever else it takes to offer the results your customers truly desire: achieving their aspirations. For there is no greater economic value you can create than to guide your customers in becoming who they want to become.

So how can your company create lasting value by helping customers reach their greatest aspirations? To start, you must answer the fundamental question, What business are we really in? Doing that intelligently requires understanding the history of economic progress.

The Progression of Economic Value

Figure 1-1 illustrates how the creation of economic value has changed over time. In the beginning were commodities: the *fungible stuff* we raise on the ground, pull out of the ground, or grow in the ground—animal, mineral, vegetable—and then sell on the open marketplace. Commodities were the basis of the Agrarian Economy that lasted for millennia. In 1776, the year Adam Smith published *The Wealth of Nations,* over 90 percent of people employed in the United States worked on farms. Today it's down to 1.5 percent. What happened in the past 250 years? Agricultural output skyrocketed! Thanks to vast technological and productivity improvements, it simply takes fewer and fewer people to produce more and more output.

So people moved from farms into factories, where they used commodities as raw material to make or manufacture physical, *tangible things.* These goods became the basis of the Industrial

FIGURE 1-1

The Progression of Economic Value

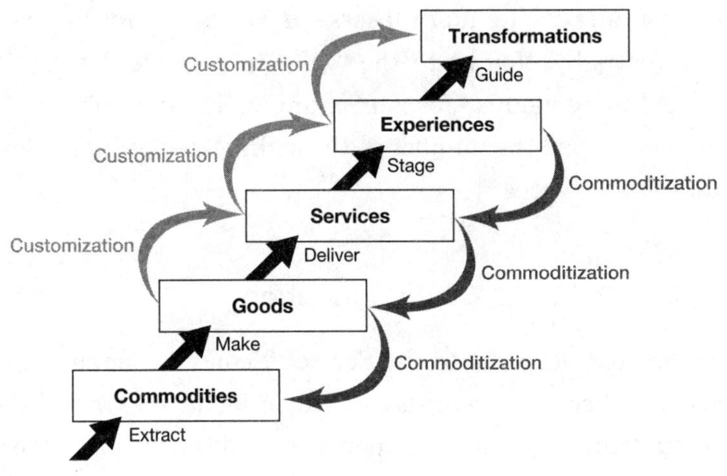

Economy, which overtook the Agrarian one in the early part of the twentieth century. Commodity extraction still employed about 40 percent of US workers, but the success of mass production soon vaulted goods manufacturing into the position of economic engine of the country (and, soon after that, the world).

As the Industrial Economy progressed, however, it became less and less of a job creator, as once again massive technological and productivity improvements meant it took fewer workers to produce more output. So people moved out of factories and into office jobs, retail, fast food and restaurants, maintenance and repair, childcare, finance, and numerous other service occupations where companies deliver a set of *intangible activities* on behalf of individual customers.

Over time, the Service Economy displaced the Industrial Economy, with services becoming the primary economic offering. In the United States, service delivery actually overtook manufacturing as the top employment sector in the 1950s, but that wasn't widely understood until the 1980s, when pundits began decrying the hollowing out of American manufacturing as such jobs increasingly moved overseas. Service employment was denigrated as "McJobs," and there was a lot of truth to that. But every economic shift creates many losers—and always many more winners. Eventually, thanks to the "gales of creative destruction" identified by economist Joseph Schumpeter, the number of jobs created swamped the number of those displaced at higher levels of salaries and wages.[2]

Commoditization

As we shifted deeper into the Service Economy, manufactured goods often became *commoditized,* meaning buyers treated them like commodities, purchasing them primarily on the basis of price and convenience. (The internet is the greatest force of commoditization ever invented, as customers can instantly compare prices from one vendor to the next.) When faced with commoditization, companies lose much of their ability to control prices, which drop down toward marginal costs and become subject to the vagaries of the marketplace.

There's nothing fundamentally wrong with a commoditized business; you can still make a lot of money in it. Generally, however, only one or two companies in any industry prove successful at doing so. And it's not a very fun situation to be in, as you must relentlessly focus on costs by, among other things, automating tasks and getting rid of as many people as possible. That's why so many manufacturers have shifted into the services business—repairs, leasing, warranty plans, equipment management, and so forth. Today many, if not most, manufacturers make as much, if not more, money from offering services as from making goods.

But services can be commoditized as well. For example, no industry has commoditized itself more than banking, as managers started to view customers coming into their banks as costing them money. So they pushed people out of branches to use ATMs, then the internet, and finally phone apps. Eliminating human contact is a surefire way to commoditize yourself.

Customization

Customization is the antidote to commoditization. Commoditization is like the law of gravity; if you do nothing to counteract it, it will just drag you down year after year. Customization, on the other hand, lifts you up. You cannot help but be differentiated if you tailor to each individual customer.

And when you customize your physical goods, you automatically turn them into services. Consider the classic economic distinctions: goods are *standardized,* while services are *customized*—done on behalf of an individual customer. Goods are *inventoried after production,* while services are *delivered on demand,* when the customer says this is exactly what they want. Goods are *tangible,* while services are *intangible.* Part and parcel of customization is the intangible service of helping customers figure out exactly what they want. Meanwhile, mass customization—efficiently serving customers uniquely—means giving people exactly what they want at a price they're willing to pay.[3]

Consider Coca-Cola's Freestyle machine. The company is a paragon of mass production, but with this device found at Five Guys, Wendy's, Jack in the Box, and many other restaurants, you as the consumer get to determine exactly what drink you want right now and have it made for you. After paying, you bring the cup to the machine, where you first select the base for your drink: regular Coke, Diet Coke, Coke Zero, Barq's root beer, Sprite, Dr. Pepper, and beyond, many with caffeine and caffeine-free options. Then you pick whether to add lemon, lime, cherry, and other flavors. Each of these options has its own container inside the machine, and when you press your cup into the mechanical lever, the machine-as-factory brings the liquid modules together to flow into your cup, just for you.[4] The next person can opt for completely different options, and the machine mass customizes their drink for them.

While Coca-Cola talks about there being over a hundred combinations, in fact there's virtually infinite possibility. What I like to do, for example, is pour Coke and lime into my cup until it's around 80 percent full, and then switch over to Coke Zero with lime, just to limit my calories a bit. You can mix anything with anything else to any degree you want (not that every set of options yields a tasty drink).

So what Coca-Cola's Freestyle machine and other mass customizers of goods do is enable customers to define what they want and then make and deliver it, turning the good into a service.

From services to experiences

In the same way, when you customize your services, devising and delivering exactly what an individual wants or needs in a specific situation at a particular point in time, then you can't help but make that customer go "Wow!" You turn it into a memorable event—you turn it into an *experience.*

The Ritz-Carlton Hotel Company, for example, aims to customize as many aspects of its services as it can for each guest. If, for example, you stay at a Ritz-Carlton hotel and call housekeeping to ask for hypoallergenic pillows, a staff member dutifully brings up the pillows and then adds this preference to your profile. The next time you stay at a Ritz-Carlton anywhere in the world, even if you have never been to that location before, hypoallergenic pillows will be on your bed before you arrive. The company never asks you questions about what you want, because it wants to create mystique about just knowing. Staff members observe your preferences across many dimensions of the stay—from how you like to be addressed, to your favorite drinks, to whether you prefer to stay on a low or high floor, and on and on the list goes—and then fulfill them again and again, with every visit an opportunity to learn more. Each time you stay, they access your preferences from the company's system, naturally called Mystique, and strive to wow you at any opportunity. Ritz-Carlton doesn't just provide hotel services; by customizing them each step of the way, it stages a hospitality experience.

Here, we define experiences as *memorable events that engage each individual in an inherently personal way.* As the Progression of Economic Value shows, experiences are built atop services, just as services are formed around goods and goods are made from commodities. With experiences, a company uses goods as props and services as the stage to engage guests in a personal way. Those are exactly the right terms: where commodities are *extracted,* goods *made,* and services *delivered,* experiences are *staged.*[5] And where commodities have *markets,* goods *users,* and services *clients,* experiences have *guests.*

Recognize that experiences are a distinct economic offering, as distinct from services as services are from goods.[6] Where goods are tangible and services intangible, experiences are memorable. If you do not create a memory within your guests, then you did not stage an experience. Further, while goods are standardized and services customized, experiences are inherently personal. No two people can have the same experience, even if they are in the same place at the same time, for the experience actually happens inside of them, in reaction to the events staged outside of them.

And where goods are inventoried after production and services delivered on demand, experiences are revealed over a duration of time. You cannot have an instantaneous experience; it must rise up to a climax and come back down again. With experiences, what customers value is the time they spend in the company's (physical or virtual) place. In fact, people *want* both goods & services to be commoditized—to be bought at the lowest possible price and greatest possible convenience—in order to spend their hard-earned money and their even harder-earned time on the experiences they value more highly.

That's why today we live in an Experience Economy. It has supplanted the Service Economy, which displaced the Industrial Economy based on goods, which overtook the Agrarian Economy based on commodities. Experiences have become the predominant economic offering, effectively causing services to be more and more commoditized, just as goods were before.

Beyond experiences

But experiences can be commoditized as well. The second time you have an experience, it may not be as engaging as the first, and the third time not as good as the second. Pretty soon customers are saying, "Been there, done that"—the hallmark of a commoditized experience, whether or not they also bought the T-shirt.

So-called theme restaurants perhaps first encountered commoditization at this level of economic offering, as once you've experienced one particular place, you've pretty much seen everything it has to offer. Such operators also failed to appreciate that in order to create an engaging and memorable experience, having lousy food and poor service doesn't cut it (the exception being Medieval Times, where eating off a messy plate with no utensils, with your "wench" or "serf" overfilling your mug and intentionally spilling your beer, is the experience in and of itself).

Think also of Starbucks, which famously styles itself as a "third place" with a coffee-drinking experience, turning a few cents' worth of beans into $4–$7 (and sometimes more) cups of coffee. Over the past decade or so, the company has been commoditizing itself by offering less space, on average, than it used to have, fewer personal interactions, and harder wooden chairs so people won't linger as long. More and more of its business is coming from drive-throughs and mobile ordering, impinging on the experience for those who want to spend time in the third place, while the other customers get none of the in-place experience but pay all the price. Brian Niccol, named CEO in September 2024, is working hard to turn much of this around, yet over the past few years, the company's rising prices have become the experience equivalent of "shrinkflation."[7]

So using the heuristic that customization is the antidote to commoditization, what happens when you customize an experience? When you design and stage an encounter that is tailored to an individual at exactly the right moment in time, you can't help but turn it into a life-changing experience that *transforms* them in some way. Here, companies use experiences as the raw material to guide customers to change, to help them in achieving their aspirations, to become who they want to become. That is, economically, a transformation.

The Transformation Economy

Many enterprises are naturally in the transformation business: health-care systems, counselors, fitness centers, financial firms, educational institutions, spiritual organizations, and coaches of all stripes, to name a few. They all work on personal transformations; many other enterprises are naturally in the business of B2B or organizational transformations, including management consulting, employee training, and outsourcing, as well as much of technology, accounting, and finance.

However, far too many view their offerings as mere services and fail to compete on guiding their customers in truly achieving their aspirations. Think of higher education, such as business schools. Why do people spend tens, even hundreds of thousands of dollars for an MBA? Is it because of the ideas they get? No, those are the commodities; every university has the same ideas, more or less. Is it because of books, computers, and other educational equipment? No. How about teaching, homework analysis, and other activities professors deliver? Not that either. ("C's get degrees," as the old saying goes.) Certainly, the in-classroom experience, knowledge sharing, and MBA environment—particularly networking—have a great deal to do with it. But fundamentally, people go to business school to gain insight and skills; to have a better career; to increase their earning potential; and to be a *new you.* They get an MBA to be transformed.

As John Quelch, former dean of London Business School, once told *Fast Company* magazine:

> We're not in the education business. We're in the transformation business. We expect everyone who participates in a program at the London Business School—whether it's for three days or for two years—to be transformed by the experience. We want people to look back on their time here as something that significantly influenced their career and possibly even their entire life.... One nice thing about declaring that we're in the transformation business is that everyone here—from custodians to deputy deans—has become much more motivated. People are eager to take part in having an impact on the students who come here.[8]

That's a different mindset, and a different economic offering. And *impact* is a great word for it, for without an impactful change there is no transformation.

Transformation distinctions

Transformations are *effectual outcomes that change individuals in a lasting way.* Where experiences are memorable, transformations are *effectual.*[9] Commodities, goods, and services have no lasting consequence beyond their consumption, and even the memories of an experience fade over time. But buyers of transformations seek to be guided toward some specific aim or purpose. Without a change in values, behaviors, purpose, or some other fundamental aspect of self, no transformation occurs. The transformation affects the very being, the identity, of the buyer.

Where experiences are inherently personal, transformations are fundamentally *individual.* While experiences happen inside of us, transformations change us from the inside out, whether we're talking about a consumer or a business. People value transformation above all other economic offerings because it addresses the *why,* the buyer's aspiration. That's also the reason companies that guide transformations ideally shouldn't refer to their customers as users, clients, or even guests, but rather as *aspirants.*

And where experiences are revealed over a duration of time, transformations are *sustained through time.* Suppose you go to a nutritionist for a six-week program to gain healthy eating habits, but three months later, you are back to your old habits. Or suppose your business hires a consulting company to stop wasteful practices, but the changes never really take. If the results of these offerings prove impermanent, then there was no transformation but merely a momentary uptick (or downtick, as the case may be) along the same old journey. Transformations must last. (For more on temporary change, see the sidebar "Quasi-Transformations.")

In sum, with transformations the customer *is* the product. Nothing you do for a customer matters unless the person achieves their aspirations and gets their desired outcome. That's what it means to be in the transformation business.

Of course, you cannot guarantee your customers achieve their aspirations. All you can do is create the conditions under which aspirants transform themselves. Therefore, the economic function for transformations is *guide.* You are an experience stager but a transformation guider, leading customers along a journey from who they are today to who they want to become.[10] Think of every transformation as a *from/to* statement: from out of shape to fit, from sick to well, from living paycheck-to-paycheck to being financially secure, from home cook to chef, from worker to manager,

Quasi-Transformations

As part of my research into experiences & transformations, I have been fortunate to work with founder Dave Norton and his colleagues at Stone Mantel on their annual program called the Collaboratives. The yearlong Collaboratives pool the time and resources of many people from various businesses to do direct customer research, both qualitative and quantitative, and then guide participant companies in designing and validating new experience and transformation strategies.

One of the intriguing results from the research in the 2022–2023 Collaborative was that many people *say* they are transformed after experiences, but note later that they did not really see or act differently. My immediate thought when encountering the data was, *They weren't transformed at all.* The result of their various experiences was not effectual, or if they were changed, it certainly wasn't sustained through time. But nonetheless, they said they were. Many research participants felt they underwent a temporary, transient, or provisional "transformation," a change that happened to them for some length of time—a morning, a day, a week, maybe a month. But then they went back to normal, without much, if any, of a long-term change in how they saw the world or lived their lives. Those results are quite common, actually; let's call them *quasi-transformations*.

from employee to retiree. Every one of these shifts is an aspiration that's difficult to accomplish well—and in some cases at all—without a guide to help.

There is no greater economic value you can create than to help customers achieve their aspirations. That's the reason the forthcoming Transformation Economy is hot on the heels of the Experience Economy—why it already comprises a large share of employment and GDP, not to mention a large share of customers' desires, needs, and aspirations.

There are many situations where people desire only temporary change. Live-action role-playing (LARPing), costume play (cosplay), and alternate reality games (ARGs) all count here; in each case people turn into a completely different persona or being for a time and then become their normal selves again. Sports fantasy camps, war reenactments, living history groups, and any game or virtual place experienced via an avatar offer similar opportunities. People also provisionally try out new careers through organizations such as PivotPlanet, where customers take a vacation from their day jobs to work for microbreweries, bed-and-breakfasts, and other organizations for a week. Actual vacations may offer the best opportunities of all for temporary change. People want to get away and see new sights, do new activities, and even try out new ways of being without any expectation of lasting difference. Some consumers enter weight-loss and fitness programs seeking only temporary change. They may have a temporary desire—"aspiration" doesn't fit for quasi-transformations—such as "I want to fit into the swimsuit I wore last summer" with no intention of making it last through the fall. Cosmetic changes also fit the bill, such as Botox, dental whitening, tanning, makeovers, and other such procedures.

There are plenty of quasi-transformations your company can sell as valuable offerings in and of themselves. Just be sure not to promote something as transformative when it is not.

It's about Time

One reality underlying the Progression of Economic Value: the most precious resource on the planet is the time of individual human beings. That's always been the case, and it's a big reason people prefer buying food rather than growing it, or paying someone to sew their clothes or fix their cars rather than doing it themselves. Moreover, as people live longer and value experiences and transformations more highly, they value their time more highly.

After all, we have only a limited time on this earth to experience all we'd like to experience and become who we want to become, and as that time is used, it can never be recovered.

What customers want from commodities, goods, and services is *time well saved*: for someone else to do something for them so they don't have to. Many companies, however, waste their customers' time. Consider how contact centers intentionally reduce the time service representatives spend on the phone by compelling people to spend more time talking to machines. Or how retail stores staff their checkouts for the least personnel cost, not for the greatest customer demand—or offer self-checkout, commoditizing themselves by violating the basic contract of service companies: do activities for me.

As shown in figure 1-2, experiences offer *time well spent*: what people value is the time they spend with a company, having the experience it stages.[11]

And transformations go beyond even that to guide *time well invested*.[12] Aspirants invest their time, with the help of the trans-

FIGURE 1-2

The progression of time

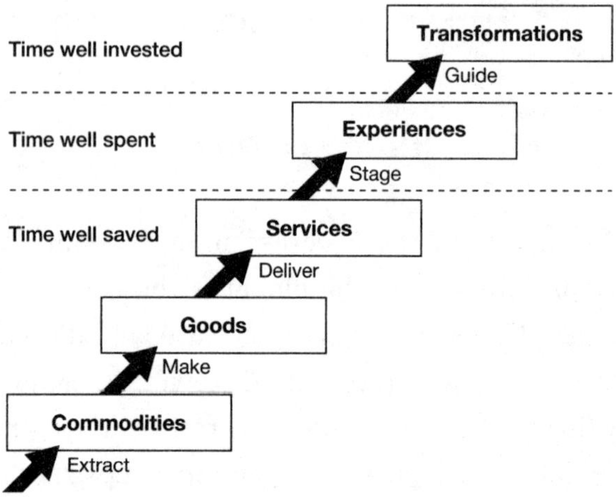

formation guider, to achieve their personal and corporate aspirations, reaping dividends now and into the future. Companies that guide transformations should of course still concern themselves with time well spent—for we are all the products of our experiences. Through transformative experiences we gain much greater value from the compound interest of time well invested. For when you guide customers to achieve their aspirations, you help them wisely spend that most precious resource, their time.

Noom presents a good example of this.[13] Originally a provider of fitness equipment, the company was started in 2008 by Saeju Jeong and Artem Petakov because they were dissatisfied with how the US health-care system "had become so focused on sick care instead of health care," and they had the vision of "helping more people everywhere live better longer."[14]

The company empowers individuals to lose weight and keep it off by changing their thought processes and behaviors. Its app offers daily lessons, customized for each customer (called "Noomers") and their weight-loss journey, on topics such as how to think about food, form healthy habits, and avoid triggers that may induce greater eating. Each lesson lasts around one to three minutes and serves as daily motivation for making progress toward personal goals. After ten days, the app lets customers access Noom Circles, groups moderated by the company that enable them to connect with other Noomers on topics of interest, including not just food and exercise but also hobbies and other subjects.

Noom further introduces you to a coaching team. First, there's "Welli," an AI chatbot that can immediately answer many questions, although not (yet) ones based on your personal goals and progress. Then there are Noom Guides, who respond asynchronously to personal queries to offer some guidance and support. And finally, there are 1:1 Coaches, who are rigorously trained on the company's psychological research and transformation methods. They interact with Noomers on a daily basis, chatting with them about their habits, hopes, and fears and helping them understand their journey and areas of improvement—all with the goal of building a relationship over time.[15]

That "over time" is key, for no one downloads Noom and immediately makes progress on losing weight or having greater well-being. The process takes an extended period, is highly dependent on coaching, and involves customized encounters. Noomers invest their time—encounter by encounter, lesson by lesson, behavior change by behavior change—to achieve their well-being goal.

As with weight loss, there are very few transformations that happen all at once. The real transformation almost always takes place after someone spends time reflecting, making meaning out of the experience, and integrating it into their life or work (something we'll talk more about later in the book). In other words, many transformative experiences are required after the allegedly life-changing one. Yet many people do not reinforce their shift with subsequent pursuits and end up in the same place as before.

To avoid that result, someone's investment must build on each experience, one after the other, to yield the achievement of their aspirational desire. Such investment also creates greater economic value. Whether selling commodities, goods, services, experiences, or transformations, the amount of money you can charge can be only as great as the value you create for customers, which is dependent on your effect on their time:

$$\text{Value created} = \text{functionality provided} + \text{net value of time}$$

In the formula's last variable, when you waste your customers' time, the net value of time is negative; in one way or another you have to discount your offerings to entice customers to buy from you. Time well saved essentially puts the net value of time at zero, a neutral result. Time well spent has a positive value, and time well invested an even greater value, enabling companies that guide transformations to gain a significant price premium. (See the sidebar "The Economic Value of Time" for more.)

The Economic Value of Time

Ben Franklin famously quipped that "time is money." That's especially true when you recognize how precious the time of individual human beings is. As author George Gilder, cofounder of the Discovery Institute, put it, "The ultimate test and measuring stick of wealth is time. What remains scarce when all else becomes abundant is our minutes, hours, days, and years. Time is the only resource that cannot be recycled, stored, duplicated, or recovered."[a]

In the book *Superabundance*, Marian Tupy, senior fellow at the Cato Institute, and Gale Pooley, adjunct professor at Utah Tech University, marshal prodigious data to measure wealth and abundance in terms of not GDP but *time prices*, which denote "the length of time that a person has to work to earn enough money to buy something. It is the money price divided by hourly income . . . expressed in hours and minutes."[b]

Measuring in time prices shows how truly much more abundance we came to have in the past century, and how much goods and services have been commoditized. In commodities, Tupy and Pooley examined forty-two grocery food items (eggs, bread, butter, etc.) between 1919 and 2019, finding the time price fell by a whopping 91.2 percent—meaning that the average blue-collar worker spent over 90 percent less of their working time to buy them. In goods, they examined thirty-five items (toasters, washing machines, pants, etc.) and found that in the same period their average time prices fell by 72.3 percent. And in services, cosmetic procedures (laser hair removals, liposuction, facelifts, etc.) saw their time prices go down 30.8 percent between 1998 and 2018.[c]

This result fits well with the analysis that Jim Gilmore and I did in *The Experience Economy*, with the hefty spreadsheet lifting done by Lee Kaplan, founder of Lee3 Consultants. It showed that between 1959 and 2009 the consumer price index for commodities and goods was significantly lower than that of

(*continued*)

the average offering, while services were slightly above, experiences above that, and transformations even higher. Employment and GDP contribution within each genre of offering followed the same pattern across the five economic offerings (with growth in employment negative for commodities and goods across those fifty years). The 1997 annual report of the Federal Reserve Bank of Dallas, interestingly titled "Time Well Spent: The Declining *Real* Cost of Living in America," included experiences & transformations that *Superabundance* didn't cover. The report found that "the work-time price of a movie ticket today is slightly *higher* than in the 1920s" and that "paying for higher education and medical care requires *more* hours of work than it used to."[d]

Such increases are not primarily about inflation as we commonly think of it, as an increase in prices due to a rise in underlying costs such as raw materials, labor, and equipment. Yes, in higher education and health care such factors have increased costs—most notably the increase in the ratio of administrators to instructors in education and the growth of technology in health care.[e] But primarily it's *valueflation*, an increase in price because of the higher value customers place on transformations (and to a lesser degree experiences), relative to the lower-level offerings in the Progression of Economic Value. That's the chief reason US college tuition has far outpaced inflation for decades and spending on health care as a percentage of GDP increased almost 2.7 times in the United States and almost 2.3 times in comparable developed countries in that same period.[f]

Time is money, and this data shows that consumers now buy goods and services at lower time prices than what they once paid for commodities. Simultaneously, they save themselves time that they then spend on the higher-level offerings in the Progression of Economic Value, with transformation offerings the greatest value: the investment of their time in bettering themselves.

Notes

a. George Gilder's foreword in Marian L. Tupy and Gale L. Pooley, *Superabundance: The Story of Population Growth, Innovation, and Human*

Flourishing on an Infinitely Bountiful Planet (Washington, DC: Cato Institute, 2022), 12.

b. Tupy and Pooley, *Superabundance*, 3.

c. Tupy and Pooley, *Superabundance*, 165, 171, and 183, respectively. Note that cosmetic procedures do have overtones of transformation but are widely treated as mere services.

d. W. Michael Cox and Richard Alm, "Time Well Spent: The Declining *Real* Cost of Living in America," Federal Reserve Bank of Dallas, 1997, 14 and 16, respectively, https://www.minneapolisfed.org/~/media/files/research/prescott/quant_macro/arpt97.pdf, emphasis added.

e. Another factor in health care is that the customers—patients—are not the ones directly paying for services. Insurance companies and governments pay the great majority, the latter dictating prices, procedures, and reimbursements. This affects price signals and incentives, offering little motivation to improve the quality-to-cost ratio—or, better, the outcome-to-cost ratio.

f. Around three times the increase in inflation over the past five decades, according to Jessica Bryant, "Cost of College Over Time," BestColleges, updated February 25, 2025, https://www.bestcolleges.com/research/college-costs-over-time/; Emma Wagner et al., "How Does Health Spending in the U.S. Compare to Other Countries?" Peterson-KFF Health System Tracker, April 9, 2025, https://www.healthsystemtracker.org/chart-collection/health-spending-u-s-compare-countries/.

What Business Are You Really In?

So if you want to get into the transformation business, recognize that *it's about time.* It's about ensuring your customers—your aspirants—progressively gain time well invested with every ongoing encounter, each one contributing to the transformation journeys they undergo.

Recognize, too, that it's about time not only for your customers but for the people employed in your company whose time can likewise be wasted, saved, spent, or invested in creating economic value for the enterprise and personal value for them.

And it's about time you determined once and for all what business you are really in. For those who decide they do not want to merely provide time well saved or stage time well spent, but rather to guide time well invested, the answer is to get into the transformation business.

Focusing on time well spent and time well invested enables you to shift up the Progression of Economic Value to offer experiences & transformations, respectively. If you do it well, and do it fully, then you can go beyond goods & services and shift the business you are in. Doing so forestalls the forces of commoditization, enables you to provide much value for your current as well as an entirely new set of customers, and thereby creates greater economic value for your enterprise.

That doesn't mean you have to stop selling your current offerings; you can subsume them into transformations. The Nicorette brand, for example, manufactures smoking cessation products in the forms of gum, patches, sprays, and more. Quitting smoking with these goods alone, however, is incredibly hard to do—because quitting smoking is incredibly hard to do, period. So the brand has long offered MyQuit, which subsumes the physical goods into a smoking cessation program that helps you plan to quit and provides customized guidance with behavioral support, progress tracking, and relapse assistance. Your favored form of Nicorette is shipped directly to you as part of the program.

In services, Vance Thompson Vision is world-renowned for the quality of the vision services it provides. Founder Dr. Vance Thompson knows patients aren't the experts, so they can't judge the quality of the service they receive, but they can judge the level of experience engagement. The company's theme is "control of light," with visual stimulation everywhere. It built its offices like an eye, with the cornea up front to let natural light stream in, and the retina—the nerve center—in back, where all exams, diagnostics, and surgeries take place. The building has a natural flow to it; there's no signage. Highlighting the distinction between on- and offstage, the exam rooms have two doors—one for patients who naturally follow the light, and the other, which goes to a backstage area, for the eyecare professionals. So engaging is the design that the local tourism board lists it as a tourist destination. But Vance Thompson Vision goes further, knowing that in the end it's in the transformation business—the business of "Changing Lives by Creating Vision," as its slogan attests. So surrounding its medical services the company works specifically to, as one example, help people who receive LASIK, new lenses, or cornea transplants get comfortable with what is not just an improvement in seeing but a significant change in their lives.

Short of directly being in the transformation business, manufacturers and service providers—experience stagers as well—can supply those who are. As discussed earlier in the chapter, each economic offering is built atop the one below, so transformation guiders require the lower-level offerings to create their own economic offerings. They must therefore integrate experiences, services, goods, and sometimes even commodities into one cohesive solution to determine and guide transformations.[16] As with any business, there's a "make or buy" decision on which elements they create themselves and which they purchase from other enterprises.

In an extreme but inspiring case, the Hogeweyk is a "dementia village" in Weesp, Netherlands, "a familiar and safe environment in which people with dementia live while retaining their own identity and autonomy as much as possible."[17] It is a real neighborhood, with houses that hearken back to various settings that the more than 180 residents remember and identify with from their predementia days, such as urban, tradecraft, religious, and Indonesian (that country being a longtime Dutch colony). All the care staff, including psychiatrists, therapists, and social workers, take on normal community roles as neighbors, clerks, servers, and so forth. The Hogeweyk hosts a supermarket for obtaining commodities and goods; services such as a hairdressing salon, a restaurant, and a handyman; and experiences such as a theater, a pub, a café, and a town square.

The Hogeweyk is basically a general contractor, bringing together a suite of offerings from outside its business for each aspirant without having to produce them itself. Note that aspirants—people as well as businesses—can act as their own general contractor and "hire" everything they need. Think of a goal to lead a healthier lifestyle. An aspirant could seek out organic foodstuffs, self-help books, fitness-tracking devices and apps, fitness centers, and a personal trainer, each one supporting them on their transformation journey. This is in fact the way most transformations occur today.

Increasingly, however, aspirants seek outside help from those who know how to do it better than they do. That is the core opportunity as transformations closely follow experiences as the basis of the economy, an opportunity best captured by charging explicitly for transformations.

You Are What You Charge For

While you can charge premium pricing with transformations, a business ultimately defines itself by what it charges for. If you charge for undifferentiated stuff, you're in the commodities business. If you charge for tangible things, you are in the goods business. If you charge for the activities your people do, you are in the services business. So, economically, you are in the experience business if and only if you *charge for the time customers spend with you*. That means using an admission fee, a membership fee, or some other way of putting a price on customer time. It's not the "time and materials" fees of so many service providers, which add up the hours workers spend on tasks, but *customers'* time, for that is what they value with experiences: time well spent. You would not imagine, for example, entering the venue of any traditional experience—movies, plays, concerts, theme parks, sporting events—without paying admission.

More than twenty-five years ago, when Jim Gilmore and I first predicted that companies never considered to be in the experience business—retailers, restaurants, manufacturers, B2B companies, and so on—would charge for time, people thought we were crazy.[18] But that's exactly what's happened. For you ultimately must align what you charge for with what your customers value, and with experiences that means charging for time.

You are what you charge for. With transformations, then, what customers value is achieving their aspirations. Inputs don't matter, only outcomes. To align what you charge for with what your customers value, you must *charge for the demonstrated outcomes* your customers desire. Even if you choose not to charge for change, you'll receive immense benefit from thinking through everything your enterprise does as though its income were dependent on customer outcomes—because ultimately it is.

A number of businesses already do so, notably consulting firms that get paid based on parameters of success, put some of their fees at risk, get bonuses based on overachievement, or take shares in clients so their income goes up (or down) with share prices. There's a marked shift to charging for outcomes in health care, where it's often called "value-based payments." For example, Omar Ishrak, retired chief executive of Medtronic, told the *Wall Street Journal* that the company was "signing supply contracts with customers that adjust prices based on how well the products work in patients, rather than simply having the customer pay a fixed per-unit cost regardless of a device's performance in individual patients."[19] He added that the company was "moving, just like the rest of health care, to a value-based model, where we get paid in some fashion for actually achieving the outcome."[20] Geisinger Health System embraces this model, "offering a money-back guarantee when we fall short."[21]

Government, education, and social nonprofits also lead the way. As just one example, the State of Texas decided to bring performance-based funding into higher education. When the heads of each college and university were asked by the chair of the Texas Senate finance committee how much of their funding they would be willing to base on the actual outcomes of their students, the nearly unanimous answer was: very little or none. The exception: Texas State Technical College (TSTC). Its response? "One hundred percent."[22]

Based in Waco, Texas, with ten campuses across the state, TSTC always received funding, like most such colleges, based on "credit hours," whether or not students actually went to class, learned anything, graduated, or applied what they learned in jobs after graduating. The state, however, sought not the input of credit hours but the *outcomes* of students who graduated and went on to contribute to society. Since 2014, TSTC's funding has been 100 percent based on a "returned value formula" that measures the contributions of graduates to the state, including in taxes paid. TSTC had to transform itself to align how it operated—including what and how it taught—to make this work, and its results include seeing the number of students placed in jobs go up dramatically, with a 34 percent increase in starting wages, a 51 percent increase in cumulative earnings of graduates, and a 136 percent increase in funding through the returned value formula (all adjusted for inflation).[23] The college's focus on student outcomes, propelled by its new outcome-based funding, proved so successful that TSTC turned around and offered students in select programs a money-back guarantee—another form of outcome-based charging—where those who didn't find a job within six months of graduation could get a complete refund.[24]

I'll cover pricing options in more depth in chapter 7, but here let me point out what outcome-based fees do. First, they send a signal that you as a business are serious in helping your customers achieve their aspirations. Second, they're a catalytic mechanism for designing your transformation offerings so that they yield the outcomes customers desire. And third, the money you make, based on the value you create, gives you the wherewithal to invest in your offerings to ensure you do everything possible in guiding each individual to recoup the time and effort they put in.

In short, outcome-based fees align what you charge for with what your customers value and put you economically in the transformation business. They yield time very well invested on *both* sides of the economic equation.

REFLECTION

Contemplate what you've learned in this first chapter through these questions:

- What really struck and surprised you in this chapter? What might hold the biggest benefit for your business?
- Where do you see your business today in the Progression of Economic Value? Can you ascend to the proposition that you can be in the transformation business?
- Where do you waste customer time today? How can you flip that into time well saved or time well spent, and even time well invested?
- How might you charge for the demonstrated outcomes your customers achieve?

PREPARATION

Guiding transformations requires understanding your customers' *why*, the aspirations behind their purchases from you. Chapter 2 is about the why behind the why: the reason people aspire at all. Answering these questions will help you embrace the lessons of the next chapter and more richly think about your business, your customers, and your life:

- What industry are you in today? If you ascend to the proposition that you are in the transformation business, how would you then describe your industry?
- In just a few words, why do you think customers buy from your business, beyond the specific benefits your offerings provide?
- Given that, what is the why behind the why of your business? Why does your business exist?
- What do you think life is mainly about? Is it something more than being happy?

2

FOSTERING HUMAN FLOURISHING

Customers buy an economic offering if and only if they believe it to be of greater value than the money they exchange for it. They must feel they'll be better off—however they individually define the phrase—with the offering than with the cash in their pocket, purse, or account. Yes, they may be wrong. They may get carried away by a bright and shiny object. They may be illogical, emotional, or short-sighted. But their goal is always to improve their existence, to progress, to be happier, to have a better life and live it more abundantly.

In short, to *flourish*.

That connection between purchasing an offering and flourishing is most direct with transformations. Customers pay for a transformation only if they believe it will help them achieve an aspiration, that it will improve their lives in some significant way. All transformations guide aspirants to higher and higher degrees of flourishing as human beings.

Understanding Human Flourishing

There has been a renaissance in the idea of human flourishing in the social sciences, philosophy, psychology, and even economics over the past thirty years or so. But it has a long history, tracing back to the Greek philosopher Aristotle in the fourth century BC. He spoke of flourishing (using the term *eudaimonia*) as the "highest good," the end goal for what it meant to live a good life.[1]

The field of positive psychology—where the work focuses on helping people live more fulfilling lives, rather than recover from trauma or deal with issues—specifically addresses human flourishing. Martin Seligman, director of the University of Pennsylvania's Positive Psychology Center, jump-started the field in 1998 when he became president of the American Psychological Association. Originally concentrating just on happiness, he realized that people needed more than that from positive psychology. In his book *Flourish: A Visionary New Understanding of Happiness and Well-Being,* Seligman writes that the field's goal "is to increase the amount of flourishing in your own life and on the planet."[2] He also asks, "What is flourishing?," although rather than defining it, he cites researchers that provide a list of features to be measured. Specifically, he mentions the three core features of positive emotions, engagement/interest, and meaning/purpose, and states that three of six additional features must be present: self-esteem, optimism, resilience, vitality, self-determination, and positive relationships.[3]

Other thought leaders and organizations have expanded this list, including Harvard University's Human Flourishing Program, which defines flourishing as "a state in which *all* aspects of a person's life are good" and similarly provides a measure of five domains: happiness and life satisfaction, mental and physical health, meaning and purpose, character and virtue, and close social relationships.[4]

These are all good elements, each one the subject of transformation offerings that would indeed help people thrive. But flourishing is not an on-off switch, where either you have it or you don't. There are degrees as it fluctuates over time, even as we endeavor to achieve higher and higher levels. Moreover, any definition of the term needs to recognize that what constitutes flourishing differs for every individual. It is not a state to be attained but a multidimensional and ever-changing picture of where we stand today in relation to our possibilities for tomorrow, one that realizes we all have, to varying degrees, aspects of our lives that are not perfect, and that far too many of us have dimensions that on any scale would register on the negative side—as struggling, languishing, even dying.

Every transformation moves people to a higher degree of flourishing, and even though few people may use the term to describe what they seek, it is precisely their aim when they exchange their money for transformation offerings, for the opportunity to achieve their aspirations.

So what is flourishing? Think of it as *the extent to which each one of us is the way we are meant to be.*[5]

This definition intentionally leaves vague exactly who (or Who) determines that meaning, which also differs for different people. Fulfilling the definition entails times of discovery as much as journeys of transformation, a pursuit that lasts a lifetime, with many, many transformations along the way. Helping aspirants reach ever-higher degrees of flourishing is the goal of all transformations: guiding people not only in changing their lives but in living them more abundantly. In improving not just who they are but the possibilities of who they can become. In not just increasing happiness but nurturing joy. In not just being human but in growing as human beings, thriving as businesses, and blossoming as communities. In transforming people in some way to be more of who they are meant to be.

At the Heart of Business

Fostering human flourishing is the true purpose of business, its raison d'être. Customers buy economic offerings to enhance their lives, and your role is to design, create, and sell those offerings. This is true even when your enterprise sells to other businesses, for that business, or the one it sells to after that, eventually reaches individuals who deserve to realize the life they want. The Swedes have it exactly right: "*näringsliv,* the Swedish word for enterprise, literally means *nurturing life.*"[6]

Supporting flourishing is not a social responsibility; it's a business imperative. (See the sidebar "Flourishing and Business.") It is core to why companies exist at all, from time immemorial. And it's imperative that we recognize this truth—and act accordingly. As my friend and colleague Stan Hustad puts it, "If a business doesn't help people flourish, it's a racket."

Part and parcel of helping people better themselves as an enterprise is working to help your employees do so, from frontline workers to professionals, managers, executives, and the C-suite. Employees should never be treated as mere means to an end; as human beings, they are always ends in and of themselves. Employment with you is a means to the end of their own betterment, as they simultaneously help you foster the betterment of your customers.

That extends to the communities in which you reside—your existence should be to each community's betterment, never its detriment. The idea extends further to society overall, the social order in which you are incorporated, for which your enterprise should be a net positive, not a negative. (And it really shouldn't be a close call.) Moreover, the idea extends to the planet of which we are all stewards, for it is the place where all human flourishing happens.[7]

To be clear: I am not saying that each of these "stakeholders" have rights on you, that you *must* take each and every one into account for every decision you make. I am saying your enterprise has *responsibilities* to them, that the true purpose of business of fostering human flourishing necessarily includes not just customers but employees, communities, society, and the planet.

This concept is not utopian. It is simply a recognition of what has always been true. It doesn't mean you can never fire or lay

Flourishing and Business

The forthcoming Transformation Economy will enable human flourishing both individually and on a scale never before seen, as people shift from purchasing lower-level economic offerings to the one genre of offering that so directly affects their ability to achieve their aspirations: transformations.

Human flourishing very much needs to be a concern in business, and it has a long economic history. It goes back at least as far as Adam Smith, who correctly concluded that societies, economies, and people all thrive when each individual "intends only his own gain . . . led by an invisible hand to promote an end which was no part of his intention."[a] Many caricature the "invisible hand" as greed anthropomorphized, but in fact, as journalist Daniel Akst put it, Smith "recognized that if commerce is to promote human flourishing, it must be guided not just by unbridled self-interest but by values and a moral imagination."[b] The invisible hand yields to a visible heart for helping humanity. It was in fact Smith's "vision of human flourishing" that "is itself the grounds for his defense of economic liberty."[c]

Edmund Phelps, 2006 Nobel laureate in economics and director of the Center on Capitalism and Society at Columbia University, provides a guide for how proper economic principles in general—and what became known as capitalism in particular—led to the namesake of his book *Mass Flourishing*. In seeking "a new perspective" on the "prosperity of nations," Phelps writes that "the modern economy answers a widespread desire for the good life" and "perfectly illustrated the Aristotelian perspective on the highest good," that of flourishing. Moreover, "flourishing is the heart of prospering," and "prosperity on a national scale comes from the broad involvement of people in the processes of innovation: the conception, development, and spread of new methods and products—indigenous innovation down to the grass roots."[d]

The shift from goods & services, which both Smith and Phelps focus on, to the newly identified economic offerings of

(continued)

experiences and transformations further enabled mass flourishing in recent times and especially will do so into the future.

It's become de rigueur in many circles to decry capitalism and the free-market economy for giving rise to inequality and social injustice—and they most certainly have their ills. But those ills can be traced in considerable measure to one fundamental issue: businesspeople not understanding that capitalism, business, and enterprises exist to foster human flourishing. Despite that, capitalism is the greatest force for human flourishing ever invented. Affluence and the thriving that comes with it have increased astronomically since the Industrial Revolution. Not by capitalism per se, but rather by the innovation to which Phelps refers, and what economist Deirdre McCloskey calls *innovism*—investment not in capital but in knowledge.[e] Among many others to make this point, economist Thomas Sowell put it well: "The cavemen had the same natural resources at their disposal as we have today, and the difference between their standard of living and ours is a difference between the knowledge they could bring to bear on those resources and the knowledge used today."[f]

The knowledge underlying innovism has always been what enables human beings to flourish, first through commodities, then goods and services, then experiences, and now increasingly directly through transformations. Thriving in the emerging Transformation Economy requires creating new economic offerings that directly increase the degree to which people become who they are meant to be.

Notes

a. Adam Smith, *An Inquiry into the Nature and Causes of the Wealth of Nations* (New York: Modern Library, 1994), 485.

b. Daniel Akst, "'Taming the Octopus' and 'The Race to Zero' Review: The Moral Corporation," *Wall Street Journal*, February 16, 2024, https://www.wsj.com/arts-culture/books/taming-the-octopus-and-the-race-to-zero-review-the-moral-corporation-2d4f1cfa.

c. Ryan Patrick Hanley, "Human Flourishing Smith," American Enterprise Institute, October 25, 2016, https://www.aei.org/spotlight-panels/human-flourishing-smith/.

d. Edmund Phelps, *Mass Flourishing: How Grassroots Innovation Created Jobs, Challenge, and Change* (Princeton: Princeton University Press, 2013), 307, 308, and vii, respectively.

e. See Deirdre Nansen McCloskey, "How Growth Happens: Liberalism, Innovism, and the Great Enrichment," Economic History Seminar, Northwestern University, November 29, 2018, https://www.deirdremccloskey.com/docs/pdf/McCloskey_HowGrowthHappens.pdf, and the "The Bourgeois Era trilogy" cited in it. McCloskey further makes the case that it wasn't really an Industrial Revolution but a "Great Enrichment" that improved living standards and flourishing for so many around the world in the 1800s.

f. Thomas Sowell, *Knowledge and Decisions* (New York: Basic Books, 1980), 47. And just consider the gains in knowledge since Sowell wrote that almost five decades ago!

off an employee, you must do everything any community member demands, or you can't make proper trade-offs regarding effects you have on the world. It does mean you should not be underhanded in your dealings, exploit your employees, or attempt to addict people to your offerings. And it means you must recognize that profits are not the goal of your business; human flourishing is. Profits are the measure of how well you contribute to that.

S.C. Johnson & Son has exemplified this view since its founding 140 years ago. Now on its fifth generation of family leadership, its stated purpose is "A Family Company at Work for a Better World."[8] The company articulated its long-held principles as a statement called "This We Believe" in 1976 and hasn't wavered on them since:

> This We Believe states our beliefs about the five groups of people to whom we are responsible and whose trust we must earn . . .
>
> - *Employees:* We believe that the fundamental vitality and strength of our worldwide company lies in our people.

- *Consumers and Users:* We believe in earning the enduring goodwill of consumers and users of our products and services.
- *General Public:* We believe in being a responsible leader within the free market economy.
- *Neighbors and Hosts:* We believe in contributing to the well-being of the countries and communities where we conduct business.
- *World Community:* We believe in improving international understanding.[9]

And S.C. Johnson is a household products company! How much more should transformation guiders be committed to working for a better world? To feel their responsibilities to customers, employees, communities, society, and the planet? To understand that fostering human flourishing is their reason for existence? And then to act as if they truly believed that?

S.C. Johnson has the luxury of being a privately held company. It doesn't have to pay homage to Wall Street. Better than most investment firms, it and other companies focused on human flourishing understand that business is not a quarter-by-quarter game; it's a long-term competition. A competition less against rivals than against short-termism, greed, stagnation, and anything else that lessens the innovation required to make their offerings worth more than the money customers hold. A competition to withstand the gales of creative destruction. A competition to, as my colleague and friend Kim Korn likes to say, resist the temptation to fall into mediocrity and eventually fail, but instead to thrive forever.[10]

Think of Amazon. From its very beginning, Jeff Bezos instilled what he calls a "Day 1" mentality. This mindset includes an extreme obsession with customers and what they need. As he put it in his 2020 letter to shareholders, "There are many advantages to a customer-centric approach, but here's the big one: customers are always beautifully, wonderfully dissatisfied, even when they report being happy and business is great. Even when they don't yet know it, customers want something better, and your desire to delight customers will drive you to invent on their behalf."[11] And even after going public, Amazon never wavered in its long-term focus—five to seven years, not three to five, and certainly not the next quarter.[12]

Truist Bank is another company that proclaims such a purpose: "At Truist, our purpose is to inspire and build better lives and communities. And we do this through real, unwavering care. Care that creates more opportunities, lends a helping hand, and encourages people and businesses to thrive. By living on purpose—and bringing others along on the journey—we can make our world better together."[13]

Perhaps the last kind of industry you'd expect to embrace flourishing would be private equity, investment banking, and other financing enterprises, but at least some such firms recognize that it's not just about the money. Many years ago, I worked with a trust company that catered to the finances of high-net-worth individuals. One of its clients was a professional athlete who led a hardscrabble life until he made it big. As he aged and his kids got into their teens, he became very worried that they would grow up to be entitled snobs. The trust executive told me they spent as much time on ensuring that the kids grew up well as on the family's finances.

Many capital firms go even further in making human flourishing core to their business. A sample:

- Wildwood Ventures, which focuses on "building and investing in human technology businesses that bring life to the full" and that addresses "America's health and wellness crisis for greater physical, mental, social and spiritual wellbeing."[14]

- Eventide Asset Management, whose tagline is "Investing that makes the world rejoice."[15]
- Commonwealth Impact Investing, which "harnesses the same entrepreneurial talent that creates wealth to create more opportunity for everyone to flourish."[16]

Monon Capital LLC, whose chair and founder, Doug Wilson, told me that the company "starts with need rather than returns" and has a forty- to fifty-year time horizon on its investments. Its "foundation is engaging with partners so that we lift people above profit, celebrate imagination over habit, and invest in futures that outlast quick returns." Monon fulfills this mission in part by investing substantially in a $100 million, 28-acre master-planned community in Carmel, Indiana, called the North End. It's a mixed-use community with light agriculture/manufacturing, retail, and restaurants, in addition to a 200-unit apartment complex and a 240-unit senior living facility, with over five acres of green space. A central element of the apartment building is a set-aside of forty of the units for people with intellectual and developmental disabilities. Wilson said,

> [Each of these businesses] were invited to become part of this community because of the unique ways they contribute to its flourishing. Rather than owning property, they lease it—an intentional structure designed to ensure their presence supports and aligns with the broader purpose of this place. We use the term "business resident" rather than "lessee" to invite a more expansive imagination—one in which their role includes actively building and sustaining a shared vision of loving our neighbors well.

Whatever your business is, your economic offerings almost certainly foster human flourishing, at least to some extent. The higher up the Progression of Economic Value you go, the more you can do for your customers, and the more economic value you create with your enterprise. When you think about the highest level of being in the business of guiding transformations, think simultaneously about how your offerings could better enable your customers to flourish, how the thriving of your employees can better make that happen, and how both of those contribute to the blossoming of the communities in which you operate, of society overall, and even of the planet.

As you do, you'll find it beneficial to better understand the territory of transformations, how exactly they foster human flourishing.

The Spheres of Transformation

Any enterprise in the business of helping people become healthy, wealthy, and wise (as the proverb says) is in the transformation business, as each of these represent different ways in which we aspire to flourish.[17] "Accidents" of birth—DNA, country, year—greatly affect your starting point and your potential for becoming healthier, wealthier, and wiser, but progress on each of these aspirations drives people to higher and higher degrees of flourishing.

These qualities express what I call a *sphere* of the Transformation Economy, a sector comprising all the companies focused on similar endeavors, business opportunities, and properties of flourishing. They each encompass huge swaths of businesses and their economic offerings, overlap to a point, and will expand over time as more and more of them embrace the value to be gained in guiding people in achieving their aspirations.

However, the straightforward phrase "healthy, wealthy, and wise" does not go near far enough in describing the opportunities in the emerging Transformation Economy. It's not just about staying healthy; it's about having *health & well-being*. It's not just about becoming wealthy; it's about having *wealth & prosperity*.

FIGURE 2-1

The four spheres of transformation

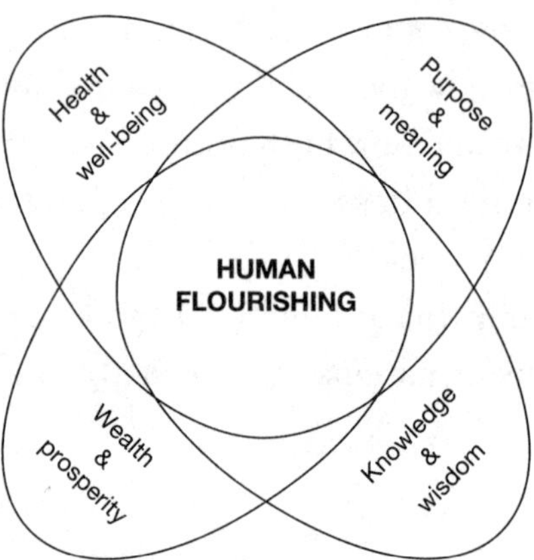

And it's not just about being wise; it's about having *knowledge & wisdom.* Additionally, I'll add one more: *purpose & meaning.* In fact, this is the most important sphere within the Transformation Economy, the one without which we simply cannot flourish. (See figure 2-1.) Let's go through each in turn.

Health & Well-Being

The health-care industry perhaps most clearly comprises companies in the transformation business. No one interacts with a health-care system unless they want to go (at the most basic level) from sick to well, to find out if they are impaired or injured, or to avoid falling ill in the first place.

We value the transformational benefits of health care to a much greater extent than most other offerings, and also much more highly than we used to, in part because of improvements in medicine in the past century. Again, it's about time. Fundamentally, we value our time in this world so much more than in the ancient past, when life was nasty, brutish, and short; the distant past, when we worked more, had less leisure time, and didn't live as long; and even the near past, when we had yet to shift into the Experience Economy, with its ability to fill our time engagingly. We don't want to be sick, encumbered by injury, or otherwise unable to fully enjoy all the experiences that offer us time well spent, nor do we want to be incapable of investing in the transformations that enable us to flourish.

Note how each of the health factors in the last sentence is negatively stated. Health care primarily involves returning us from negative circumstances to positive ones. More and more, though, we desire higher levels of not just health per se, but well-being. Well-being encompasses the positive circumstances of and within ourselves that let us enjoy life and all the experiences—economic and noneconomic—afforded to us in this world. In other words, to flourish.

The general aspiration for well-being drives consumers to increasingly pay out of their own pockets for such offerings. Here I don't mean copays, Medicare Advantage policies, or insurance add-ons. I'm talking about paying for massages and spas; fitness centers and personal trainers; yoga, meditation, and tai chi; health and wellness coaches; medical tourism and transformational travel; and on and on the list could go. And that's not to mention devices such as Fitbit, Apple Watch, Oura, and Whoop, nor apps such as Noom, Aura, Calm, and Hallow, which allow us to track elements of our well-being and improve them.

Such apps and devices aren't full transformation offerings, but they are transformation*al*, an element that individuals can bring into their life to have greater health & well-being. Many companies recognize the value in this, with fast-food chain Chipotle selling "lifestyle bowls" that it describes as "feel good, taste good, are good"; cosmetics retailer Rituals adding spas to its stores; and CVS shifting from pharmacies to health and wellness services, such as clinics under the brand CVS Healthspire.[18]

HEALTH & WELL-BEING: This sphere encompasses all of health care, including hospitals, clinics, doctors, pharmaceuticals, medical devices, and everything else—not just transformations themselves but commodities, goods, services, and experiences—involved in the diagnosis, treatment, and care people need to deal with, recover from, and even prevent illnesses, injuries, or conditions. It also includes activities having nothing to do with illnesses or injuries but contributing to the ongoing condition of people across factors physical and mental, emotional and social, things tied to life quality and contentment. Such well-being offerings that facilitate human flourishing—although often sold as experiences, not transformations—include spas, fitness centers, classes, therapists, coaches, and mind-body practices such as meditation, mindfulness, yoga, and tai chi.

Other companies are innovating new-to-the-world transformations in this sphere. Equinox has expanded from fitness clubs to not only spas and "regenerative" hotels but a longevity program, called Optimize by Equinox, for which it charges a tidy annual fee. Remedy Place is a social club focused on "enhancing your health and social life through human connection and self-care."[19] Corvas Brinkerhoff, cofounder of immersive art company Meow Wolf, is creating an entirely new form of public bath house, called Submersive, focused on being therapeutic, "an exploration of what's possible when art, science, and human connection come together to transform lives," as he puts it.[20]

Health & well-being is easily the largest sphere of the Transformation Economy. It includes everything people buy to achieve health outcomes and have greater well-being, such as the transformational elements and full transformation offerings above. As delineated in the box, it also includes all the experiences, services, goods, and even commodities subsumed within transformations. Transformation guiders must integrate these together into their offerings to effect the change desired by their customers, though many people, as we saw in chapter 1, use them piecemeal, acting as their own general contractors to achieve their aspirations.

There isn't a firm line as to what constitutes health and what constitutes well-being, but on the whole, health is the means to which well-being is the end. Where health care is largely objective, well-being is largely subjective. Health care commonly treats the disease or condition; well-being proactively impacts one's whole life. And, in general, if someone else pays for it directly, it's about health care. If you pay, it's much more likely to be about well-being.

Wealth & Prosperity

Wealth is the domain of banks, credit unions, wealth management, and other firms that go in the general category of financial service providers. Financial firms ostensibly are in the transformation business, fulfilling aspirations people (and businesses) have for money, and especially for what wealth can do for them. But few such firms recognize this. They all seem to describe their offerings with the phrase "products and services," so often pronounced as if it were a six-syllable word: "productsandservices." All such enterprises should banish that term—as well as the phrase "financial *services*"—from their vocabulary and instead recognize the value in offering financial transformations.

People value wealth precisely because it enables most everything they want to have, benefit from, experience, and be. Money is a means to an end. If financial firms ascertained and offered the *ends*, rather than merely advising on the *means*, they would create so much more value. But they must understand the *why* of each individual aspirant, the reasons they desire to increase and use wealth. Such aspirations include having a new child, affording a house, renovating a home, taking an annual vacation, covering college tuition for the kids, starting a business, caring for parents, and retiring, with every specific aspiration as individual as the person—or family or business—desiring it.

Unfortunately, the endemic mindset of the industry focuses companies on their productsandservices rather than the desires, needs, and aspirations of their customers. If they instead were customer-focused, they could both charge more for their existing offerings and create many more to supply the outcomes customers truly desire.

Now, there may be no sectors more regulated than banking and insurance, and wealth management can't be far behind. If you're in one of these industries—and if your business solely focuses on the commodity of money, then "industry" is an appropriate term—you probably can't imagine how you could get around regulations in order to focus on aspirations, as more than one person has told me. Well, I'm no financial regulations expert, but I do know that if you don't move beyond productsandservices, you will eventually be commoditized and become a supplier to those that form relationships with people based on their aspirations rather than their money.

You can start by creating sister firms or partnering with those that recognize your clients as aspirants and offer them the achievement of their aspirations while you focus on their wealth. I worked with one wealth management firm, for example, that partnered with Carefull, a financial safety fintech that protects people—especially seniors—from fraud, scams, identity theft, and even their own mistakes. The company incorporates its capabilities into the offerings of wealth advisers, banks, credit unions, and insurers, and lets them handle the relationship with clients. As Todd Rovak, CEO and cofounder, told me, "In addition to the benefit of clients who are and feel financially safe, it helps financial advisers have conversations with their clients that they never otherwise would, treating them holistically as human beings.

WEALTH & PROSPERITY: This sphere begins with the entirety of so-called financial services, including banks, credit unions, credit cards, payments, insurance, investments, brokers, wealth management, and everything else related to financial instruments, as well as tax planning and preparation, accounting, and real estate. In other words, basically anything that has to do with money. But not solely money, for the sphere offers myriad ways for what gives us human beings prosperity—what gives us a good life. The possibilities here are innumerable but include hobbies, sports, and other leisure pursuits; family, friends, and socializing; freedom, liberty, and peace. To be even shorter: prosperity is a life lived well. A life full of experiences (both economic and personal) that enable us to flourish.

And they include in those conversations and extend the relationship to the next generation of clients, those who do or will care for their parents, who so often go elsewhere after inheriting money."

Of course, financial safety—plus financial stability and money management skills—provides the bare minimum for shifting to wealth transformations. Recall all the aspiration topics given above: children, homes, vacations, businesses, parents, retirement, plus many more you could think of. What kinds of conversations would such topics engender, what types of goals would they elicit, and what sorts of differences would they make in gaining, managing, and growing the accounts, portfolios, and insurance policies that would ensure aspirants have ways to achieve their aspirations across these arenas?

The umbrella term for such beyond-money aspirations is *prosperity.* In thinking about prosperity, consider the Hebrew word *shalom.* Its primary meaning, of course, is "peace," but from biblical times to today it's been used as a greeting or salutation to mean "Peace be upon you," wishing someone to have a nice life, to be prosperous. There's certainly some overlap between prosperity and the previous sphere's well-being, which simply means that human flourishing can be approached from many different angles. And you can have such prosperity at whatever socioeconomic level you are at. It is not the sole province of the rich, nor is helping people with their wealth the bailiwick solely of those who consider themselves to be in financial services today.

Look at how Apple, Amazon, and Walmart all moved into these businesses, catering to people across the socioeconomic spectrum. Of the latter two in particular, think also of how much money they save families—almost certainly yours included—because of their relentless focus on bringing down the costs of retail goods, money that you can spend on experiences & transformations or whatever else it is that you desire for you and your family. Over Walmart's more than sixty-year existence, think of the millions of families that benefited from shopping there to help them afford to send their kids to college, buy a better home, retire early, or build the wealth required to achieve their personal aspirations for prosperity, however they defined it.

Pundits already view Walmart, Amazon, and Apple as disrupters in health care and financial productsandservices. The myriad other companies innovating new technologies and economic offerings are, potentially, too. They further increase the competition—and chances of commoditization—for those who still view themselves as being in financial services rather than the transformation business.

Recognize that, as with all the spheres, the first term in *wealth & prosperity* leads to the second. Where wealth is largely objective, prosperity is largely subjective. Financial firms manage money; prosperity impacts the life of the individual and family, and in B2B it impacts the core concerns of the business. In general, if the conversation starts with money, it's about financial services. If it starts with you, it's much more likely to be about prosperity.

Knowledge & Wisdom

Education is also fundamentally a transformation industry. Parents have aspirations for the education of their children, from preschool to elementary school to high school to (often) college, each one a stage in the progression from childhood to adulthood. They may pay for many classes, courses, and programs outside of school based on the personal interests and tastes of their kids and themselves. Governments have great interest in transforming citizens into productive and contributing members of society through education, spending a lot of money to do so. Education affords individuals—as people, as consumers, as workers—greater possibilities for their futures as their knowledge grows. They want actionable knowledge and practical wisdom that actually improves their lives, that fulfills their aspirations for learning, working, living, and being.

Wisdom is not about acquiring knowledge in and of itself; it is about the outcomes we derive from that knowledge in our lives, outcomes that yield flourishing. It's about applying what we learn with perspective and judgment, about shifting from knowing to doing. Wisdom is not the sole realm of the learned—scholars, academics, experts, intellectuals, and the like. Everyone seeks knowledge that improves their work, home life, and relationships with families and friends. Over time that practical knowledge turns into principles, applications, and decisions that reflect everyday know-how.

Knowledge & wisdom is the proper, most expansive name for this sphere of transformation, of helping people gain knowledge, turn it into wisdom, and thereby reap an impact on their lives. It's what education, however gained, is for.

Consider Cardinal Kung Academy in Stamford, Connecticut, which offers a classical Catholic high school education. Unlike at many private schools, attendance is not seen as just a rung on the ladder to success. As principal Alexander Miller says, "Most high schools are designed to quantify student achievement, so it's easily digested by college admissions departments. Ours isn't like that. Ours is geared toward student flourishing, which doesn't lend itself to quantification."[21]

This sphere isn't just about the intellectual; we gain knowledge & wisdom outside of formal education, including the kinetic/embodied, know-how, emotional, and other forms of experiential learning. For example, I am the least handy person you will ever meet. (Well, almost. My wife once entered me into a Home Depot contest for "least handy husband" and, somehow, I didn't win.) But even I have learned to fix and install a few things around the house by watching YouTube videos. Others use such content as a springboard to become experts, and some of them then post their own videos filled with practical wisdom.

Consider Fender Musical Instruments Corporation, known for its guitars. Many people buy a guitar to learn how to play it as a hobby, but after fits and starts, the instrument just gathers dust. So in 2017 Fender created an app with thousands of its own song-based video lessons that enabled people to quickly play the music they listen to and then advance their skills. The fee-based program took off during the Covid-19 pandemic, with subscribers and guitar sales exploding. As Paul Dunn and Ronald Baker explain in their book about subscription pricing, "Ultimately, Fender understood it wasn't selling guitars—it was selling the ability to play them—*musicianship*."[22]

Wisdom derives from knowledge, just as knowledge derives from information. Knowledge is *experiential information*, intelligence gained from and applied through experiences. And knowledge & wisdom necessarily reside in the brains of human beings. If something can be represented in symbols—or *codified*, residing

---

KNOWLEDGE & WISDOM: This sphere involves everything having to do with education, and not just formal education in schools at any level (public, private, or parochial), but tutoring, teaching, and training wherever and whenever it might occur, whether in classes or outside of them, in physical environments or online, at home, at work, or out in the world. It's not just about facts, figures, and bits of information; it should go far beyond that. Knowledge requires an understanding that is learned from and applied to experience, including the kinetic/embodied, know-how, and emotional. Wisdom comes from the ability to apply the proper aspects of knowledge to situations in the right way, making appropriate, effective, and impactful decisions that advance flourishing. This sphere usually, therefore, requires not just parents and instructors but mentors, coaches, advisers, and guides. In addition to education, the sphere of knowledge & wisdom includes companies and professions in libraries, publishing, legal, accounting, many creative businesses (including experience and transformation design), and management consulting.

---

in computer code—and embedded with context in technology (from books to computers to AI), then it is neither wisdom nor knowledge until someone reads, absorbs, and learns from it. It's mere data, which with context becomes information, pure and simple, no matter how "artificial intelligently" it might be derived. (Artificial intelligence should really be called IA, *intelligent augmentation.* IA helps us gain wisdom & knowledge, while alleviating us from lower-order work.)[23]

Knowledge is the means to which wisdom is the end. Where knowledge is largely objective, wisdom is largely subjective. Education institutions focus too much on imparting instruction rather than impacting lives, as all who understand they are in the sphere of knowledge & wisdom should be doing. And in general, if it involves the acquisition of intelligence, it's about knowledge; if it involves application of that knowledge, it's about wisdom.

Purpose & Meaning

The final sphere of transformation is *purpose & meaning.* These have been enormous factors in human flourishing throughout history. People not only desire but *need* to have meaning in their lives; it is core to who we are. And it is often in fulfilling our purpose that we gain meaning.

Meaning is innate to being human, and a sphere in which people commonly seek transformation. Without it, people perish, as the psychologist and Holocaust survivor Dr. Viktor Frankl made clear in his seminal book *Man's Search for Meaning.*[24] He found that the primary determination of which Jews survived concentration camps during World War II and which did not was whether they found meaning even amid the most depraved of circumstances imaginable. He further argued that "the quest for meaning is the key to mental health and human flourishing."[25]

In Abraham Maslow's famous hierarchy of needs, the highest-order one is self-actualization, which he wrote "might be phrased as the desire to become more and more what one is, to become everything that one is capable of becoming."[26] In other words, self-actualization is all about flourishing through transformation. The lowest-order need is the physiological, particularly the body's need to maintain itself through food and water, and above that comes safety, then love, and above that esteem, before reaching the level of self-actualization. But Frankl argued that meaning is in fact the essential, basic, lowest-order need, one for which we often require guidance.

Human beings have long gained meaning from religion and spirituality through organizations including churches, synagogues, mosques, temples, and all other places of worship.[27] Despite the transformational benefits, these organizations are not by nature businesses—although many operate as such (and parachurches—separate entities operating alongside churches—often are)—and I hesitate to suggest they should be run by the principles of a business book.

There is no doubt, however, that people seek and gain transformations from religion. As the late novelist David Foster Wallace said in a 2005 commencement address at Kenyon College, "In the day-to day trenches of adult life, there is actually no such thing as atheism. There is no such thing as not worshipping. Everybody worships. The only choice we get is *what* to worship."[28] Who or what you worship and serve gives your life meaning. So choose carefully.

People do find meaning in many other pursuits, though, especially in family and other relationships. What we buy, use, and experience also reflects our individual searches for meaning. And we often look to businesses as well. Think of companies that offer a percentage of profits to charitable organizations, or products made from recycled goods for those more sustainably minded. Each of these areas offers opportunities to contribute to meaning and purpose for customers.

Given how much time they spend at work, people of course find meaning in their occupations too. Work has a certain dignity, being a core element of what it means to be human. Helping employees discover and act on their personal sense of purpose benefits them not just as workers but as people. Think back to the statements from S.C. Johnson, Truist, and even the investment companies. In addition to providing lasting value for customers, such *meaningful*

PURPOSE & MEANING: The most obvious category in this sphere is family, relationships, and communities. People also seek to define and live out their purpose & meaning through myriad other means, including religious organizations; memberships and affiliations; contributions of money and time; what they buy, use, and experience; and, certainly not least, work. People seek flourishing from this sphere via guidance from pastors, spiritual advisers, gurus, counselors, coaches, shamans, mentors, elders, and so forth.

purpose statements, when implemented well, can give work meaning for employees, and thereby help them flourish.

In general, if it entails how you impact the world, it's about purpose; if it entails how the world impacts you, it's about meaning. Purpose & meaning thus go hand in hand. As with each of the spheres of transformation, the first term is the means to which the second term is the end. Health is the means of well-being. Wealth is the means of prosperity. Knowledge is the means of wisdom. And purpose is the means of meaning.

Embracing the Spheres

If your enterprise fits anywhere among the four spheres of transformation, then you need to think about how you design and depict transformations, how you create and guide them, how you help customers achieve their aspirations and thereby flourish. And if you do not already guide transformations today, consider how you can bring one or more of these spheres into your business, extending your offerings—commodities, goods, services, or experiences—into transformations focused on why people buy whatever you sell today.

You might find that at least some of your business(es) have elements that lend themselves to guiding transformations across one or more of the spheres. Even if you never sell transformations per se, you can contribute to human flourishing by being transformation*al* through offerings that guiders or customers themselves can integrate into a full-fledged transformation. Consider just some of the possibilities: In commodities, organic produce can boost health & well-being, while working the land can help in finding purpose & meaning. In goods, financial instruments help attain wealth & prosperity, while books—nonfiction and self-help volumes among them—assist with gaining knowledge & wisdom. In services, banks, credits cards, and financial apps help attain wealth & prosperity, while classes, videos, and tutoring support knowledge & wisdom. And in experiences, fitness centers, spas, and yoga boost health & well-being, while religious gatherings, retreats, and communal memberships help with finding purpose & meaning.

Remember, too, the Progression of Economic Value: each offering subsumes the ones below it. Transformations are only ever guided through experiences; experiences are staged atop service activities; services are delivered using physical goods; and goods are manufactured out of commodities. You and your business can contribute at any of these levels, and can contribute more effectively and create more value by recognizing the outcomes for which people buy your offerings. The greatest opportunities lie in shifting up to guiding transformations as your economic offering.

Moreover, you need not confine yourself to any one sphere. Intentionally embracing multiple spheres and doing so more fully can magnify the value of what you sell. For example, the Massachusetts Institute of Technology embraces all four spheres with its Whole Student initiative. In the university's quarterly *Spectrum* publication, chancellor Melissa Nobles speaks of it this way: "There are three key elements in our approach: supporting academic success, fostering community and well-being, and cultivating personal and intellectual growth. We want students to gain a deeper understanding of themselves and the world around them as they drink from the proverbial MIT firehose. We help them uncover new passions and embrace new experiences as they learn to care for themselves physically, emotionally, and spiritually."[29]

Right there you can see health & well-being, knowledge & wisdom, and purpose & meaning. In terms of wealth & prosperity, Nobles adds that MIT seeks "to ensure that an individual's financial situation does not create a barrier to experiencing all that MIT has to offer."[30] While the initiative is new, embracing the spheres of transformation is not, for as she says, "We are building on decades of transformative work across MIT seeking to improve the student experience and ensuring academics and research, especially in science and technology."[31]

As you endeavor to shift up to guiding transformations, simultaneously work to identify your enterprise within these four spheres, somewhere. If you see opportunities in more than one—great! After all, the four overlap and support each other. Knowledge enables prosperity. Prosperity facilitates well-being. Wealth and health govern and influence the pursuit of purpose. Having that purpose fuels the pursuit of wisdom, engenders well-being, and shapes a personal sense of what it means to be prosperous. And around and around we could go.

For again, at the intersection of the four spheres, at their very heart, lies their shared commonality: they together foster human flourishing. They are what business is for.

REFLECTION

Think about human flourishing as the raison d'être of business and how it flows through the four spheres of transformation, and then reflect on these questions:

- How is your business today contributing to human flourishing? Are there any ways in which you are detracting from it?
- No matter the level of your current offerings, where are you operating in the four spheres of transformation? How can you intensify, deepen, or expand your offerings in your current sphere(s) of operation?
- Where might you provide value for current or new customers in one or more of the other spheres?

PREPARATION

Now that you understand the great opportunities to contribute to human flourishing by guiding transformations, let's take a moment to understand aspirants and their aspirations more fully. Before reading chapter 3, ask yourself these questions:

- How would you describe your current customer mix? Do you sell directly to individual customers (B2C), to other businesses (B2B), or something else?
- Put yourself in your customers' shoes. *Why* do people buy from you? What are their aspirations, and what are the transformations they desire?
- What might cause customers to have those aspirations? What might contribute to their desire to transform?

3

UNDERSTANDING ASPIRANTS AND ASPIRATIONS

All transformation is identity change. Which is strange, if you think about it, for the word "identity" comes from a Latin root meaning "same" and is closely related to the term "identical." By definition, an identity can't change.[1]

And there is a sense in which you are the same as you were a decade ago, as a youth, as a child, even at birth. Some essence of *you* never wavers. For instance, the expression "You can take the boy out of the country, but you can't take the country out of the boy" (said perhaps disparagingly of someone else, and with pride about oneself) speaks to unchanging identity.

What we're really talking about with transformation offerings, though—with their economic distinction of being fundamentally individual—is a change in *self-identity*.[2] In how you, as an individual, describe your own being. This concept of a sense of self is how *Psychology Today* defines the term: "Identity encompasses the memories, experiences, relationships, and values that create one's sense of self. This amalgamation creates a steady sense of who one is over time, even as new facets are developed and incorporated into one's identity."[3] I love how Suzy Ross, transformation expert and professor at San Jose State University, expresses identity, calling it "all the ways you can complete the statement 'I am . . .'"[4] How many ways can you complete it? Scores, hundreds, probably thousands if you thought about it long enough.

A transformation, then, occurs any time you can complete the statement "I was X, now I am Y." The Y of how you now think about yourself is often expressed with adjectives: "I am fit," "I am not sick," "I am generous," and so forth. (You can easily imagine which X words would precede these in a transformation statement.) But it might also be done with nouns: "I am a gardener," "I am a sailor," "I am a vegan," "I am an optician," "I am a pianist." Since our agency and our sense of self are very intertwined, people often use agent nouns to express identity. And we often use adjectives to express the extent, degree, or level to which we have an identity: "I am an avid gardener," "I am a novice sailor," "I am a committed vegan," "I am an excellent optician," "I am a professional pianist."

Of course, we can complete the transformation statement in ways that do not signify lasting change or that regard trivial matters: "I was tired, now I am energized," "I was cold, now I am warm." Such prosaic changes do not rise to the level of the economic. They represent changes in *state*, not changes in being.

Those changes that do denote a lasting, significant shift in being, however, always involve some aspect of identity. It may be a central aspect of self, some part of your essence that no longer works for your current life, as so often happens when beginning a new life stage, such as becoming an adolescent, heading to college, entering the workforce, getting married, becoming a parent, going through a midlife crisis, or retiring. It may be an attitude, behavior, or action that you wish to change. It may be your values. Maybe even your mindset, worldview, or personal purpose of why you exist.

Transformations within each of these aspects can lead to greater flourishing in your life, but they can be difficult to achieve on your own. People so often need help, someone to guide them through the shift from X to Y.

In order to effect such transformations within your customers, you need to know much more about them, aspirant by aspirant and aspiration by aspiration. This chapter, then, focuses on understanding who your customers are (the X) and what they aspire to become (the Y).

Varieties of Aspirants

Ask yourself, Who are you guiding? There are in fact four varieties of aspirants for which you can guide transformations:

- *People:* Individual consumers, employees, or members of a community
- *Businesses:* Enterprises, including such entities as nonprofits, religious establishments, and governmental institutions
- *Organizations:* A set of employees with a collective identity within a business or other institution
- *Communities:* Groups not affiliated with any of the businesses above, such as associations, neighborhoods, and other sets of loosely affiliated people, scaling up to include societies, countries, and the world

While most examples I've described thus far have been of guiding human beings who aspire to transform themselves, not all aspirants are individual people—those are but one variety, though a very common one. Anyone who comes to you with a goal to change themselves falls into this category. Most businesses cater specifically to this group and stop there.

But companies also have aspirations and need guidance in transforming themselves. This provides the entire basis of the consulting industry and many others that work to help enterprises become better businesses, including outsourcing, banking, and technology. Think of it as the *new biz* business, where companies can help their B2B customers become organizationally healthy, financially fit, wise in how they approach their objectives and customers, and purposeful in how they operate.

Indeed, every company that sells to other companies should be on the lookout for transformation opportunities. No customer buys your offering—whether a piece of equipment, hours of a consultant's time, or facilitation of a team-building offsite—for the offering itself. It is always a means to an end. Sell the *end*—operational efficiency, the new strategic direction the consultant helps you develop, or better relationships between team members—rather than the *means,* and you will both transform your customers and gain greater economic value.

As one B2B example, Flavorman—a beverage consultancy that has created over seventy-four thousand beverage formulations, including for Jones Soda, Ocean Spray, and Sunsweet Growers—saw an opportunity in the growing market for craft beers and spirits. So in 2013 Flavorman created Moonshine University to teach entrepreneurs about distilling methods and running a business. Up to thirty people at a time can enroll in a five-day distilling course, and attendees have opened close to two hundred distilleries, many of which in turn became clients.[5]

B2B2C models also offer possibilities for transformations, where businesses help other businesses help their consumers flourish. Symplany is a plan-driven investing company that supports financial advisers in guiding their clients to become prosperous. Founded by chief strategist Jeff Landt and CEO Alex Korn, with my friend and colleague Kim Korn as the chair of the board, Symplany is the rare company that explicitly recognizes that it fosters human flourishing as well as starting at the topmost, transformation level of the Progression of Economic Value, only then designing the experiences and services required for its business model and offerings. The company transforms the practices of advisers by enabling them to instantly show their clients, in both data and visualizations, how they would fare financially under various circumstances using the Symplany Indicator, a number representing the viability of a plan to meet a client's wealth & prosperity aspirations. When someone sees how their assets could optimally be invested in support of their spending needs and legacy objectives, synchronized year by year, it yields understanding and confidence in the credibility and integrity of the process. The conversation then leaps over the conventional discussion of investment selections and instead focuses on envisioning the opportunities the client's means make possible. The advisers help people discover and act on the aspirations they have for themselves, their families, and their legacies, guiding them with real, valuable, and illuminating information that supports their life-changing decisions.

When your aspirants are businesses, all the ideas, principles, and frameworks in this book still apply. Recognize that companies have a vested interest in not only the capabilities of their employees, but also their health & well-being so they can apply those capabilities; their wealth & prosperity so they desire this particular employment; their knowledge & wisdom so they can perform, innovate, and improve the business; and their purpose & meaning, which nurture intrinsic motivation and advance organizational alignment.[6]

Accomplishing the transformations for which businesses so often hire consultants almost always requires altering not just the business itself but the organization, the third kind of aspirant. Being an assembly of individual employees with a collective identity (often framed as "culture" or "DNA"), the organization is not the same as the business. Organizational transformation often must precede business transformation, especially when an organization seeks its own preservation rather than that of its customers.[7] So while businesses do desire transformations to be better equipped for changing times and new opportunities, often they must first pursue remedial transformations when the organization is too bureaucratic, sclerotic, and product-centric to become open, agile, and customer-centric.

BetterUp, for example, offers customized coaching, immersive learning, and personal insights to enterprises, particularly when undergoing a business transformation. Billing itself as "the Human Transformation Platform," its work for learning and development departments draws on a transformative journey model, a three-stage framework of "learning to doing to being."[8] It works with B2B aspirants to determine what employee coaching would best position the organization to effectively transform, and then employees use its app to select a personal coach to help them in their own particular circumstances.

Communities form the final variety of aspirants and can scale from neighborhoods to societies. People buy 4ocean bracelets not because they are special in and of themselves, but because the organization promises that each purchase enables it to remove five pounds of trash from the ocean, making people feel like a part of a community that cares for the environment and does something about it. Dutch consulting and design agency includi specializes in turning public settings into third places. Its design of the youth library Deichman Biblo Tøyen and its sister library Deichman Tøyen helped rejuvenate the Gamle district of Oslo, Norway, aiming to overcome high vacancy rates and adverse social issues while attracting new businesses such as coffee shops, bakeries, and creative enterprises. As founder Aat Vos told me, "The transformative power of third places is evident in the impacts they have on users, cultural and social organizations, and society as a whole. Inclusive and dynamic third places foster social cohesion, economic revitalization, and community well-being."

Or consider Dignity Made, a company that sells coconut oil for cooking and other purposes. Its stated aim is to help coconut farmers and their communities in the Philippines. Founders Stephen Freed and the late Don Byker did Christian missionary work in the country and were astounded by the scale of human trafficking and other ills, crimes so prevalent in the least developed areas of the world. They met parents, for example, who felt they needed to sell their daughters into slavery or online sexual exploitation to have enough money to get out of debt and feed their families. Selling the family farm and having no income isn't a much better choice, nor is leaving the family to get work elsewhere, which itself often leads to abuse and exploitation.

As Freed told me, "It was an economic problem, and it needed an economic solution." What the communities lacked were jobs—good-paying, local jobs. The one plentiful thing in the area was coconuts, so Freed and Byker's team built a coconut factory. Dignity Made—its purpose right there in the name—was born with "the heart of a nonprofit" and committed to buying the coconuts of local farmers at a fair price, turning them into coconut oil and selling them around the globe.

And it worked. CEO Erik Olson told me that the efforts transformed several rural villages, with the company supplied by over 150 thriving farms, some families of which now send their daughters to high school and even to college. The company employs more than 110 people in the factory and in distribution, with weekly work and life skills training. Some employees and neighbors have even started their own businesses to support the factory workers, including general stores, restaurants, and building material suppliers. Olson summed up the community transformation by relaying that "2,200 families are healthier through clean water and multiple medical and dental clinics—many adults say it's their first time seeing a doctor. After super typhoons and Covid, they are stronger because we rebuilt 336 homes, gave food and cash to farmers who lost crops, planted 26,000 trees, and gave a total of 250,000 pounds of rice from house to house."

What's more, each jar of coconut oil sold comes with a transformation story. Customers can scan a QR code and learn of how they, thanks to their purchase and those of thousands of others, made a material difference in people's lives.

Dignity Made explicitly went into business to help communities in the Philippines. Based on the most prevalent local commodity, it created physical goods (its factory, not to mention its coconut oil offerings), service activities (employment, distribution, etc.), and experiences (training, community events, etc.) to transform a local community from poverty to flourishing.

Of course, that community didn't pay for its transformation; it wasn't the company's customer but its *mission*. By definition, customers are the ones who pay you money—but they are not the only ones for whom you can guide transformations. Often customers have aspirations for someone else and are willing to pay for a transformation for such a beneficiary. Parents, for instance, often pay on behalf of their children, whether for tutoring, tae kwon do classes, or guitar lessons. Businesses pay for employees to take courses to learn new skills, take time off to enhance their well-being, and even take retirement.[9] Learning and development departments exist solely for employee transformations, with benefits to the enterprise in higher-skilled employees and to the workers themselves in gaining knowledge and abilities to further their careers.[10] In all such situations where a customer hires you to transform a beneficiary, recognize that you must satisfy *both* parties, guiding the beneficiary in achieving the aspiration—no matter who originated it—while meeting the desires of the one who's paying for it.

People flourish alongside other people, as part of organizations, inside businesses, and within communities. No matter what business you are in, whatever genre of economic offering you sell is for one or more of these varieties. And pretty much every customer you have today aspires to change one or more aspects of who they are. By shifting up the Progression of Economic Value to guide transformations, you can foster human flourishing both individually and collectively. You can lead businesses in thriving. And you can help communities blossom.

Catalysts for Change

Aspirants across these categories perceive something in themselves that they want to change, formulate an aspiration to define that change, and, if they need help in making it happen, hire a business to guide them, creating economic opportunities.

Which raises a question: Where do aspirations come from? Understanding the catalyst for the desire to transform helps you design the right transformation offerings, and can even spark aspirations that people, organizations, businesses, and communities decide they would like to achieve.[11]

Major changes are perhaps most often instigated and planned by aspirants themselves. Such *directed* catalysts include going to college, getting a job or joining the military, and getting married, or in the world of business, entering a new market, becoming more agile, or acquiring another company. You recognize that you want change, and initiate, plan, and go on a transformation journey that is completed long after its instigation.

While emotions remain significant in every decision, you generally need to make more of an intellectual pitch to directed aspirants to show you have what it takes to get them to the other side. Having a point of view about *how* aspirants should change, as management consultants typically do, can be of great benefit.

But directed transformations are not the only way people are pushed to change. My research reveals three other catalysts, as seen in figure 3-1: disruptions, deviations, and discovery.

Many transformations that people undergo are catalyzed by a shock or trauma in their lives.[12] On the personal side, such disruptions could include a diagnosis of heart disease or other health scare, a death in the family, or the loss of a job. In business, it could be a

FIGURE 3-1

Catalysts for change

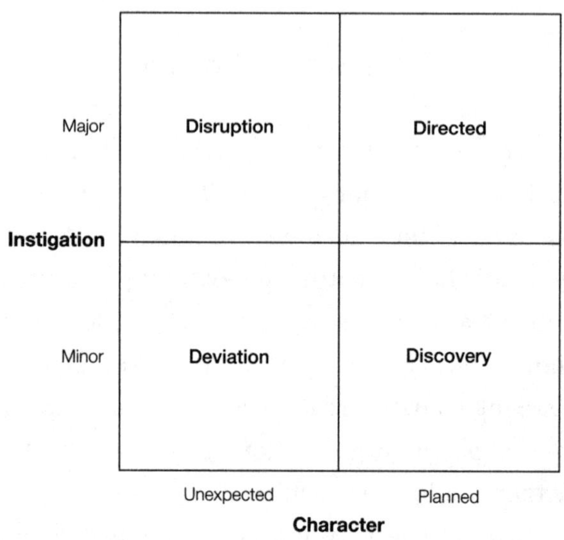

large financial hit, being sued for illegal trade practices, or disruptive innovation in an industry. These may seem to come out of the blue and can prove to be of enough magnitude to change how we live or manage, often instantly. If we then don't let the disruption just happen to us but take control of it and transform positively, we can use the event as a force for good—for us, our family or friends, our organization or business, our community, even society at large.

With disruptions, think about referring to aspirations not with the typical *from/to* statements but with *transforming/into* statements, such as transforming pain into purpose, devastation into determination, or distress into opportunity. The goal should be not just eliminating the effects of the disruption, but working through them to find a new, higher level of flourishing, especially in finding meaning in it.

Also unexpected are *deviation* catalysts, when something happens to you, often suddenly, as you go about your everyday life, and ends up stimulating an aspiration. Deviations include such seemingly minor events as seeing a TV show that inspires you to modify your behavior, finding a book in the library that shifts your thinking, or meeting someone at a coffee shop who opens up a new pursuit. Professionally, deviations could be an unexpected promotion or stretch opportunity, research that changes how you approach a project, or the proverbial watercooler conversation (or Slack interaction).

A deviation catalyst might immediately spark desire, but it may take a while for the aspiration to form, and even longer for the person to seek help from a transformation guider. When the aspiration does come, it may still be ill formed, so collaborate with the person to draw out its nature and extent, resulting in a concrete, individual from/to statement. Also be careful not to scare off aspirants with too grandiose a transformation plan. Over time an objective that started small can take on greater and greater magnitude and become a major change.

The final category, *discovery* catalysts, happen during some planned experience you sought—all experiences contain within them the possibility of transformation—with its instigation usually immediate but not nearly as major as a disruption. Such discoveries can happen in areas as varied as attending a thought-provoking play, hearing an enlightening message, traveling to a stunning destination, or visiting an inspiring museum—each one a potential spark of aspiration. Professionally, discovery catalysts can come into play when you encounter something you have not seen or thought of before, such as a new technology unveiled by your R&D organization or another company.

As a transformation guider, you can often prompt people to make a discovery that instigates a transformation that you can then lead them in. Trade shows, conferences, and other events prove great vehicles for discovery, as do travel, conventions, and retail outlets—especially flagship experiences—for consumers. (For more on this, see the sidebar "Invitational Transformations.")

Invitational Transformations

Transformational desires can be intentionally sparked by companies. You can stage experiences that create the conditions under which people develop that desire, via deviation or discovery.

For instance, if you've never been, get thee to an Eataly. It's the most vibrant retail experience in the world, even though it's a grocery store chain. Oscar Farinetti, who in 2007 founded the company in Turin, Italy, didn't just set out to create a supermarket stocked with Italian products; he envisioned an immersive experience that would embody the Slow Food philosophy: high quality, locally produced, traditionally crafted, and intentionally eaten. Wanting to entice people to join the movement, Farinetti scoured the Italian countryside for exactly the right suppliers, themed the store experience as a journey, and ensured that consumers would be enriched by learning about the produce, meat, and packaged goods as well as how to prepare them. Now with over forty locations—twelve in Italy and the rest in major cities around the world—Eataly has a bustling marketplace atmosphere, complete with winding routes, cafés, and restaurants that cater to those who find meaning in the simple art of cooking. The entire place invites customers to find that meaning. No one visits Eataly expecting a transformation—unless it's at the admission-feed cooking school through which guests can become Italian chefs—but they're encouraged to incorporate the Slow Food philosophy into their lives.[a]

Such *invitational transformations* build atop marketing experiences, as they do the job of marketing by generating demand for a company's core offerings.[b] Think of how much more customers buy from Eataly once they discover and become devoted to Italian foodstuffs and cooking, even more so if they intentionally embrace Slow Food. Bob Rogers, onetime Disney Imagineer and founder of experience designer BRC Imagination Arts, introduced me to the term, saying invitational transformations "include brand experiences, museums, cultural attractions, and other visitor experiences that share with you a subject they hope will interest you. Such experiences initially present as a pleasant way to spend an hour or more, but the best of them are designed to connect emotionally with the guest in a way that causes the guest to discover a lasting interest and fall in love."

This approach is not forced, nefarious, or underhanded; it engages you in time well spent through a marketing experience while simultaneously exposing you to new possibilities and letting you discover if you would like to invest your time in them. Rogers's team, for example, designed the Abraham Lincoln Presidential Library and Museum, which won one of the Experience Stager of the Year awards we have given at Strategic Horizons.[c] Rogers told me that BRC's goal was to "create a lasting memory connection between the guest and the subject that would cause guests to acquire a permanent interest in the life and times of Abraham Lincoln." And many visitors do in fact become Lincoln enthusiasts and even devotees.

A less lofty but equally valid and greatly enjoyable example is the Johnnie Walker Princes Street experience in Edinburgh.[d] Its owner, Diageo plc, obviously wants to sell more Johnnie Walker whisky and would love it if more people became regular consumers. So to invite them to do so, BRC designed the flagship experience to expose people to Scotch whisky, and Johnnie Walker in particular. Some consumers arrive without a great affinity for it; they come for an engaging, ninety-minute visit that includes theatrical special-effects presentations of Johnnie Walker's heritage, whisky making, and the art of blending, with at least three drinks. The place uses AI to customize the visit based on each guest's unique flavor preferences. People never leave disappointed—the company turns novice whisky drinkers into whisky buffs, and whisky drinkers into Johnnie Walker aficionados. According to Rob Maxwell, head of experience for Johnnie Walker Princes Street, 82 percent of visitors say they were "likely" or "more likely" to consume the

(*continued*)

company's whisky after their visit, with a 91 percent "brand conversion score," meaning they now identify with the brand. That may not have been something visitors sought, but they gladly ascend to such identities because of their engagement with the experience. BRC's lead designer, Christian Lachel, explains that "brand conversion leads to long-term loyalty. It is the measurable change in preference and the deepening of brand love. And this means lifelong value for a brand well beyond a single visit to a brand home or on-site purchase."

Those are exactly the sort of effects that marketing experiences around the world create by inviting people to come in, be engaged, and, just maybe, transform.

Notes

a. Eataly actually supplies all five genres of economic offerings: *commodities* of meats, grains, cheeses, and other Italian foodstuffs; packaged *goods* and kitchen appliances; the retail *service* of merchandising and quick-service meals; *experiences* through shopping, discovery, socializing, and so on; and, finally, lifestyle *transformation*, as each of these has an effect on customers.

b. For more on marketing experiences (which Jim Gilmore and I also call "placemaking experiences"), see our book *Authenticity: What Consumers Really Want* (Boston: Harvard Business School Press, 2007), 147–177.

c. For more details on the place (and much more on museums), see B. Joseph Pine II and James H. Gilmore, "Museums & Authenticity," *Museum News*, May–June 2007, 76–80 and 92–93, available at https://strategichorizons.com/wp-content/uploads/MuseumNews-May07-MuseumsAuthenticity.pdf.

d. Like Eataly, Johnnie Walker Princes Street has a transformational offering, the Learning for Life Academy. It's a training facility with classes teaching how to mix drinks, plus programs for those looking to become bartenders/mixologists but facing barriers to education and employment.

Ah, but all roads lead to *desire*. In every case, the catalyzing incident results in a transformational desire, an intention, an aspiration. With discovery you may have to reflect on your experience and internalize it before a desire sparks; with deviation you may feel that spark almost instantly; with disruption you may have to unpack your emotional responses before that desire arises; and with directed catalysts a major decision in your life or business may yield not just one but perhaps a cascade of aspirations.

Each of those desires sets transformation journeys in motion through the aspirations of individuals.

Types of Aspirations

As noted at the beginning of the chapter, transformation always entails identity change, a shift in how you think of yourself. When philosophers analyze the subject, though, only deep and personal changes count, such as those in central beliefs, worldview, purpose, and values, or what might be called core aspects of identity. In her book *Aspiration: The Agency of Becoming*, for example, Agnes Callard, associate professor of philosophy at the University of Chicago, focuses on transformation as a deep change in values in particular. For her, true aspiration involves—and true transformation ensues from—only such life-altering change. Everything else remains shallow, with Callard identifying as a marker of shallowness "whether we're inclined to preface it with 'mere.'"[13]

However, as long as they change one or more aspects of identity, changes that are shallow and mere are just as much transformations as those that are deep and core. They simply arise from different types of aspirations. By understanding the nature of aspirations, you can determine what type of transformation you can offer, and how to guide it.

Thinking epistemically

When the transformation is deep, highly personal, and substantial, involving profound identity change, the aspiration is best called one of *metamorphosis*. The word is used in biology to refer to a change ("meta") in form ("morph"), such as frogs going from egg to tadpole to adult, salmon transmuting physiologically to move from fresh water to salt water (and back again), and caterpillars becoming butterflies (which comprises multiple metamorphoses, actually: from egg to caterpillar to chrysalis and finally to butterfly).

The term "metamorphosis" was first used, though, to refer to human transformation, particularly that done by "magic" or "witchcraft."[14] Today it's not about such mystical and fictional means; aspirations of metamorphosis refer to a longing for identity change, which as we shift to the Transformation Economy often entails the guidance of companies. (And can, as in biology, involve multiple and occasionally seemingly back-and-forth identity changes, such as becoming a long-term cancer patient and later a cancer survivor.)

For Callard and other philosophers, this sort of change is so great—it affects your values and sense of self so much—that *you cannot even foresee* what it would be like to undergo it. For example, L. A. Paul, professor of philosophy and cognitive science at Yale University, argues in her book *Transformative Experience* that only if such an event "changes you enough to substantially change your point of view, thus substantially revising your core preferences or revising how you experience being yourself" is it "a personally transformative experience."[15] She goes further to say that some episode is truly a transformative experience only if it involves "epistemic change," affecting how you see and know yourself:

> [If something] is a radically new experience for you, it means that important features of your future self, the self that results from the personal transformation, are epistemically inaccessible to your current, inexperienced self. A radically new experience can fundamentally change your own point of view so much and so deeply that, before you've had that experience, you can't know what it is going to be like to be

> you after the experience. It changes your subjective value for what it is like to be you and changes your core preferences about what matters.[16]

Meaning that after such a transformation *you no longer recognize* the person you once were.

Paul gives the example of deciding whether to have a baby.[17] Before you have a child, the future experience of creating a human life is so unfamiliar that you simply cannot know what it is like to be a parent. No matter how much you think back to your own parents and see other people taking care of their kids, the experience of actual parenting remains a mystery to you, because it changes your values and identity so very much.

Such transformations start at the physical level. It's well known that pregnancy entails significant chemical changes in women, but remarkably it affects the brain as well. One study noted that "few regions [are left] untouched by the transition to motherhood."[18] The changes directly impact maternal attachment to a baby and are so great "that a machine-learning algorithm could tell mothers and nonmothers apart by their brain scans alone."[19] Surprisingly, the same effect, although less pronounced, applies to the male brain and paternal attachment. As one researcher, Darby Saxbe, a professor of psychology at the University of Southern California, makes clear, this effect both changes identity and enhances human flourishing along at least three of the four spheres of transformation:

> Most men have told us that they derive tremendous meaning and purpose from their connection to their children. Contemporary fathers are almost as likely as mothers to say that parenthood is central to their identity, and men are even more likely than women to report that children improve their well-being. And the newest data suggests that parenting may promote long-term brain health; among older men

and women, a brain-age algorithm estimated that the brain looked younger among people who had children.[20]

Having a baby, of course, is very much an economic decision. It involves numerous purchases of goods (diapers, clothing, cribs, more diapers, strollers, car seats), but also purchases of guidance in health & well-being, including both the personal and the medical. Often prospective parents take preparation classes, sometimes hire midwives or doulas, maybe even start with fertility clinics. So while parenthood never improves one's wealth in the short term, in the long term it definitely influences prosperity and offers a greater understanding of life itself.

Although becoming a parent is truly a change in biological form, it is not the only metamorphosis individuals have. For most, getting married, getting divorced, having a religious conversion, starting a first job, graduating from college, permanently departing home, joining the military, becoming a professional athlete, being promoted to manager, going beyond a mom-and-pop shop to convert into a franchiser, becoming a homeowner, leaving a salaried job to become an entrepreneur, retiring, experiencing the death of a spouse, dealing with a serious illness (and recovering from a long battle with it). All of these can change one's identity not just personally but epistemically. And in all these highly significant and sometimes traumatic cases and more, aspirants seek out transformation offerings that can help them work through them and achieve such aspirations of metamorphosis.[21]

For businesses, the same can be said of pivoting a startup growing into a full-fledged enterprise, or an organization becoming less bureaucratic or more agile. Communities and societies can also change their core identities, which usually takes decades but sometimes happens with revolutionary fervor and speed. They may, for instance, convert farmland into housing, turn crime-ridden neighborhoods into safe ones, or shift from a Rust Belt town to a technology-based one. In all such cases, economic transformations come into play.

Thinking economically

As you can tell from the prior examples, metamorphoses that involve a wholesale change in identity are real, impactful, even momentous—but remain relatively uncommon. The vast majority of transformations do not change core aspects of self. So even though the idea of the only true transformation being one of metamorphosis may be perfectly appropriate in philosophy, in business it is much too strict. In thinking about transformations as a distinct economic offering, people want not just deep but shallow change—and everything in between. And aspirations for identity transformation need not involve such sweeping change that you no longer even recognize your former self (whether as individual person, organization, business, or community).

So understand aspirations as having two primary dimensions of change: *quality* and *scale*. With the former, aspirations can range from differences in kind to differences in degree. Changes in kind do indeed transform your identity epistemically, in core aspects such as essence, values, and purpose. Such aspects are about being in the world. Changes in degree, on the other hand, shift noncore, more peripheral aspects of identity, as with attitudes, behaviors, and actions, but also including aptitudes, capabilities, skills, and other ways of acting in the world.

Aspirations for changes in both kind and degree can range in scale from large to small.[22] Large-scale aspirations seek to affect us greatly, endeavoring to shift the trajectories of our lives. But we also long for those on a smaller scale that nonetheless affect us in important ways. There's no need to denigrate these aspirations with terms such as "shallow," "superficial," or "mere," for they still represent human longings for life changes; they also represent

FIGURE 3-2

Types of aspirations

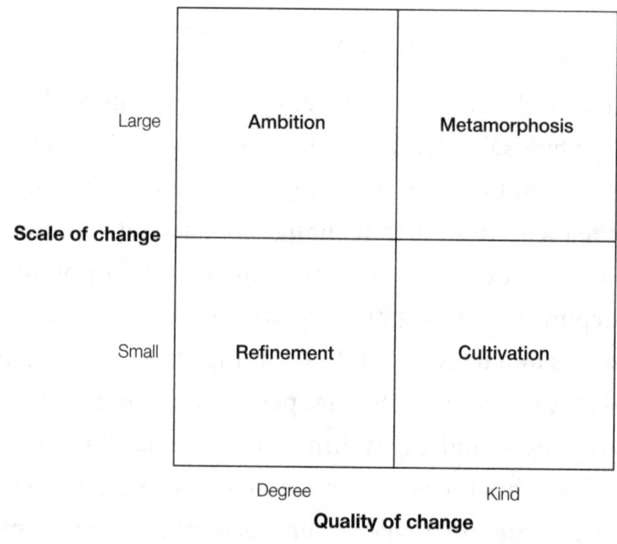

economic opportunities for businesses that can guide individuals through them.

These two dimensions, then, yield four different types of aspirations, as seen in figure 3-2.

METAMORPHOSIS. For the many examples of large-scale changes in kind discussed previously, aspirants do largely approach them with their eyes open to the transformations desired. In such cases, the *conception of self* may precede the *transformation of self*. Transformation guiders then need to work on the actual transformation as well as help aspirants reconcile the two over time.

In other cases the change in the conception of self comes after the actual transformation, as with impostor syndrome, where, say, you graduate from law school, pass the bar to officially become a lawyer, join a firm, and yet feel deeply inadequate to the tasks you're expected to do, because you've never done them. You feel like an impostor, unable to get comfortable in your own lawyerly skin. So you fake it 'til you make it by *acting as if* you know what you're doing, until eventually, one day, you realize you no longer think about the disconnect and can say, "Well, now I *am* a lawyer!" You already were a lawyer in the eyes of the bar, your company, your clients—everyone but you.[23] Not all conceptions of self reflect reality. In such cases the transformation guider—the law school in this case, but in others it could be coaches, HR departments, and so on—should prepare aspirants for exactly this eventuality, and continue to guide long after the transformation *seems* fulfilled, at least until aspirants actually complete their identity change. (More on that in chapter 7.)

CULTIVATION. There are other facets of identity change that don't involve wholesale, comprehensive changes but nonetheless remain differences in kind. These are *cultivation* aspirations.[24] They include such economic actions as joining a fitness center or becoming a vegan to cultivate a healthier lifestyle ("I am a healthy person"), shifting your savings from a bank to a wealth management firm to cultivate financial well-being ("I am financially set"), taking community educational classes to cultivate a new interest in, say, theatre ("I am a theatre maven"), or becoming a member of a museum to build an appreciation for modern art ("I am an art devotee"). These same sorts of cultivations exist in businesses, where companies may focus for a time on programs that, say, foster learning organizations, raise emotional intelligence, or enhance creativity, all as means to serve the ends of improving the business itself.

Whether within people, businesses, or other entities, such cultivations can embed themselves into core identity deeply enough that they become major changes over time. They can deeply affect values ("Financial stewardship is important to me," "All employees should have access to well-being resources"), beliefs ("Everyone should eat healthy," "Downtime makes for more productive employees"), and essence ("I am a professional athlete," "We are a learning organization").

AMBITION. Many changes are in degree, not of kind, denoting aspirations for transformation in noncore, more peripheral facets of self. You have an existing element of self and decide you want to improve, boost, or enhance it. When large in scale, such aspirations are ones of *ambition*.[25] While not like those of metamorphosis, they can still lead to great changes in one's life.

Your ambition may be to greatly improve at tennis, and so you take lessons and practice, play, and practice some more until you reach the level of your ambition. Maybe you're a programmer and recognize the explosion of generative AI, and so you enroll in courses and earn certificates to prepare for and then take advantage of the career possibilities. Perhaps you're a follower of a particular religion and have the ambition to grow deeper in your faith, and so you read books, attend services regularly, join affiliated clubs or groups, and go to conferences to learn more, and to be more. Or maybe you've always enjoyed dabbling with filming and decide you want to get better at it—not to become an auteur but an accomplished amateur—so you see more movies to study technique, take classes on the subject, and experiment with longer and more involved filming.

Businesses have their own sets of ambitions, such as to work with greater efficiency, produce fewer defects, create better marketing, sell more offerings, devise better channels, innovate more quickly, or generate a smaller environmental footprint. Each one of these involves changes in degree, not in kind, as with the personal ambitions above.

Ambitions can slip into changes in kind over time, at least within particular identity contexts (and constructs). A core facet of your identity in tennis may shift, for example, from "beginner" to "average" to "advanced," or in business from "mediocre manufacturer" to "high-quality producer" to "best-in-class enterprise." And while for you those may be core facets, for others they remain peripheral. You need to look out for such shifts when fulfilling ambition aspirations.

REFINEMENT. Finally, in other cases you want small-scale change in some facet of your identity, merely desiring a *refinement* in it. You enjoy gardening, so you start to read magazines, talk with others who garden, and watch videos to learn more. Such small-scale changes in degree could apply to anything you enjoy, relish, care for, delight in, or even love—wine, coffee, Italian food, cigars, running, reading, and more.

Refinement transformations lack a desire for large-scale change, but rather involve honing, polishing, sharpening, upgrading, or otherwise improving some element of your current identity. Indeed, there isn't an example of ambition I've described, whether of a personal or professional nature, that couldn't also have the smaller-scale nature of refinement. They can easily bleed into each other, with some gray area in between, depending on the level of desire. In some senses, then, when designing and guiding the transformation, it may not make that much difference in discerning whether a particular aspiration is of small or large scale, for either the aspirant or the company. But if an aspiration does shift over that line into ambitious territory, there may be some psychological aspects that are worth understanding and addressing, such as being unsure of actually being able to achieve the aspiration or guide the transformation, as the case may be. Some aspirants simply may not have the innate talent, ability, or suitability to achieve certain ambitions, while levels of refinement remain available to all.

Thinking transformationally

While metamorphosis may take the lion's share of thought among philosophers and other academics, cultivation, ambition, and refinement prove equally valid types of aspirations, each one representing a longing for change and therefore an opportunity for companies to guide them. Though metamorphoses remain the most impactful and valuable, the other three types of aspirations offer more business opportunities.

Metamorphosis aspirations are clearly the outlier, distinct from the rest. These are so often instigated by trauma or other causes that so greatly disrupt people's lives. They call for deep transformations that, even if the catalyst happens in a flash, generally require quite a long time.[26] Almost by its very nature, wholesale change engages the whole person, so often proving emotionally gripping, physically engrossing, intellectually stimulating, and even spiritually invigorating. But not always in a positive way; it can also be emotionally laden, physically strenuous, intellectually intimidating, and even spiritually challenging. As such, wholesale change places a high degree of responsibility on you as a transformation guider to act in the best interests of your aspirants, and deal with them as whole people, not collections of identity facets or aspirations.

Ambitions generally take a long time as well, depending on the starting point, the end aspiration, and the aspirant. Here you don't want to neglect the whole person, of course, but you need a greater focus on those aspects of them that affect the ambition. Such large-scale changes in degree tend to be concentrated, centering in one of the four ways of engaging people—emotionally, physically, intellectually, and spiritually—as well as in only one of the four spheres of transformation, although they often expand beyond these precisely because of their large-scale nature.

That is much less true of cultivation and refinement aspirations. Both are much more limited in scope, and even though cultivation affects core elements of identity, it doesn't reach the essence that causes people to question who they are. Cultivation and refinement can be treated more in isolation, enabling you as a transformation guider to be more focused on the aspiration at hand and the means to achieve it.

So when you determine that transformations are the business you are really in, consider, too, what aspirations you want to guide aspirants in achieving based on what catalysts spark the desire. Then you must determine which transformative experiences you can best use to do so, how best to stage those experiences, how to create full transformation offerings designed for each type of aspiration, and how to design the right series of experiences to not only effect the transformations but sustain them through time—and even how to charge for the economic value you create within each aspirant. And that is exactly what you will learn from the next four chapters.

REFLECTION

This chapter discussed identity change and how to better understand your aspirants and their aspirations. Consider these questions:

- Recall that all transformation involves identity change, going from "I was X, now I am Y." How might your customers complete that statement? Come up with a number of possibilities.
- What variety of customers do you sell to today—and who might you sell to tomorrow? Are you focused on one group in particular, or more than one?
- For what types of aspirations might you create transformations? How do your current offerings fit into these ideas?

PREPARATION

As you contemplate what you've learned about aspirations, think, too, about your current and potential offerings and how you can use those to create transformations:

- If you aren't yet in the experience business, how might you stage experiences that will effect change?

- If you stage experiences, what more can you do to make them truly transformative?
- What reinforcing activities might you undertake to help your customers sustain the effects of transformation over time?

4

SHIFTING FROM EXPERIENCES TO TRANSFORMATIONS

While tourism has always been in the business of helping people experience that most abundant of commodities, land, it has evolved in a way that perfectly illustrates the Progression of Economic Value, including creating transformative experiences.

From a physical goods standpoint, to experience places you need the right gear, such as clothing, shoes, backpacks, suitcases, walking sticks, mountain bikes, and so forth. Moreover, tourism has long operated as a production-oriented industry, catering to the more tangible need for shelter. The focus was on offering concrete and well-defined aspects of travel, such as convenient accommodations, reliable transportation, and other material comforts. The industry's main goal was to produce and deliver a standardized package that met the fundamental and straightforward requirements of past consumers who appreciated stability, familiarity, and value.

As the Service Economy displaced the Industrial one, tourism transitioned to a more benefit-oriented approach, emphasizing quality, standardized processes, and amenities. In today's Experience Economy, the focus has further evolved to meet the desire for memorable and authentic experiences, with such trappings as luxurious lobbies, blissful beds, spacious showers, and signature scents. More and more the focus has become experiences that connect with travelers, impart meaning, and instill wonderment.

And now the travel industry—the biggest in the world in terms of employment, according to the World Travel & Tourism Council—is already shifting to align with the forthcoming Transformation Economy.[1] In fact, what's known as *transformational travel* is one of its fastest-growing segments, creating experiences that are not just extraordinary but that promote personal growth and leave a lasting impact.

The shifts can be seen in many areas. Virtually every high-end hotel or resort has added spas, wellness experiences, and classes of various types. In April 2023, Accor hotels named a global vice president of well-being. That August, Canyon Ranch—long known for its transformative wellness-focused experiences—launched a new program focused on longevity. And in October of that year, Ritz-Carlton sent an email to all its members to promote how "Transformative Moments Begin at the Ritz-Carlton." The concept was colorfully illustrated by the phrases, "You arrived a bud, you departed a bloom," "You arrived a shell, you departed with wings," and "How will your stay leave you?" (It's yet to be seen how much or how intentionally Ritz-Carlton makes transformation happen for guests.)

Another type of travel involves going to other countries for health care—as over twenty million people crossed borders for medical treatment in 2023, according to Patients Beyond Borders.[2] Thailand is a leading destination worldwide, with Bumrungrad International Hospital, the largest private hospital in Bangkok, perhaps the first to focus on attracting patients from around the world.

Many places specialize in well-being journeys, such as REVĪVŌ Wellness Resorts in Bali. Meaning "I live again" in Latin, REVĪVŌ offers guests a "unique journey to self-discovery and ultimate happiness."[3] Before booking a stay, guests ("aspirants" would be the better term) complete an eighty-question survey about their physical, mental, emotional, relational, and health needs, and the resort wellness team analyzes the data to design a "custom wellness journey."

There's even a Transformational Travel Council (which I advise) that seeks to inspire, promote, and convene around the concept, while also offering education on transformations for travelers as well as travel designers, hosts, hospitality organizations, and communities. Its manifesto focuses directly on the drives and needs of today's consumers, beginning with this statement: "Travel is ripe with the POSSIBILITY of transformation."[4]

Tourism thus perfectly exemplifies the Progression of Economic Value from bottom to top and offers a prime example of discovery catalysts for individuals roaming around the world seeking experiences. And transformations are only ever effected by the experiences people have. Determining and guiding them, therefore, not just leans heavily on but *requires* creating experiences—transformative ones.

Levels of Experiences

The art and practice of guiding transformations subsumes that of designing and staging experiences. It begins by recognizing that experiences are not monolithic and can have different levels of engagement that themselves progress upward to successively offer more value. This extends from merely *memorable*, to highly *meaningful*, to deeply *transporting*, and finally to truly *transformative*. These experiences can then be subsumed within full transformation offerings that guide customers in achieving their aspirations.

Memorable experiences

Recall the definition of experiences as distinct economic offerings from chapter 1: memorable events that engage each individual in an inherently personal way. Note that first word: "memorable." For an offering to be a true, distinctive experience, it must create a memory, the remnant that lingers long after it is over—and the longer, the better. If there is no memory, there was no experience. Period.[5]

To be memorable, you must be *engaging,* reaching inside of people and creating the experience within them. Commodities, goods, and services exist outside of us, while experiences happen inside of us, which is what makes them inherently personal. When people think of being engaged, generally they think only of *emotional* engagement—triggering happiness, sparking surprise, building suspense, and so forth. But as mentioned previously, you can engage people not only emotionally but physically, intellectually, and spiritually. All four contribute to human flourishing, so when designing experiences never confine yourself to simply designing for emotions. Think of such traditional examples as sporting events, concerts, plays, and museums. Or more recent varieties, including movies, TV and radio programs, user-generated videos, and digital games. Entirely new genres pop up every year, such as the recent innovations of escape rooms, game cafés, esports centers, axe-throwing venues, immersive art exhibits, competitive socializing nights, and on and on the list could go. Each of these offers something engagingly memorable.

Meaningful experiences

Meaningful experiences add a level of significance to us as individuals.[6] Such experiences connect with us more strongly, particularly in appealing to our humanity, to our personal sense of purpose, to our identity in some way.[7] As Colorado State University psychology professor Michael Steger writes, "Life without meaning would be merely a string of events."[8]

Some events have more potential for meaning than others. Seeing a blockbuster movie with friends can be a pleasurable way to spend the evening and give you something to talk about later. But watching a documentary that offers insight into historical events that impacted you or your family can have much more significance and consequence. Attending a class in college can be memorable for any number of reasons (one of which hopefully is to prepare you for the test). But taking a community education class because you want to learn about photography, engine repair, or welding can have more lasting significance. Playing golf on a summer Saturday with your buddies and recounting it afterward on the nineteenth hole can be most satisfying. But taking a once-in-a-lifetime trip to play golf in Scotland, including a round at St. Andrews, makes much more of an impact on your psyche. And walking into an art gallery as you stroll down a city street may be memorable for what you see and discuss. But experiencing a beloved Vermeer painting in the flesh after only ever seeing it in books proves so much more meaningful.

What gives meaning to each of us is, of course, highly subjective. We individually determine how significant something is based on who we are and our personal identities. So a gray area forms between these first two levels of experiences, where a particular event may be memorable for some but meaningful to others; naturally, anything relating to the sphere of purpose & meaning proves inescapably meaning*ful*. Indeed, meaning is created by the individual in reaction to and in concert with the experience.[9]

Transporting experiences

When you create memorable and meaningful experiences, you have the further opportunity to make them *transporting*. Transporting experiences instill wonderment, shift you beyond the present moment, and move you metaphorically to another realm, to a transcendent and liminal space and time.[10] They do not by themselves change who you are, but can greatly change your state of heart, mind, body, and spirit while more easily leading to the truly transformative.

One way to be transported is through what psychologist Abraham Maslow called "peak experiences," which create "moments of highest happiness and fulfillment" and are "rare, exciting, oceanic, deeply moving, exhilarating, elevating experiences that generate an advanced form of perceiving reality, and are even mystic and magical in their effect."[11] Peak experiences enable individuals to transcend their daily lives through euphoric events, including getting a "runner's high," having a eureka moment, undergoing a religious encounter, feeling a burst of love, reading an inspirational book, or playing moving music.

Even going to a theme park can suffice. Wendy Heimann-Nunes, an entertainment attorney focused on location-based and immersive experiences, gave me the term "transporting experiences" when, in writing an article together for *Attractions Management* magazine, she told me of an amazing encounter she had on a theme park ride. While it was not transformative, she excitedly said it "transported" her. In the article, we explored this idea further:

> Take, for instance, Star Wars Galaxy's Edge. Here, lifelong fans aren't mere guests, but experience full euphoria as integral parts of the narrative—donning a costume; being a character in a galaxy far, far away; exploring new facets of their own identity in a universe that captivated them for years. Through these attractions, guests leave their daily lives behind and try "new versions of themselves with the agency to be a force for good or evil," as Scott Trowbridge, Senior Creative Executive at Walt Disney Imagineering, told us.

> People also undergo peak experiences at Pandora—The World of Avatar, The Wizarding World of Harry Potter, One World Observatory at the World Trade Center in New York—as well as numerous relatively immersive attractions without the big budgets of a Walt Disney or Universal Studios.[12]

Such phenomena extend beyond memorable moments and meaningful events to elevate our existence and offer transcendence, at least for a time.

Another way to be transported is *flow*. Psychologist Mihaly Csikszentmihalyi named this type of phenomenon and described it as an "optimal experience" where the challenges you face are relatively balanced with your skills.[13] When the challenge exceeds your skill level, you grow anxious, while having too high a skill level leads to boredom. But by striking the right balance, you shift into a state of elevated engagement and face the endeavor with passion and persistence. Csikszentmihalyi's research found that flow "provided a sense of discovery, a creative feeling of transporting the person into a new reality."[14] It further changes our perception of time, bestowing "freedom from the tyranny of time."[15] I love that phrase—freedom from the tyranny of time—and in gaining that freedom we escape the routine, shed the mundane, exhilarate our emotions, excite our senses, energize our bodies, and elate our minds.

A third way of having and creating transporting experiences, one that deserves special attention, is *awe*. While the word originally referred to great fear (once upon a time, anything "awesome" terrified people), it came to mean "solemn and reverential wonder," an experience of smallness in the face of greatness.[16] While I wrote earlier about transporting experiences taking us out of present space and time, the key element of awe is taking you outside of your *self*. You lose yourself, sometimes to then find yourself again.

Dacher Keltner, professor of psychology at the University of California, Berkeley, and author of *Awe: The New Science of Everyday Wonder and How It Can Transform Your Life*, defines the word as "being in the presence of something vast and mysterious that transcends your current understanding of the world."[17] Think of instances when you have experienced awe. What was the setting, the time, the spark? What thoughts sprang to mind? How long did the feeling last, and how long did it *seem* to last? Did you feel transported?

Keltner's research is based on more than 2,500 stories of awe that he and his colleagues gathered across twenty-six countries. This led him to a categorization of awe, to the "eight wonders of life," as he calls them. In order of frequency (with multiple categories possible in each story), people derive wonder, amazement, and/or reverence from these things: moral beauty, collective effervescence, nature, music, visual design, spiritual faith and religion, life and death, and epiphanies.[18]

Think again of your own experiences of awe and see how you would spread them across the categories. Then consider how Keltner concludes his introductory discussion of these eight wonders:

> It also merits considering what was *not* mentioned in stories of awe from around the world. Money didn't figure into awe. . . . No one mentioned their laptop, Facebook, Apple Watch, or smartphone. Nor did anyone mention consumer purchases, like their new Nikes, Tesla, Gucci bag, or Montblanc pen. Awe occurs in a realm separate from the mundane world of materialism, money, acquisition, and status signaling–a realm beyond the profane that many call the sacred.[19]

Yes, and no. Yes, the transporting experience of awe is the epitome of immateriality, but no, in that money and material things lie intertwined within awe experiences, explicitly or implicitly, as businesses provide economic offerings that fully and unavoidably prove part of experiencing awe, whether directly or indirectly. People pay plenty to experience the collective effervescence arising from "weddings, christenings, quinceañeras, bar and bat mitzvahs, graduations, sports celebrations, funerals, family reunions, and political rallies," as Keltner delineates.[20]

Consider some of his categories of awe. People travel to and stay in *nature* (a large proportion of transformational travel intentionally endeavors to be awe-inducing), not to mention protect themselves from its potentially harmful aspects (sunburn, burrs, rocks, cliffs, etc.). In addition to paying for concert tickets to hear *music*, we customarily buy musical instruments, not make them from scratch; the same with Bibles and other *spiritual* texts. *Life and death* so often happen in hospitals, with attendant bills. And *epiphanies* arise from research, study, and contemplation in classrooms, laboratories, offices, homes, and other places, with all the acquired accoutrements necessary to build up to the moment of insight.

Most of the awe-filled stories you read in Keltner's book, hear elsewhere, or encounter yourself (particularly those involving moral beauty—"other people's courage, kindness, strength, or overcoming") do not arise from staged experiences per se.[21] Yet it is entirely possible to design and depict awe-inducing experiences—just as with peak and flow experiences and any others that transport us.

Transformative experiences

While memorable experiences engage who you are, meaningful experiences connect with who you are, and transporting experiences move you beyond who you are, transformative experiences *change* who you are. It can happen with a single, life-altering event—in which case that experience is highly likely to first be transporting—or, more likely, a series of them that can encompass the memorable, the meaningful, and the transporting.

I know scores of experience designers who work across the spectrum of possibilities (the World Experience Organization, or WXO, seems to do a particularly good job of attracting them), and not a single one wants to stop at the memorable level. And almost all of them recognize the power and value of transformative experiences. One is Heather Gallagher, who bills herself as a strategic leader in immersive experiences and transformative events. But in Burning Man circles she is known as "Camera Girl," or "CG," an early handle that stayed with her as she became the head of technology for the annual art and music event in the Black Rock Desert in northwestern Nevada (as well as its year-round operations), supporting its growth into a nonprofit that fosters a global cultural movement.

When Gallagher presents on Burning Man, she notes that one of the reasons it's world-renowned is that attending is a tremendous ordeal, with huge obstacles participants—called burners—must overcome.[22] The process begins with buying tickets and continues with obtaining supplies, getting to the desert, setting up camp, and on and on. These tasks are part and parcel of the series of experiences before, within, and after the eight-day-long event. But, of course, there is much more across the spectrum of experiences, as Burning Man is exceedingly memorable, incredibly meaningful, highly transporting, and universally transformative. The WXO summarized one of Gallagher's talks thusly: "Despite all the inconveniences, burners keep coming back because it's also a sea of miracles. They come out with stories they'll tell for the rest of their lives, and new friends to share them with. They come back because they know that 'in the most wild and unimagined of places, you can still find beautiful things.'"[23]

Beautiful things such as peak experiences, flow, and awe. Such as the moral beauty of so many participants collaborating (particularly when things go wrong, especially the weather); effervescence collectively created; lovely natural environs framing

Black Rock City; wonderful if temporary structures, art, and performances; and epiphanies galore.

And it is transformative.[24] Although Burning Man is an "ultramarathon of inconveniences," as Gallagher puts it, "the payoff is profound." Her payoff list includes increased self-awareness, expanded consciousness, self-sovereignty, more authentic living, emotional growth, new behaviors, a shift in perspective, and a sense of agency.[25] At the end of each event all burners declare, to a person, *Burning Man changed my life*. New participants add a new aspect to their identity: "I am a burner"—a very strong aspect, in no small measure because of the tribulations they overcame to become it. In fact, Burning Man recommends participants not make any major life decisions for at least two weeks afterward.

Ah, but what happens after those two weeks? When participants get back into their daily routines, when the memories diminish, when the payoffs begin to dissipate, when the lessons, growth, new behaviors, and other changes get crowded out by life?

Recall the definition of transformations as a distinct economic offering from the first chapter: effectual outcomes that change individuals in a sustained way. There's a difference between a transformative experience and a true transformation: the outcome has to last. For aspirants to truly transform, you must continue to work with them on the changes effected by the experience(s) you stage so they incorporate those changes into their lives in an enduring way. In any transformative experience, it's what you do afterward with what happened to your aspirants that determines whether they truly transform, to what degree, and of what type.

Even without being sustained through time, transformative experiences have their place. They are more memorable, more meaningful, and more transporting than any lower-level experiences, with the greatest personal impact. They are worth having in and of themselves—but have so much more value when you guide guests in changing their lives.

Leading the Way to Lasting Change

So what does it take to turn transformative experiences into transformations? How do you guide aspirants in "bringing home" what they did, what they learned, how they grew? And how do you make it last? By *encapsulating* the experience with three activities: preparation beforehand, reflection afterward, and integration on an ongoing basis, as seen in figure 4-1.[26]

The best way to sustain a transformation is to get people ready for it in advance. *Preparation* involves helping them imagine the experience before it happens by picturing its sequence of events, thinking about what it will be like, ideally even envisioning what effect it may have on them and how that relates to their aspiration. Such contemplation before the event engages guests in anticipating it, primes them to have an even better experience, and puts them in the right frame of mind, opening them up to the possibility of transformation.[27]

For in very many cases, customers are not yet aspirants. They may only be seeking memorable, meaningful, or transporting experiences—even quasi- or short-term transformations, where

FIGURE 4-1

Encapsulation

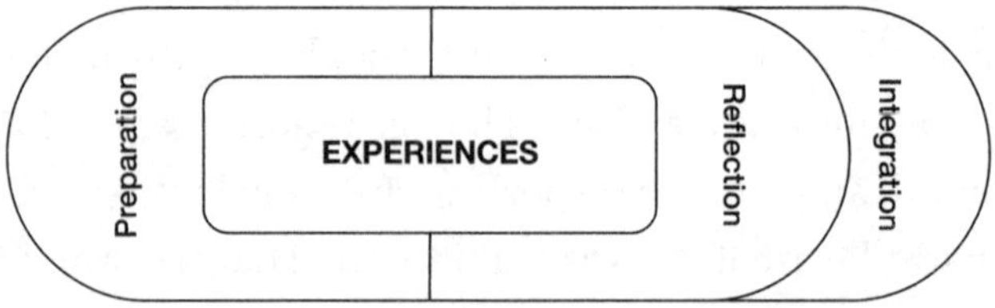

Preparation
EXPERIENCES
Reflection
Integration

they want to change but only temporarily before heading back to their normal lives. They may not have considered the possibility of lasting change. But they may indeed discover a catalyst for it in the midst of being transported, or they may accept your invitation to transform, embracing the possibility to achieve the actuality. Sometimes, too, they recognize the changes they see in themselves after the experience and want to incorporate them into their lives, or desire to go further with an even greater aspiration.

The second step of encapsulation, *reflection,* happens when guests look back on an event not just to remember it, but to ponder it, perhaps to discuss it with others, and always to consider its impact on them as individuals. People don't reflect on all their experiences, and companies don't do near enough to encourage, instigate, or participate in reflection. But when it happens, it cements the memories of the experience, aids people in viewing it as meaningful, gets them to relive what was transporting, and advances the transformation journey.

While thinking back on any experience, people can simultaneously look forward. Doing so pushes them to contemplate who they are in light of the event just encountered. It connects what they underwent to their identity, testing for a sympathetic vibration that resonates with who they have been—and who they might become. It can also lead them to desire new change, to formulate a new aspiration, even to commit to another journey of transformation.

Integration takes that reflection and puts it into action. This is where people—if they were mere guests before, they are full aspirants now—go beyond mere experience to begin serious work on the transformation itself, with your guidance.[28] It often starts with an understanding of the size and nature of the gap between what they now aspire to become and where they are today—their personal from/to statements. Help them explore various ways of behaving and being, noticing when and where they fall short, and endeavor together to close the gap with each opportunity, while realizing that regress sometimes follows progress. The work of integrating their experiences into their lives also resides in a liminal place and time—betwixt and between the *from* of who they were and the *to* of who they can become. In situations where people have been pursuing a transformation on their own, this is often when they seek help, a guide who can make integration take place more effectively, more surely, and perhaps more efficiently.

Transformation expert and professor Suzy Ross emphasizes integration in her book *The Map to Wholeness*, writing that transformations have first a transformative cycle and then an integrative one, with the latter taking far longer than the former. She presents them as two loops forming a figure eight, and notes:

> The integrative loop of the Map to Wholeness . . . represent[s] the hidden part of transformation . . . because much of what happens during it is unseen by others and occurs deep within your interior. Regardless of whether your life-changing event occurred at work, in a hospital, on a sports field, or while visiting a distant country, the lower half of the figure eight begins when you literally return home, whatever "home" is to you at the time. At the place you call home, you begin integrating your life-changing experience by relaxing into the comfort and relief of all that is familiar to you.[29]

As the last of Ross's four quick examples indicate, transformational travel is a class of experience where encapsulation can be most rewarding—and mandatory if you truly desire lasting change. When people participate in Burning Man, for example, they have opportunities for reflections in its programming, including coloring exercises, tea and cookie sessions, sharing circles, and access to multiple-year participants who serve as coaches.

The Transformational Travel Council (TTC) guides all its members in encapsulation. Founding member Eric Rupp wrote

The Transformational Travel Journal to help people make their own lasting changes—and to help destinations and travel companies guide them. He introduces it by writing, "Making travel 'transformational' is up to you. It may happen by chance, but you need not leave it to luck. You can forge your journey toward growth and change."[30] To forge that journey, Rupp offers this PATH structure:[31]

- ***P**repare:* Shape the impact of your journey before you step out the door.
- ***A**dventure:* As you observe, explore, absorb, and interact, you are creating your experience.
- ***T**hink:* Make time to consider, discuss, and ponder.
- ***H**onor:* Intentional transformation occurs when you honor your insights and integrate them into your life. . . . Affect the lives of others and radiate out into the world.

You can directly see in these the three steps of encapsulation: preparation, reflection, and integration.

Travel design company Explorer X operationalizes this idea. Founded by Michael Bennett and Jake Haupert—both of whom, not coincidentally, helped found the TTC—the company is "dedicated to crafting customized travel experiences that have a profound and lasting impact on your life. We believe that traveling like true explorers—with curiosity, courage, resilience, and an open heart and mind—allows us to learn and grow from our adventures. In doing so, we are inspired to live with more joy, intention, mindfulness, and meaning."[32] Never merely memorable, the highly customized travel experiences that Explorer X designs, books, and encapsulates for its clients—called "explorers"—are meaningful at a minimum, almost always transporting, and frequently transformative. As Bennett, who essentially designed the company as his doctoral dissertation, told me, "What we've found over the years is that, in terms of desired outcomes, most people don't have specific goals or intentions in mind for their travel experiences before they embark. What they do know is that when they approach travel with a curious heart and open mind, *something* inevitably will happen along the way that invites them to consider new ideas, perspectives, and ways of living." The catalyst for the transformation, in other words, is usually not instigated in advance, but comes via some discovery made along the way.

Encapsulation is key to the company's success, for as Bennett told me, "By far the most important element of a transformative experience is the traveler's mindset before, during, and after their adventures." After booking but before the trip commences, Explorer X provides a Mindful Travel Toolkit & Guide to help travelers both prepare for and deepen their travel experience, and challenges them to answer these preparatory questions:[33]

1. Why are you going on this Journey? What is your "Call to Adventure"?
2. What is your intention for this Journey? What would you like to get out of this experience?
3. What questions, opportunities, and/or challenges would you love clarity around?
4. What will you DO to make the most of this Journey?
5. How are you going to BE on this Journey?

The company then urges its explorers to reflect as they travel, not waiting until the end of the trip. Ideally, they write their thoughts daily in a journal, and then use the Journey Reflection Guide, which the company encourages as the trip nears its end, and afterward as well.[34] This tool elicits reflection and integration by inviting the traveler to write down a description of the trip in detail. It asks such reflective questions as "What people, moments, or experiences will you remember?" "Who/what inspired you?" and

"What did you learn (or relearn) about yourself?" followed by three integration questions that solicit one new action, one new behavior, and one new mindset the traveler should now practice. The Mindful Travel Toolkit & Guide helps people reflect and integrate by guiding each one to "make sense of what you experienced, identify things you learned, and begin to take actions—big or small—that will positively impact your life, your community, and the world around you." To help with these two all-important transformation tools, it further offers support in the way of "community conversations, mastermind groups, introductions to coaches and consultants, and loads of recommended resources and tools."[35]

You should similarly create opportunities for your guests to prepare for, reflect on, and integrate their experiences, for encapsulation is the crux of turning transformative experiences into full transformations. Like Explorer X, encapsulate your offerings with questions that would best assist your guests in turning any level of experience—memorable, meaningful, or transporting—into a fully transformative one. Then determine how best you can ask those questions, get customers to answer and act on them, and guide them through the entire journey.

When you do this, you can transform your business from being an experience stager to a transformation guider. The next chapter offers a number of techniques, beyond encapsulation, for staging experiences that effect transformations.

REFLECTION

Here are some questions to reflect on about moving through the levels of experiences to full and lasting transformations:

- Think of experiences in your own life that exemplify the four levels: memorable, meaningful, transporting, and transformative. What distinctions between the four do you perceive?

- How do these distinctions help you identify, define, and clarify the types of experiences your company could stage?
- Does your company perform any of the elements to encapsulation today? What's missing, and how can you add that to your customer journey?

PREPARATION

In the next chapter you will find ideas, principles, and frameworks that will enable you to design and stage memorable, meaningful, transporting, and transformative experiences. Before moving on, think through these questions about your current offerings:

- Is your organization aligned in how it approaches customers, and are the experiences they have with you unified in such a way that they perceive one holistic journey?
- How much effort do your employees generally put in to satisfy customers? Do they tend to go beyond the norm to create higher levels of engagement and loyalty? If not, why?
- Are your offerings pretty much the same for everybody, or do you go to lengths to appeal to each customer individually?
- Do the interactions that customers have with your business and employees tend to be consistent each time, or do they ever take on an intensity that excites and engages?

5

STAGING TRANSFORMATIVE EXPERIENCES

Given that transformations comprise a series of experiences staged to guide customers in achieving their aspirations, every idea, principle, and framework for experience design applies to transformation design as well. To that end, this chapter offers four key elements of experience design. Turning the memorable, meaningful, and transporting into the transformative requires making it:

- *Cohesive:* Establishing and applying a theme, the organizing principle that determines what is in the experience and what is not. With flourishing the raison d'être of business, as a transformation guider you need to go beyond a theme to determine your *corporate* raison d'être, the meaningful purpose that gets to the heart of why you are in the transformation business.
- *Robust:* Hitting the sweet spot within the four realms of experience—entertainment, educational, escapist, and esthetic. With transformative experiences, you need to use these realms to transform each aspirant's viewpoint, understanding, capabilities, and appreciation.

- *Personal:* Reaching inside people to engage them by mass customizing the components of goods, services, and experiences that integrate into the offering. With the rise of digital technology and AI, you especially need to consider creating digital platforms that mass customize their offerings to individual aspirants on demand, at point of need.
- *Dramatic:* Directing workers to act on your business stage, plus designing the experience to rise up to a climax and come back down again through dramatic structure. For most transformation journeys—given the ups and downs, the progress and regress, and the inherent uncertainty of how people react to guiding—you should embrace street theatre as the model for work and employ the hero's journey as the dramatic structure specifically attuned to transformations.

While these four elements originate in experience design, in the following sections I'll extend them in ways particularly helpful to guiding transformations.[1]

Cohesive

Theming often gets a bad rap because many theme parks and attractions go over the top with it and because the decor and costumes at virtually every theme restaurant are so in your face. A theme, however, is simply the organizing principle of an experience. It is your intention for everything you design and stage, serving as a two-edged sword for determining what is in the experience and—perhaps even more important—what is out. You then design all the components—physical, human, and digital—so they unite to keep guests engaged. With a great theme, your experience becomes cohesive. Without it, experiences so easily devolve into "everything but the kitchen sink."

Whether you intentionally give your experience a theme or not, it ends up having one.[2] Your guests will surmise an organizing principle from their own encounters, consciously or otherwise. Therefore, the first thing you should determine is that theme. And if you already stage experiences but have yet to explicitly use a theme, determine what organizing principle would best harmonize the positive aspects of each one, and then eliminate whatever doesn't fit.[3]

Since most transformations happen not at once but with a series of experiences that lead aspirants from where they are today to what they want to become, your theme needs to encompass each event in the series. These may be very different from each other—in weight-loss programs, think of the initial orientation meeting, weighing sessions, counseling, app check-ins, and so forth—so you very well may benefit from having a different theme for every experience. App check-ins may have an entertaining gaming motif, for example, while individual counseling is more serious and straightforward.

This in turn means you may need a guiding principle, or *meta*-theme, for your complete transformation offering. The overarching meta-theme unites all the individual experiences into one cohesive whole, creating a unified journey for aspirants.

For instance, in health & well-being, a number of years ago Heartland Health embraced as its meta-theme the three-word phrase "Live Life Well." The health-care system's leaders didn't want to just treat symptoms and conduct procedures, but desired that everyone who came to Heartland would experience the phrase's intention, no matter their entry point or connection. They wanted patients to be able to live life well, their family members to live life well, the entire community to live life well, and—core to the whole endeavor—its caregivers to live life well, so out of that abundance they could care for everyone else. They wanted everyone to not be treated as cogs in the machine of a health-care system, but to individually flourish as human beings. Live Life Well became so important as the organizing principle that CEO Dr. Mark Laney, now retired, renamed the company Mosaic Life Care and transformed the organization to enact it. That manifested in different ways for distinct transformative experiences in different hospitals, clinics, and offices while unifying them together.

From meta-themes to meaningful purpose

For Mosaic Life Care, since its meta-theme of Live Life Well encompassed the entire enterprise, it became the enterprise's *meaningful purpose*. This is the corporate raison d'être, the enterprise's reason for existence, *why* the business exists beyond making money, with profit being the measure of how well an enterprise fulfills its purpose. As Jim Gilmore and I wrote in our book *Authenticity: What Consumers* Really *Want,* a sense of purpose "gives work meaning, defines why the enterprise is more than an accumulation of processes and an aggregation of employees, and points workers toward a common goal."[4]

Purpose brings together the interests of employer, employees, and customers while defining the company's overarching intention. It guides, inspires, and unifies those affiliated with, contributing to, and impacted by the enterprise. And purpose manifests outwardly through your economic offerings, cohesively aligning them around why and how you create economic value. Your meaningful purpose should be inspirational, aspirational, and timeless, providing ongoing stability internally even as everything else shifts around you externally.

While some companies have long been led by their meaningful purpose—think of S.C. Johnson in chapter 2—the vast majority have never thought about it. Nonetheless, individual enterprises (and business units within them) generally *have* a purpose of some sort; it's just never been brought into the open and intentionally expressed. Unless you're a new company, you generally don't want to simply pull a purpose out of thin air, but instead *uncover* what your purpose already is. (For an example of how one enterprise did it, see the sidebar "Meaningful Purpose Case Study: Crown Worldwide Group.")

To then make that purpose meaningful to the entire organization, it must be declared, promulgated, upheld, and lived in a way that ideally:[5]

- Enriches greater humanity to foster human flourishing
- Simultaneously enriches the workers within and other contributors to the enterprise, so they also flourish
- Aligns all contributors—whether employees, contractors, suppliers, community members, volunteers, and sometimes customers themselves—in doing the work and producing the offerings of the enterprise
- Is inspirational, aspirational, and timeless
- Functions as a theme, determining what is in and what is out
- Works for everyone who chooses to be a part of it (whether or not others view it as silly, trite, or unworkable)
- Is concise, evocative, and memorable

As with an experience theme, a meaningful purpose faces inward and manifests outward. It inspires, aligns, and directs workers in order that the organization can create economic value for customers in ways that fulfill the purpose. All companies should embrace this concept for the meaning it offers employees (beginning, not ending, at the top!), as well as to enable the business to thrive through the ongoing value it creates for customers.

Embracing it is particularly crucial for transformation guiders because of the deep emotional labor that your employees naturally put into their work, and the deeply individual nature of transforming aspirants from the inside out. You want all

Meaningful Purpose Case Study: Crown Worldwide Group

In January 2020 Crown Worldwide Group realized that its people were not as aligned as they should be. Recognizing that research pointed to the success of enterprises with a strong purpose and employees who are connected to it, Crown embarked on a journey to define its meaningful purpose. A privately held $600 million company with around four thousand employees across a number of logistics brands—covering records and information management, private and corporate relocations, fine art, workspaces, and other industries involving moving things around the world—Crown didn't put top executives together to determine what its purpose *should be*, but smartly sought to unearth what it already *was*. Led by Norah Franchetti, group vice president for marketing, in concert with Crown's HR group, employee engagement and experience agency FathomXP, and corporate and brand storytellers Insight Agents, the effort engaged around 150 employees across its brands and geographic areas, from executives to frontline personnel.

The approach "focused on sourcing and articulating the purpose from within, planting the seeds of purpose-focused conversation across the organization and supporting those conversations to enable them to grow and translate into purpose-led work," as FathomXP cofounder Charlotte Dewar put it to me. The process involved reviewing Crown's sixty-year history, conducting linguistic analysis of company materials, gathering information and feedback from employees, and conducting a series of workshops. Taking into account its long-held values—being caring, being there, being determined, being open-minded, and sharing—this deep dive revealed a meaningful purpose that likewise was long-held but newly articulated: *We make it simpler for people to live, work, and do business anywhere in the world.*

Once articulated, Crown's leadership team and executive board enthusiastically embraced this statement as the company's meaningful purpose and began to promulgate it throughout the organization. Franchetti told me that its simplicity and straightforwardness was easy to understand, which was important as Crown's business is quite complex, so the quest to make the purpose simple for both external and internal customers really resonated. Aligning around it became a unifying force, transforming the organization from focusing on its own complexity to centering on customer simplicity.

Crown has seen tangible results from understanding and living the purpose. Franchetti credits it with enhancing collaboration and innovation, with many new ideas generated for making current and new offerings simple for customers. For example, during the Covid-19 pandemic the company began to scan and digitally deliver documents rather than physically store and ship client boxes, reducing both complication and environmental impact. Crown further expanded into new services such as office design and relocation consulting.

It also introduced a Net Simpler Score (NSS) to measure its impact on customers, which has steadily improved as the organization has become more driven by its purpose. Employee engagement has similarly gone up, with a high correlation between greater engagement and better NSS.

Overall, Crown's focus on meaningful purpose has transformed the organization, making it more aligned, customer-centric, and innovative. Its well-articulated and thoroughly understood purpose has taken root within its culture. As Franchetti related, "Crown has never been through such a period of transformation. Purpose has been at the heart of that—enabling us to connect better with our teams, opening up new conversations, and reducing complexity to help decision making. Purpose will continue to be pivotal to how we learn and adapt as a business."

contributors to ascend to the proposition stated in your purpose, even if it means some leave, and all new hires, partners, suppliers likewise should know and agree with the purpose before they join. Without that, alignment is lost and meaning is muddled.

You also want your aspirants to viscerally *feel* the purpose emanating from your guides, who must live it with every interaction, encounter, and step along the journey. This, too, must be the case at the top of the company and everywhere in between. If the C-suite focuses on finances above all else, purpose loses its meaning. The organization will realize it, corrode from the inside out, lose its way, become mediocre, and eventually fail. The meaningful purpose must inform and guide everything employees do and everything customers experience.

And that purpose should never be a vision, a mission statement, or a tagline, all of which necessarily change with changing times. Rather, it should be composed to last. Decades ago, for example, Mark Scott, then the CEO of Mid-Columbia Medical Center (now known as Adventist Health Columbia Gorge), marshaled into place a three-word meaningful purpose still operative today: "Personalize. Humanize. Demystify," or "PHD." Every decision made in the enterprise, from the board and CEO on down, is based on whether it better personalizes, humanizes, or demystifies health care for patients and their families. Thanks to the power of PHD, this small hospital went from serving two sides of the Columbia River Gorge to having patients travel to it from over twenty states.[6]

In conversations with Scott, other executives, and associates, including visits to Mid-Columbia, I could tell what a real difference the purpose made with employees at every level, and how that manifested in turn with patients, their family members, and the community. Meaningful purpose is a wonderful way to foster flourishing with everyone the organization touches. Imagine what a difference it would make in your business to be that intentional about the work everyone does. And what a difference it would make across the world if every other enterprise did as well.

Robust

The second core element of experience design is to make your experiences robust by exploring how to make them broader, more substantial, and have greater engagement. To do so, recognize that guest participation in any experience can vary from *passive*, where they do not affect the experience much, to *active*, where what they do decidedly influences it. The connection guests have with the experience can also vary from *absorption*, where it comes into them, to *immersion*, where they go into the experience. These dimensions are continuums along which the experience always has aspects of being active and passive, immersive and absorbing.

You can take advantage of these continuums to design your experiences to be more engaging, and therefore more memorable, by employing the four mutually compatible realms, as seen in figure 5-1:[7]

- *Entertainment:* Passively absorbing the sights and sounds presented to you. Watching TV or movies, listening to music, taking in plays, and other such events count as the entertainment realm, which captivates *audiences* who *enjoy* the experience.
- *Educational:* Actively wrestling with what is presented to you. Taking a class, listening to an informative presentation, watching a video to figure out how to fix something, and other such actions fall into the educational realm where it engrosses *learners* that, naturally, *learn* from the experience.
- *Escapist:* Actively joining what is happening around you. Cross-country skiing, puzzling through an escape room,

and touring a city or destination all employ the escapist realm, which involves *participants* that *go* to some location and *do* activities within it.

- *Esthetic:* Passively immersing yourself in a place. Walking in a park, visiting a museum, and sitting in a café gain from the esthetic realm, which connects with *selves* that sit down, hang out, and just *be.*[8]

While the examples given for the four realms all have their "center of gravity" in specific quadrants of the framework, all four are always in play and therefore should be factored into the design of virtually all experiences. The most engaging, most memorable, and most robust draw richly from all the realms by hitting the sweet spot in the center. Escape rooms, for instance, clearly have a center of gravity in the escapist realm, yet participants immerse themselves in a place designed with a theme whose esthetic aspects create a desire to come in, and then are educated in how to escape by exploring those aspects, all the while being

FIGURE 5-1

The four realms of experience

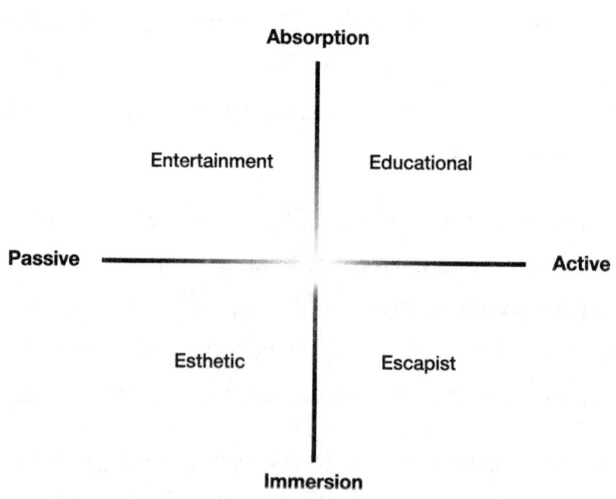

entertained by seeing fellow participants (and themselves) repeatedly try to figure out hidden clues, with the entertainment realm heightened more by failures than successes. So whatever you design and stage, incorporate all four realms to hit the sweet spot and thereby create more value for your guests.

It's easiest to employ the four realms within different aspects of the experience. Jin Li Street in Chengdu, China, exemplifies this concept (as well as so many other principles of experience design and rendering authenticity).[9] Its center of gravity lies in the escapist realm, for it is a world apart from modern Chengdu. Once you enter its gates, emblazoned with the Chinese characters "Jin" and "Li," you are transported back in time to the period of the three kingdoms (220–280 AD). While the shopping street looks as if it has always been there—an oasis in the middle of the city—it in fact arose from the dirt, partly due to funding from a nearby museum of this period in China's history. Its meaningful purpose entails saving the ancient handcrafts from the Szechuan province and sustaining the modern artisans who carry on these trades.

Jin Li Street further extends the escapist realm with, for example, games you can play that were popular 1,800 years ago. The esthetic environment—again, built from scratch—immerses you in the era, especially at night when lantern lights fill your view from above. One part of the street that did precede the current place incorporates deep-rooted temple gardens that bestow a respite in your day, while also being the home for such entertainment offerings as a flautist. Puppetry and other shows also involve elements from the entertainment realm, while the many educational aspects include information, exhibits, and interactions on both the time of the three kingdoms and the modern artisans in the shops, from whom you can buy goods made right there, such as clothing handcrafted on looms.

Though you can encounter numerous aspects from each realm in any visit to Jin Li Street, there is one activity—the place's signature moment—when all four come together simultaneously: the daily parade. Here, guests explore further into the past while watching characters come alive. They actively participate in the show and its movements, learning more about the period and what people did there, while enjoying the people-watching of fellow guests and hanging out with their families, friends, and the characters. It is passive and active, absorptive and immersive, all in the same place at the same time. That's truly hitting the sweet spot.

As I found during my visits to Jin Li Street, robust experiences can become deeply transporting!

The four realms within transformative experiences

Robust experiences are broader, more substantial, and have greater engagement than those more typically encountered. With transformative experiences, this means expanding them to encompass the heart, body, mind, and spirit; going beyond what aspirants say to what they mean or have yet to discover; and guiding the whole person, not just acting on appearances, superficialities, or symptoms.

The four realms naturally serve as stimuli for and lend themselves to specific sorts of changes. The entertainment realm most readily yields a transformation of *viewpoint*. Film directors, for example, often create movies just to get across a certain perspective that they want others to understand, accept, and even embrace.[10] Plays, concerts, and other forms of passive absorption—books most especially—can affect experiencer viewpoints. While much of this involves *pushing* a perspective out into the world, you can use entertainment aspects to *pull* a viewpoint aspiration from an individual to help effect most any desired transformation.[11]

The educational realm encompasses a transformation in *understanding*. Any transformation requiring that someone comprehend new levels of information and knowledge requires a center of gravity within that realm. This of course includes schools from kindergarten on up to higher education, but also lifelong learning opportunities, employee experiences managed by learning and development departments, and any other transformative experience involving the attainment of knowledge & wisdom.

The escapist realm grants great possibilities for transformations in *capability*, whether new or improved. Immersive environments enable people to gain such capabilities in the places they would then apply them, such as with sports: it's hard to get better at skiing without going down the slopes. Simulators and virtual reality also let people increase their capabilities at not only sports and games but mental health, physical rehabilitation, training, and work.

Finally, the esthetic realm suits itself to transformations of *appreciation*. By walking or hiking through a state or national park, you can come to appreciate the awesome wonder of nature. By visiting an art museum, you can grow in admiration for art objects, artists, and art in general. By sitting in a café, you can feel gratitude for a moment of peace, thankfulness for time with a friend, or simple pleasure in the small joys in life, a cup of coffee not the least of them.

No authors discuss the esthetic realm as applied to transformations more, or better, than Susan Magsamen and Ivy Ross in *Your Brain on Art: How the Arts Transform Us*. It's a beautifully written compendium of the science of neuroaesthetics, research into how the brain responds to art, architecture, reading, and so many other stimuli, and how our responses change us. As they open the book:

> You know the transformative power of art. You've gotten lost in music, in a painting, in a movie or play, and you felt something shift within you. You've read a book so compelling that you pressed it into the hands of a friend; you heard a song so

> moving, you listened to it over and over, memorizing every word. The arts bring joy. Inspiration. Well-being. Understanding. Even salvation. And while these experiences may not be easy to explain, you have always known they are real and true.[12]

Within the context of business, consider the work of David Putrino, director of rehabilitation innovation at Mount Sinai Health System. Magsamen and Ross write that Dr. Putrino "marries aesthetics and the arts with technology to treat people who have suffered serious injury or illness such as stroke, ALS, and traumatic brain injury."[13] He stresses that "you shouldn't just rehabilitate a stroke survivor to the point they were at before they had the stroke, you should be pushing them along the wellness spectrum, beyond where they were."[14]

What surprised me in reading *Your Brain on Art* was how very much of it applied to the three realms of experience besides the esthetic. As just one example, Magsamen and Ross report on Adam Gazzaley, executive director of Neuroscape, a neuroscience facility at the UCSF Medical Center. Focusing on ADHD, Dr. Gazzaley and his team worked on immersive video games to improve user attention. The games start easy and get harder as people play. One such game, EndeavorRx, was approved by the FDA as a Class 2 medical device to treat children with ADHD.[15]

You can gain more powerful outcomes if you intentionally design aspects of all four realms into your transformative experiences. Hit the sweet spot by asking yourself these questions:

- How can you use the entertainment realm to help an aspirant enjoy the experience and thereby influence their *viewpoint*?
- How can you use the educational realm to enable an aspirant to learn from exploring new activities that yield greater *understanding*?

- How can you use the escapist realm to guide an aspirant to go and actively do in order to gain or improve *capabilities*?
- How can you use the esthetic realm to get an aspirant to sit down, hang out, and just be, to affect their *appreciation*?

Increasing the robustness of the transformative experiences you create, design, and stage will increase the level of engagement your aspirants have, and thereby greatly increase the chances of transformation.

Personal

As discussed in chapter 1, customization is a route up the Progression of Economic Value. Experiences become transformations when they're tailored to exactly what customers need at this moment in time, based on who they are and what they want to become. Experiences are inherently personal, but again, transformations are fundamentally individual, changing us from the inside out based on what we undergo. So you can shift from simply personal to deeply individual by customizing transformation journeys, experience by experience, for each aspirant.[16] And when you *mass* customize them with low costs and high volume, you efficiently guide customers uniquely.

Modularity is the key to mass customizing anything. Think of LEGO bricks. What can you build with LEGOs? *Anything you want*, because of the bricks' variety of sizes, shapes, and colors, and because of the linkage system that snaps them together. That's what modularity is—modules + linkage system—and you can use it to mass customize not only physical goods but service activities (often by modularizing processes) and, of course, experiences.[17] Your modules + linkage system defines the modular architecture from which you mass customize your offerings on demand, at point of need for individual customers.

LEGOs use what's called *sectional* modularity, but for experiences the more useful type is *bus* modularity.[18] The term comes from transportation buses, where differing people get on and off at different times, so between every stop there can be a different configuration of people. With experiences, time is the bus. It's the linkage system on which different experience segments can be placed, creating a mass-customized journey through time, and customizing it for each individual can make it time well spent. (For a third kind of modularity and its implications, see the sidebar "Digital Modularity and AI.")

For example, Princess Cruises, a unit of Carnival Corporation & plc, designs a mass-customized itinerary for each guest using its Princess MedallionClass program. (Disclosure: I have worked with Carnival in an advisory capacity.) The program centers on an internet-of-things device dubbed the Medallion, which enables every onboard employee to identify each individual guest. Based on responses to a pre-cruise query about favorite experiences and pre-embarkation bookings, the company puts together a personal itinerary for every guest that can be modified in real time, adapting to changing desires. This itinerary covers the entire cruise, representing the bus of time each person has. Guests can access and update it through the Princess Cruises app on their phone, tablet, or stateroom TV, or on public monitors throughout the ship. As the system learns more and more about the guest—through direct responses, how they rate their activities, and even such external factors as the weather—it sends personalized experience invitations that match people's interests and the time they have available. Crew members can even presciently deliver a drink to someone, using MedallionClass to remember that when they are on the pool deck with their kids, their favored beverage is an iced tea with no lemon; when they're in the bar with their buddies, it's a mojito; and when they're in a restaurant with their spouse, it's a glass of shiraz.

Each potential on- and off-ship experience has a module that MedallionClass links together to mass customize guest experiences. And "mass" is a key property of it: Princess can offer much more personal experiences while lowering costs and increasing efficiencies across its total offering. As the creator of Medallion-Class, John Padgett, former Princess president and Carnival chief experience and innovation officer, likes to say, it "allows us to take the service delivery burden off our crew members so they can do what they do best—make our guests happy."

That feeling, over time, yields true loyalty. Most companies seem to think loyalty is about rewarding customers by giving them free stuff they would have bought anyway. That's not loyalty; it's bribery. Moreover, such loyalty programs are self-commoditizing by focusing customers on price—"The company must be overcharging me on my purchases to have the money to give it away for free!" Instead, true loyalty comes from understanding your customers better than anyone else and customizing to their personal desires, needs, and aspirations. Think of every interaction with customers as an opportunity to learn about them individually. The more you learn, the better you can customize. The better you customize, the more they'll benefit. The more customers benefit, the more they'll interact with you. And every interaction is an opportunity to learn.[19]

Experience and transformation platforms

Princess Cruises is in the experience business, offering time well spent in a highly personal manner through what I call an operational *experience platform*.[20] Walt Disney World's MagicBand+ is another such platform—which is no coincidence since John Padgett was one of the five members of the team that created it there.[21] Other platforms include Grip for events, Like Magic in hospitality, and Attractions.io for theme parks, zoos, and other such experiences. But they are not just for consumer experiences. In B2B, commercial real estate landlords and property managers can use HqO's REX Platform—for real estate experience—to

Digital Modularity and AI

While platforms today connect all genres of economic offerings to customers, they themselves are built entirely out of bits. They use *digital modularity*, the most powerful type, with much greater capabilities for mass customizing than even the sectional modularity of LEGO bricks. Anything you can digitize, you can customize, for once it enters the realm of zeroes and ones, you can change a zero to a one and vice versa instantly, costlessly, frictionlessly, and seamlessly.[a]

Digital modularity is the foundation of generative artificial intelligence. It works by using large language models (LLMs), in which each data point is a module at the disposal of the AI, whether that data point is a word, a number, a pixel, or a frame. These can be grouped into higher and higher clusters of each, such as phrases, images, and video segments. Generative AI chooses, or *generates*, each digital module in turn based on which one has the highest probability—according to the LLM created from its training, ongoing use, and feedback—of completing the prompt asked of it. Prompts are answered (almost) literally bit by bit, pixel by pixel, symbol by symbol.

AI supercharges mass customizing capabilities. It enables companies to learn individual desires, needs, and aspirations, as well as to determine what offering modules—goods, services, or experiences—would best be used in a situation to create customer-unique offerings, whether those are digital, physical, or fuse the real with the virtual. LOOP, for example, is a public benefit corporation that offers car insurance to underserved communities. It avoids standard insurance metrics to instead collect individual driving patterns, using AI to develop a personal driving score, based on which it can lower or raise rates as appropriate. Its AI-driven app suggests ways to drive more safely and thereby increase the driving score and lower rates. As a *Harvard Business Review* article about the company explains, "LOOP not only helps create safer roads; it lowers the chances that its customers will get into an accident and file a claim, increasing their lifetime value."[b]

Each of the transformation platforms mentioned in this book already uses artificial intelligence—if not the generative kind, then machine learning, its more mature, less capable cousin—with much more to come thanks to continuing progress in the field, including recognizing the power of intelligent augmentation. For example, in 2025 BetterUp, the transformation platform that connects employees and individuals to coaches, enhanced its offering with AI coaches customized to "personality, preferred learning style, and organizational culture" as well as "strategic business metrics, aligning with leadership frameworks, competencies and employees' professional journeys." The professional coaches aren't automated by the AI; rather, they together offer a "dynamic blend of support—from AI-powered insights available 24/7 to deep, meaningful connections with expert human coaches." At its announcement, CEO and cofounder Alexi Robichaux remarked:

> For over a decade, BetterUp has led the way in showing how coaching transforms lives and businesses. With this launch, we're taking that transformation further—scaling coaching to meet every employee where they are. By weaving together the always-on access of AI and the deep human expertise of our coaches, we are proud to be the only platform to offer a complete approach to development—one that scales growth, deepens connection, and empowers organizations to thrive.[c]

Whether you use a platform or not, or whether you take advantage of AI or not, embrace the power of modularity to mass customize your experiences in order to efficiently, uniquely guide transformations that are fundamentally individual.

Notes

a. We first used these four watchwords of mass customization in B. Joseph Pine II, Bart Victor, and Andrew C. Boynton, "Making Mass Customization

(*continued*)

Work," *Harvard Business Review*, September–October 1993, https://hbr.org/1993/09/making-mass-customization-work.

b. Julian De Freitas and Elie Ofek, "How AI Can Power Brand Management," *Harvard Business Review*, September–October 2024, https://hbr.org/2024/09/how-ai-can-power-brand-management.

c. All quotes are from "BetterUp Launches AI Coaching: Bridging Human Expertise and AI Innovation to Transform Organizational Impact at Scale," Business Wire, January 21, 2025, https://www.businesswire.com/news/home/20250121963707/en/BetterUp-Launches-AI-Coaching-Bridging-Human-Expertise-and-AI-Innovation-to-Transform-Organizational-Impact-at-Scale.

enable tenants, employees, and visitors to discover, book, customize, and stage building amenities, special events, local restaurants and gyms, and other physical and digital experiences.

Similarly, there are operational *transformation platforms*. These incorporate experience platforms but go beyond time well spent to yield time well invested. Each experience must be appropriately customized, through learning about and responding to personal preferences, and built atop previous experiences to yield the desired transformation.[22] For instance, Symplany, the B2B2C plan-driven investing company we met in chapter 3, provides a transformation platform that financial advisers employ to dynamically and spontaneously orchestrate ongoing discussions with clients, experience module by experience module, within the flow of conversation. For example, a client can "test out" a goal—such as saving for the kids' college funds, buying a cabin, selling a piece of property, or working another year before retiring—and the adviser can treat it as a new module in the overall plan and show its potential impact. The platform further gives them various ways of examining and visualizing whatever issues arise, depending on the depth of financial knowledge the client demonstrates. Advisers can thereby instantly handle whatever concerns, questions, or opportunities come up. Symplany's powerful visualization tools, built via sophisticated algorithms using mountains of data, enable customers to visually see the results of any aspirational decisions under consideration, as well as the continuing outcomes of those decisions once made.

That is key to differentiating transformation platforms from experience ones: mass customizing journeys across time for individual aspirants. It means doing whatever it takes to get there, including handling backsliding or other obstacles with remedial, rousing, and/or recommitment experiences staged on demand, even in the moment.

Other such platforms include the wonderfully named Outcomes4Me to support cancer patients; Betterment, which helps consumers manage every aspect of their finances with on-demand access to financial coaches; and Benevity, which helps companies engage their employees in charitable giving and volunteering that enhances business purpose and offers employees meaning. To look at one transformation platform in detail, Echo360 offers a customizable eLearning platform that works with educational, corporate, and government institutions to better engage learners and ensure greater educational outcomes. (Disclosure: I work with Echo360 in an advisory capacity.) The company recognizes that it has three distinct constituencies: administrators, instructors, and learners. Administrators—the customers who buy the platform—want courses that help instructors effectively create, stage, and assess learning experiences for the benefit of the people who consume the content. Echo360's platform mass customizes for each constituency to inspire learners to achieve their educational goals, encourage instructors to get into flow and improve their performance, and enable administrators to create collaborative environments that yield the educational outcomes they value most for their organizations.

President and CEO Murad Velani joined the company in 2021 amid the shift to online learning due to Covid-19. He and his team faced a challenging marketplace, with education, business, and government enterprises trying to make sense of myriad and often disparate technologies purchased in a panic to keep workers engaged. As Velani told me:

> It had been an arms race to develop and sell remote learning engagement technologies, with little eye toward longer-term outcomes and residual impact for the different types of customers and users around the world. When we developed our "trilogy" of stakeholders and started helping them achieve the transformations they were seeking, we started delivering on each one's exacting use case, which in turn unlocked better learning outcomes as well as growth for our company. Adopting a transformation mindset not only changes the narrative, it changes the very approach you take to investing, serving, partnering, and growing with customers.

If you have ongoing relationships with customers, or desire to create them, then think about how to create such transformation platforms that let aspirants access your company, your people, your capabilities, and your guidance on demand, at point of need.

Dramatic

Creating dramatic experiences matters in two ways. First, when you stage experiences, work is theatre. It's not a metaphor—work *as* theatre—but a model: work *is* theatre. Whenever workers are in front of customers, they are on stage. You must therefore direct your workers to act in ways that engage customers, the audience of their performance. Theatre alone can turn mundane interactions into engaging encounters, and engaging encounters into transformation journeys.

With transformative experiences, though, aspirants aren't just an audience and workers aren't just actors; your employees are also guides. They must watch and cocreate performances with aspirants, helping them just as acting coaches help actors. They must treat each aspirant—including individual people within organizations and communities—as a whole person, engaging them not just emotionally but often physically, intellectually, and spiritually.

Most importantly, they must guide each aspirant *individually,* recognizing the unique person, organization, business, or community whom they have the privilege of leading to aspiration achievement. This again means that not only the economic offerings but the *encounters* workers have with aspirants must be mass customized.

When directing workers to act, then, embrace street theatre, the mass-customized form where performers have a large set of routines or "bits"—experience modules—that they call on in response to every reaction of the audience.[23] And whenever you encounter something you haven't seen before, you must turn to improv theatre to improvise the proper response. Modularizing employee performance in this way enables you to efficiently guide individual transformations through every encounter with an aspirant.

Second, transformative experiences must pay attention to the structure of performances, how the business intentionally arranges and stages everything. Recall that goods are inventoried after production, services are delivered on demand, and experiences—transformative ones included—are *revealed over a duration of time.*[24] As the late experience architect Jon Jerde put it, "What we do is design time. . . . The primary design focus is not an object, but time itself. It's designing what happens to people in time, in a place."[25] Exactly. To create drama, you must intentionally design the time customers spend with you to be both time well spent and well invested.

This means embracing dramatic structure. With any drama, the complication or intensity of the experience changes through time—rising to a climax and coming back down again—and thus do experiences become memorable.

The hero's journey

While there are many models for enacting dramatic structure, the one framework perfectly suited to staging transformative experiences is known as the hero's journey.[26] Delineated by literature professor Joseph Campbell in his seminal book *The Hero with a Thousand Faces,* it is based on research into world mythologies.[27] It's not only a dramatic structure; it's a *transformation journey.*

I think the best representation of it, seen in figure 5-2, comes from movie story consultant Christopher Vogler in his book *The Writer's Journey.* Vogler describes how a seemingly ordinary individual, living a normal life, encounters something unexpected that calls that person to an adventure. Hesitating, the individual meets a wise old man as mentor/sage/wizard/Jedi.[28] With help, the hero crosses a threshold from their ordinary world into a "special world" where they confront dangers, undergo ordeals, and face the threat of death, if not death itself, before saving the world/Middle-Earth/a galaxy far, far away. The hero leaves the "special world," still needing to prove their worth, and with a reward to offer others, finally returns home, transformed.

Now, it's rare that a customer comes to you for help in saving the world. But everyone is the hero of their own transformation journey, the protagonist who with the forming of an aspiration must leave the comforts of their present self to set forth on a journey—with the help of a guide—to face many experiences that move them toward that point when the aspirant can proclaim, "I was X, now I am Y." Transformations do not come easy. To get there, aspirants must overcome obstacles and go through ordeals, dig deep within themselves to learn what is possible, and recognize that the point of proclamation is not the end of the journey. They must return to their daily life with the transformation integrated into their identity.

FIGURE 5-2

The hero's journey

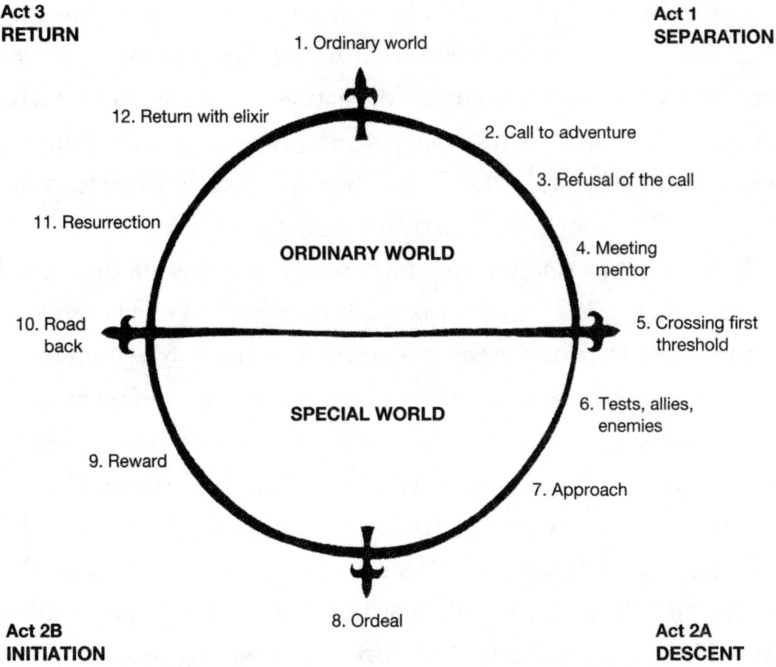

Source: Graphic from *The Writer's Journey, 25th Anniversary Edition*, by Christoper Vogler, provided courtesy of Michael Wiese Productions, www.mwp.com.

Think about how you can make your customers the heroes of their own journeys. In health & well-being, for example, consider the months, even years, that people with cancer spend being treated for and recovering from the disease. Thanks to the emotional impact of the diagnosis, they separate themselves from their normal lives, crossing a threshold and descending into the trials of treatment after treatment under the guidance of a health-care provider. They lose their hair, have good days and bad, see progress—but you are there not just to provide treatments, but to guide them in actively partaking in their personal care plan *outside* of the time they spend in your health facilities, enlisting the full participation and support of their fellowship of family and friends. Thanks to your thorough, holistic guidance—treating the patients as whole people rather than a collection of symptoms—you see them through to the other side physically, emotionally, and even spiritually. When their treatments end and they experience the catharsis that entails, they identify not as someone who's merely completed treatment, but as someone who *conquered* the disease, restored to a new, cancer-free life. And yet, while the physical treatments may be done, you continue to guide them back into normal life, a transformed person.

In wealth & prosperity, one end to which money is but the means is retirement. It's a journey that one (hopefully) starts decades in advance, but there are many ups and downs and maybe even trials and travails. And its impact affects not only the expectant retiree, but their family as well. The climax of that journey, however, should not be the day of retirement; it's the day when the retiree knows, without a doubt, that they *can* retire! That is the day that you, as the guiding financial transformations firm that's been there from the beginning, celebrate the retiree as hero, for it is a day that reduces stress, induces calm, and enables dreams to come true. Even if this path does not follow the stages of the hero's journey all that closely, it honors it in spirit, with aspects of the journey along the way: the initial goal-setting meeting as a call to adventure; the crossing of various thresholds; and the helping of the retiree, after the you-can-do-it! climax, to be "The Master of the Two Worlds," as Campbell put it, in this case meaning current work and future retirement. The fully funded retirement accounts become the metaphorical "elixir," "boon," or "special knowledge" the hero brings to their family after the transformation. If you applied the hero's journey, how much better would your financial experiences be and how much more would you enable aspirants to achieve their dreams?

This form of dramatic structure can of course play out in the other two spheres, knowledge & wisdom and purpose & meaning. In the former, think of every grade level in K–12 schools, as well as those in college and postgraduate work, as its own journey where students "level up" every year. Each level occupies a "special world" of learning, contrasted with the "ordinary world" outside of school, and every teacher is a "mentor." With the latter term, imagine you work for a consulting company that helps enterprises transform their businesses. As the mentor, you guide the aspirant in entering the special world of the engagement and, through many tests and trials (watch out for the organizational antibodies!), lead the client out the other side as a renewed, regenerated, even "resurrected" enterprise, transformed and extraordinarily prepared for the ordinary world of business.[29] Just remember: as a consultant, *you* are not the hero of the story; your client is.

All of these examples, note, involve aspirations of metamorphosis, as it is from such transformational stories that Campbell developed the hero's journey and is how virtually everyone applies it in storytelling across mediums. But the other types of aspirations can benefit from it as well; transformations don't have to be large-scale changes in kind. For example, many apps for fitness tracking, healthy living, stress relief, and so forth use gamification to help keep users on task over time; why not make it more of an *actual* game derived from the hero's journey?[30] There are many experiences without games or even any dramatic structure—immersive art exhibits, museums, trade shows—so you could use this structure to provide that story, giving guests an alternate reality in which they become the hero—at least for the day.[31] One of the reasons that parents spend a ton of money taking their kids to a theme park is to be a hero in their eyes. If you knew that, what could you do differently to make it happen?

Applying the hero's journey

Whatever your business, think of how different your transformative experiences would be if you designed and depicted them using the hero's journey.

I worked with Clint Carnell, founder of boutique advisory firm and accelerator Greyspace, to do exactly this when he was the CEO of Hydrafacial, a company that offers a facial treatment that is the "queen of the facial category." This process, conducted by aestheticians, has three simple steps: cleanse, extract, and hydrate. In thirty minutes, the client has a wonderful experience and can see the "gunkie" extracted from their face (blackheads, dead skin, etc.) in a vial. Afterward, their skin *glows*, an effect that lasts for weeks.

New consumers may come into salons, med spas, or dermatologists for a seemingly modest Hydrafacial treatment, but once they experience the glow it brings and hear compliments galore, they so often come back time and time again. It may not qualify as permanent, long-lasting change—it's more of a quasi-transformation—but customers view it as a facet of fulfilling their health & well-being aspirations, and it can spark new ones as well.

Eddie Yoon, Clint's partner in Greyspace and author of the book *Superconsumers,* identified a core group of Hydrafacial consumers, generally women, who not only loved and bought a lot of treatments during the year, but were also superconsumers of other aesthetic and skin care treatments, cosmetics, gyms and fitness centers, and shoes. Superconsumers are distinct from heavy users who simply buy a lot; as Eddie explains, they "are characterized by their attitude as well: they are passionate about and highly engaged with—and maybe even a little obsessive about—a category. . . . They're emotional buyers who base their purchase decisions on their life aspirations."[32]

Clint and Eddie found that 78 percent of aesthetic consumers are looking for something new, yet the vast majority purchase only one type of treatment. These superconsumers aren't just looking for a beauty transformation; they love the journey itself. The treasure hunt for new treatments and combinations is fun and reflects their deep belief that as their skin—and life—progresses, so too must their therapies.

In one meeting Eddie said, "Every superconsumer is on a quest."[33] We worked together on defining the Hydrafacial encounter as a hero's journey, with the company defining the quest as "extraordinary outcomes for your skin." The quest spreads across four parts that we named adventure, initiation, transformation, and return. Each of these was further delineated into three steps with a verb-object format, collectively defining the transformative Hydrafacial experience, as seen in figure 5-3.

As with all hero's journeys, it begins with the hero living her life when, like a call to adventure, she hears about the Hydrafacial treatment, usually from friends or her aesthetician, and makes an

FIGURE 5-3

Hydrafacial hero's journey

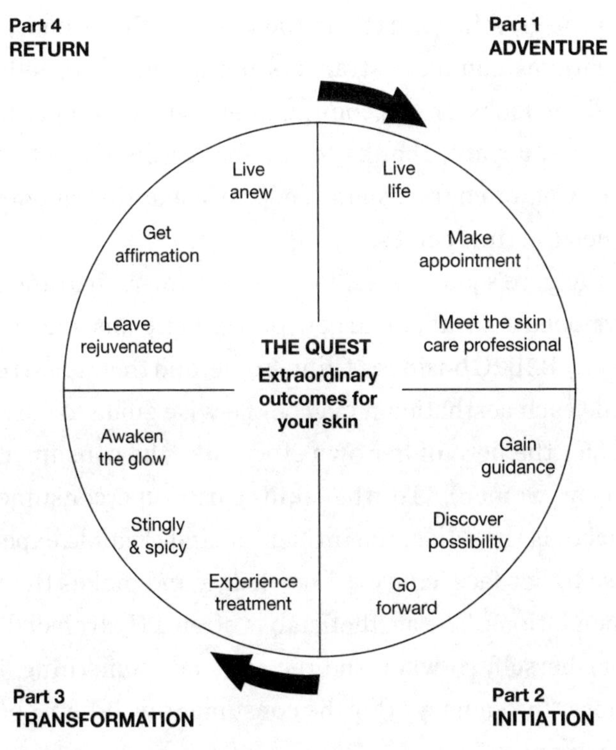

appointment. The customer meets the skin care professional who serves as her guide and explores what's going on in her life and how Hydrafacial can help. Part 2 initiates the consumer-as-hero into the possibilities, learning what Hydrafacial is all about as well as customizing treatments.

The transformation happens in part 3, where the consumer experiences the treatment, starting with a light exfoliation to cleanse the skin and then a light suction that causes her skin to get all "stingly" and spicy. This process gently extracts all the blackheads and dead skin and puts it into the "gunkie" vial that is shown to the client. The third step is to saturate the skin's surface with moisturizers and nourishing custom ingredients, which creates the signature moment where the customer sees herself aglow in a mirror, amazed at the transformation of her face from minutes before.

In part 4 she leaves rejuvenated, usually catching another peek or two at the glow in a mirror on the way out. Her friends, family, and sometimes complete strangers notice the glow, telling her how good she looks. In the coming weeks she feels more healthy, upbeat, and buoyant, thanks to the extraordinary outcome for her skin. And, of course, she's ready to make that appointment again when the time comes.

With the hero's journey set for the consumer, Hydrafacial further developed a parallel journey for aestheticians, one with lessons for any B2B2C business. Clint, Eddie, and their team realized that while each aesthetician may be the wise guide to customers, she's in fact the hero of her own story (like the consumers, they are largely women). To the skin care superconsumer, the aesthetician is the guide, the influential and credible expert who gets close to her face, conveys knowledge, and makes thoughtful recommendations. The aesthetician is often a Hydrafacial superconsumer herself, so when she recommends something, it feels much more "missionary" (for the consumer's well-being benefit), never "mercenary."

Clint built training processes not just for the treatment but for running the business itself, including marketing and pricing. He led the creation of HFX, a training institute, to transform "mere" aestheticians into full entrepreneurs running their own businesses. The Hydrafacial offering combined with the training have helped providers go from making tens of thousands of dollars to hundreds of thousands.

These dual transformations had a massive impact. When Clint took over as CEO in 2016, Hydrafacial was a small company called Edge Systems with modest growth. He rebranded the company to its current name, created an ecosystem of powerhouse brands that added boosters to the treatment, and, in an unprecedented move, put the aesthetician at the center of the category. Clint also bet big on marketing experiences such as the GLOWvolution world tour, where a tricked-out bus with multiple Hydrafacial systems traveled to cities to give people free treatments, resulting in many physicians, spa owners, and others buying machines on the spot.

Hydrafacial more than quintupled its sales during Clint's tenure, growing top and bottom lines at a 50 percent compound annual growth rate. He also led it through the pandemic, when having to lay off nearly 90 percent of the staff meant nearly everyone wrote the company off. But with perseverance, Clint was able to pierce through the noise by recognizing the aesthetician was the hero and coming alongside her on her quest. Hydrafacial is now the second-best-known brand in aesthetics after Botox, and Clint led it to become the fourth most successful special purpose acquisition company in 2021, going public at $1.1 billion and trading up to $4.5 billion when he left the company in late 2022.

The transformation journey

Think now of how you can design the drama in your sequence of transformative experiences through the hero's journey. Modeled after Christopher Vogler's insightful rendition, figure 5-4 illustrates a transformation journey that incorporates many of the ideas and principles in this book. It entails twelve stages over four parts, beginning and ending in the ordinary world of life as it passes through the transformation world, a liminal space and time where the aspirant is neither the original individual nor the fully transformed one. Consider how your business would apply the steps along the journey, recognizing that you need not follow it slavishly, but can adapt it to your perspective, circumstances, and language.

Metamorphosis aspirations are perfect for this form of dramatic structure, but the other types can benefit from it as well. Here's how the transformation journey proceeds:

FIGURE 5-4

The transformation journey

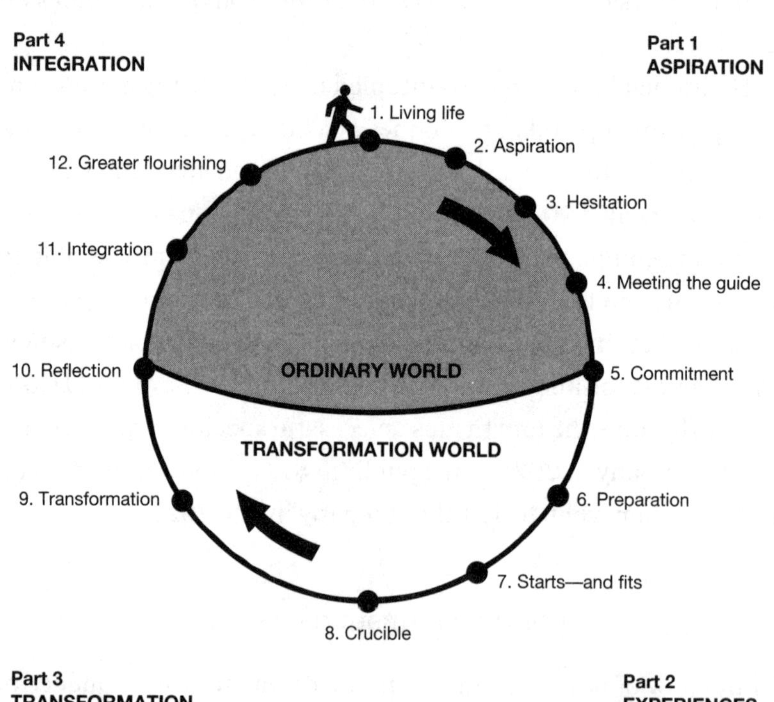

PART 1: ASPIRATION

1. *Living life:* An individual—which could be an organization, a business, or a community, not just a person—is going about their ordinary life, lacking any desire for transformation.

2. *Aspiration:* Something sparks a desire for change. Eventually that aspiration coalesces into one of refinement, ambition, cultivation, or full-on metamorphosis.

3. *Hesitation:* The aspirant may hesitate or outright refuse the call to transform, realizing they don't have the time or resources to go on the journey, or decide the aspiration is too difficult or even unachievable. It may take another catalyst to encourage the aspirant to embrace the journey of transformation—and sometimes that spark is the guide.

4. *Meeting the guide:* Having a mentor turns the journey from an individual pursuit into an economic offering—and thereby greatly increases the chances of success. This encounter could come in the first two steps, as with invitational transformations, and could result from the aspirant seeking help, not just the guide offering it. Whatever the case, it's time to develop the individual from/to statement and design the series of transformative experiences, properly encapsulated, for the journey ahead. (This process should be informed by matching the type of transformation to the type of aspiration, as will be discussed in the next chapter.)

5. *Commitment:* The transformation begins in earnest as the aspirant "crosses the threshold" from the ordinary world to the transformation world. Commitment proves crucial to doing so successfully, for without it the aspirant doesn't put the work in. You'll learn more about commitment and its power in the next two chapters, but with that in place, the

set of transformative experiences required to achieve the aspiration can proceed.

PART 2: EXPERIENCES

6. *Preparation:* This step encompasses imagining the entire journey before it happens, picturing its sequence of events, thinking about what it will be like, and envisioning life with the aspiration achieved. Doing so sets up each aspirant for success, and the more arduous the journey, the greater the preparation needs to be.

7. *Starts—and fits:* After preparation comes the first experience, then the one after that, and the one after that. Most will progress the aspirant toward the aspiration, while some may necessarily be remedial experiences to handle regress that occasionally—and for aspirations of ambition and metamorphosis, inevitably—happens. In some cases, this step may even be filled with trials and tribulations, especially for those with a disruption catalyst.

8. *Crucible:* This step is often named *ordeal* in the hero's journey, but *crucible* is a much better term for the transformation journey, for out of the most difficult of experiences comes a new creation, a changed identity, a transformed aspirant.

PART 3: TRANSFORMATION

9. *Transformation:* The aspirant achieves the aspiration, going *from* what was *to* a new identity, finally able to say, "I was X, now I am Y." If the aspiration is one of metamorphosis, the part of the journey through the crucible into this third part is like a chrysalis, the place of transformation from which emerges someone or something new.

10. *Reflection:* As the aspirant heads from the transformation world toward living life anew, the question arises: Will it last? To ensure that the transformation endures and does not dissipate under the pressures of daily life, the aspirant must be guided to reflect on the journey. Helping them look back on what transpired, and simultaneously look forward to contemplate who they are in light of the transformation, will reveal how it will likely impact the rest of their life.

PART 4: INTEGRATION

11. *Integration:* This step completes the overarching process of encapsulation by taking reflection and putting it into action. The aspirant is guided on how to incorporate the transformation into their daily life, seeing how it impacts and is impacted by other aspects of identity. Their perspective then broadens out to include how the transformation affects and is affected by relationships with others, for it is often the pressures, considerations, and impacts of the external world that cause the internal change to lessen, regress, or dissipate.

12. *Greater flourishing:* With integration the aspiration is achieved, the identity change is complete, and the transformation is sustained. As the guide, you have fostered greater flourishing for the aspirant, who can return to living life until the next aspiration starts the cycle of the transformation journey anew.

As mentioned earlier when discussing Vogler's illustration, in every hero's journey the hero returns with a reward that benefits others. With the Transformation Journey model, this naturally happens for any organizational, business, or community transformation, since the aspiration always involves employees, customers, or members, respectively. And it is often the case with individual people, but you should explicitly convey the benefits of having a positive impact on others, including helping them flourish, into the overarching encapsulation process.

Given the transformation journey results in greater flourishing, note that the return to step 1 means living life on a higher plane, if you will. Think of this as the third dimension of the Journey, rising up from the paper as a helix, spiraling up and around with each transformation, guiding aspirants in progressing closer and closer to who they are meant to be. That is the promise of the Transformation Economy, that as a guider you can, aspirant by aspirant, foster human flourishing and thereby fulfill the purpose of business.

Of course, not every step on this transformation journey is needed for every aspirant nor every guider, and there can be a lot of variation, such as where the guide comes in, when commitment happens, and how deep the crucible is. Feel free, as with the sphere examples earlier, to take professional and poetic license to design a journey that best fits your or your aspirant's needs. And realize you don't have to do it all—you can buy from or partner with other businesses and integrate their offerings into your transformation, or specialize in aspects of the journey that you can provide to other companies.

Moreover, this transformation journey is not the only way to approach dramatic experiences, and it may not be appropriate for everyone. But when it is, this structured framework, modeled on a quest, can be a powerful tool for designing and depicting, staging and guiding your experiences and for turning them into full transformation offerings.

. . .

Cohesive, robust, personal, and dramatic. In designing and staging transformative experiences with these elements in mind, you will create far more engaging and compelling experiences on which to build your transformation offerings. You will significantly enhance the likelihood that your aspirants achieve their aspirations and sustain them through time. You will contribute far more to human flourishing. And you will create greater economic value, with the flow of profits as the measure of how well you engage, transform, and contribute.

REFLECTION

This chapter was all about designing the transformative experiences that form the basis of any transformation journey. Consider these questions:

- Which of the four elements—cohesive, robust, personal, and dramatic—did you have the most affinity for? How might you use its ideas, principles, and frameworks to enhance the experiences your company stages?
- Think about the other elements as well. Are there ideas in there that you could apply?
- Look back to the transformation journey of figure 5-4. See if you can map your offerings onto its steps. What more do you need to do to guide your customers in completing their journeys?
- What might give your business the greatest economic value over the long term?

PREPARATION

Now that you're equipped with the ability to design memorable, meaningful, transporting, and transformative experiences, chapter 6 shows you how to create true transformation offerings atop them, and how those offerings differ by type of aspiration. Mull over these questions before you read it:

- Recall the four types of aspirations—refinement, ambition, cultivation, and metamorphosis—and think again about the *whys* of your customers, the aspirations behind their purchases of your offerings. Which of the aspiration types do you think best represent your customers?
- What impediments do you think your aspirants might face while trying to achieve their aspirations?
- I've been referring to those who help aspirants as guides. Considering your offerings, what other words would apply to your employees who are helping them to achieve their aspirations?

6

CREATING TRANSFORMATION OFFERINGS

Experience designer Zach Adamson had just graduated from the most transformative experience of his life, a birthday present he received from his brother-in-law.[1] It was "Essential EQ Leadership Development," a training program conducted by the ChoiceCenter Leadership University in a nondescript office building just outside the Las Vegas airport. According to founder and CEO Robyn Williams and COO Corrine Clement, this program has guided transformations for hundreds of people every year since 1998.

Zach, a longtime friend and colleague of mine, began with personal remote sessions with a coach a month before the in-person sessions started. His coach wanted to understand his personal and professional life and what path he was on, and prepare him for what he would encounter in Las Vegas. Zach went for two four-day workshops over consecutive long weekends with a cohort of about seventy-five people plus additional coaches—all past-participant volunteers—who work with six participants apiece. The focus of the ChoiceCenter offering? Asking Zach and his fellow students to determine their own, very personal aspiration: "What do you want in your life, more than anything, that you haven't been able to figure out?"

The first weekend focused on discovery, supporting participants to unpack their lifetime experiences that developed their emotional intelligence (EQ) and shaped how they face the world today. Zach found this freeing, enabling him to reframe his story, identify his self-worth, and begin to reshape his beliefs and behaviors—his reactions to setbacks in particular.

The second weekend was one of breakthrough, and like the first it consisted of a large number of experiences that built on each other: role-playing, games, and activities, along with group and solo discussions with coaches and contemplation time, resulting in what Zach said were many "aha moments." Breakthroughs come from breakdowns, and so this weekend looked internally within each participant, including candid feedback from the coach and cohort. Feedback allowed Zach to see himself as others do. With clarity around his current values and behavior, he determined which new values and behaviors would generate the results he wanted and immediately started practicing them. The last half of the workshop involved "a journey through self," and after the graduation ceremony (with his brother-in-law in attendance), Zach said, "I now understand myself better than ever before."

Ah, but the program was not over! Zach still needed to integrate it into his life. ChoiceCenter's next step was the one-hundred-day "Living EQ Leadership," where Zach's life now became the classroom. These three months were the most impactful, as he returned home with a set of transformational tools and a commitment to accomplish his personal strategic plan. Each week involved a cadence of coaching and remote meetings, adding in Zach's five cohort members, and a stretch assignment for the following week. He committed to focusing on unconditional self-love, time-blocking the use of his phone when with his family, and, as an extended goal, becoming a general partner managing a fifty-unit-plus apartment complex. This became his overarching aspiration, one he achieved through his new company, the We Choose Good Group, of which he is chief experience officer.

But the ChoiceCenter program still was not over! It concluded with a three-day weekend retreat where students acknowledged themselves and each other for the deep transformational and behavioral results they created in their relationships, families, careers, health, finances, and more. After already meeting what seemed like impossible goals, Zach and his fellow students determined new goals to achieve on their own and signed contracts they made with themselves. These always began with those two words of identity, "I am," with Zach's being "I am a loving, vulnerable, and inspiring man!" Having turned such an impactful transformation into an ongoing journey, Zach continues to work with his coach and cohort to this day. Meanwhile, just four months after graduation Zach began implementing his "We Choose Good experience" at multifamily apartment complexes across the country, which, he says, "creates an intentional place that consistently reminds people of the good within themselves—and provides invitations to act on it daily. Over time, this steady rhythm of reflection and action shifts how residents see themselves and the world, turning everyday life into a natural expression of doing good." He's also developing a product line around it so anyone can have this same experience in their home and using social media to inspire others to "choose good" on a regular basis. In Zach's words, "It made such an impact on me that I, only partially joking, refer to myself as B.C. Zach (Before Choice Zach) and A.C. Zach (After Choice Zach)."

As his example shows—and as you may have already gathered—ChoiceCenter Leadership University exemplifies most everything I have written about thus far, including addressing multiple spheres of transformation, changing participants in one or more aspects of identity, incorporating encapsulation across multiple levels of experience, embodying the Transformation Journey model, and fostering flourishing for each and every participant.

Moreover, it's a full transformation offering that ChoiceCenter designs across three physical and numerous virtual encounters—each one encompassing its own series of experiences—to lead aspirants in both developing and achieving truly life-altering aspirations of metamorphosis, with coaches as long-term guides and cohorts as accountability partners. Each participant can say along with Zach, "I have been transformed!" They are no longer aspirants; they are achievers.

The Delta Model

ChoiceCenter Leadership University didn't just stage a set of transformative experiences for Zach and his fellow participants. It guided a *transformation offering*. Everything that happened followed a process honed over decades. The program began with extended preparation, before participants ever came to Las Vegas. Next, the discovery weekend consisted of a series of experiences, some merely memorable, such as a get-to-know-you session; some meaningful, as participants worked to discover who they really were; and at least one transporting, when ChoiceCenter drew out of them who they *really* aspired to become, as most everyone came with no more than a vague idea.

The breakthrough weekend enabled aspirants to fully gauge the gap between their newfound aspiration and their current self—their individual from/to statements. That gap led to the breakdown when they realized how very far they were from their aspiration, and to the breakthrough when they committed to achieving a "new you," with different values, distinct behaviors, and a metamorphosis in core identity, and then immediately began working on it.

The offering would have been incomplete, however, without integrating these changes into the aspirants' lives, each one continuing to be guided for one hundred days by ChoiceCenter coaches with a defined, common approach, until each and every one could look back at who they were before the program and say "I was X, now I am Y"—and viscerally believe it.

The Delta Model in figure 6-1 shows how all such guiders can build up from experiences to transformations as distinct economic offerings. With the Greek uppercase letter delta (Δ) being the universal symbol for change in math and science, and more generally used to denote transformations of any kind, this model comprises three segments. The bottom represents experiences with three levels: memorable, meaningful, and transporting, each one offering progressively higher value to guests.

Both the middle and top segments comprise transformations as their own economic offerings, fully incorporating transforma-

FIGURE 6-1

The Delta Model

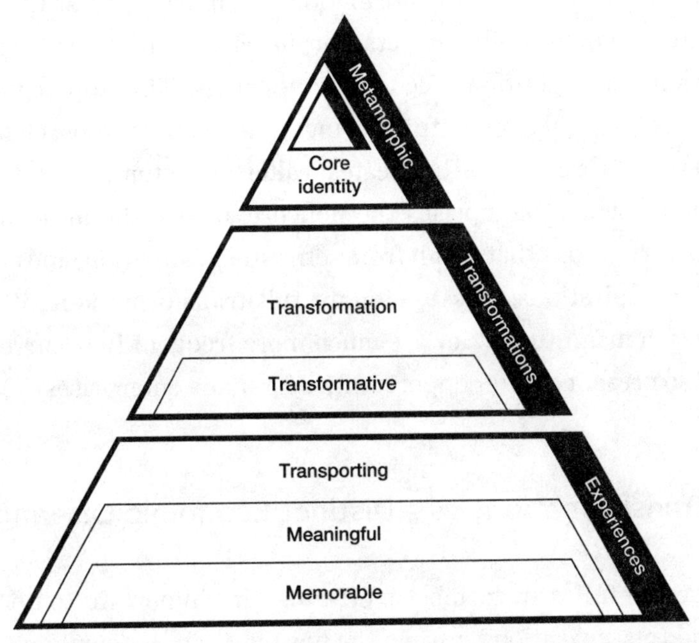

tive experiences, which are built atop the bottom segment. Transformative experiences, however, are a necessary but not sufficient condition for a transformation offering, which is why they are only a part of the middle segment. As seen with ChoiceCenter's program, a full transformation needs a stated aspiration, an affirmed commitment, and completed encapsulation (particularly the integration step, without which the change won't be sustained through time).

The top segment of the Delta Model is a step above. It represents those transformations so significant, so life-altering, so unlike the rest that they warrant being represented as such. These are *metamorphic* transformations, those that change us at our core, altering who we are by achieving aspirations for large-scale, wholesale change in identity, as we saw in the upper-right quadrant of the types of aspirations 2×2 in figure 3-2. I signify the nature of this highest level of transformation by placing "Δ Core identity" in the top segment, and that segment is itself, fractal-like, a delta symbol atop the Delta Model.

To be clear, while transformations such as Zach's at ChoiceCenter are indeed ones of metamorphosis, they are still transformations, not additional economic offerings. This top segment represents highly impactful offerings that create the most change, and therefore can have the greatest value for customers, while the middle segment comprises the noncore, or peripheral, identity transformations that result from refinement, ambition, and cultivation aspirations. These, too, are full transformations. While lesser in magnitude, they are much more frequent in occurrence and so present greater opportunities for many enterprises.

Transformations as a Distinct Economic Offering

To design full transformation offerings, it's important to understand the separation between the bottom Delta segment and the top two. In chapter 1 I wrote about the three key economic distinctions of transformations that distinguish them from mere experiences. Let's review them in more detail here.

First, transformation offerings are *effectual*. They make an impact on the aspirant that effects the desired result, achieving an aspiration. Sometimes the outcome arises from one life-changing experience, often by serendipity (a deviation or discovery catalyst). As an illustration, I once spoke to the annual conference of the American Alliance of Museums, largely consisting of curators and managers. I asked the hundreds of attendees if they worked in the industry today because of an experience they had in a museum when they were young. About 40 percent raised their hands. I've used this anecdote with clients in all manner of immersive experiences, themed attractions, and the like to assert that they, too, have sparked many kids and not a few adults to join art, attractions, and other experience businesses as artists, designers, and creators.[2] Not to mention those who acquired lifelong avocations for gardening, history, science, and so many other subjects as a kid or adult.

In the vast share of cases, however, it's not one transformative experience but a series of them that an aspirant undergoes to effect, over time, the outcome desired. And that's why the economic function of transformations is not to change, modify, or regenerate, but to *guide*—to come alongside customers and do everything you can to lead, steer, direct, encourage, urge, persuade, cajole, and whatever else required to further aspirants along the path they desire, and pay you to achieve.

Second, transformation offerings are *individual*—whether individual people, individual organizations, individual businesses, or individual communities. Aspirants are the ones who transform and bring about their own aspirations. The customer is the product; you are the guide.

You must therefore get very individual with each aspirant. No two transformations are alike, simply because every customer is unique. It's certainly possible to have one standard transformation process—army boot camps come immediately to mind—but everyone reacts to that process in their own ways. Even drill sergeants know they can't yell in the same way at every recruit all the time. When mass customizing your offerings to create personal transformative experiences, you should customize the entire *series* of experiences (along with the supporting service activities and physical goods). Each one is a module within your architecture of modularity that you can bring "off the shelf" when you determine that *this* is the exact right experience needed at this step in the series. And then within that module you further mass customize its elements to ensure you create *the* memorable, meaningful, transporting, and/or transformative experience *this* individual aspirant needs to undergo at *this* moment in time.

Recognize, too, that transformations rarely form a straight line from where an aspirant is today to achievement. As seen in the Transformation Journey model, transformation offerings entail hiccups to handle, setbacks to deal with, personal nemeses to vanquish, deterioration to offset, hindrances to overcome, impediments to restrain, regressions to reverse, obstacles to rise over, stumbling blocks to surmount, and backsliding to counteract. Some combination of these proves almost inevitable. Any such issues must be managed, and you must have modules in your offering to continue the journey onward and upward. Each episode serves as a trigger—as with street theatre—to call the proper module, on demand in time of need, to get your aspirants back on track.

Third, transformation offerings must be *sustained through time*. Many of the issues I've described in fact happen after the putative transformation seems finished, causing aspirants to fall short of their aspirations. Unless the transformation sticks, the individual wasn't truly transformed and it was not a complete transformation offering. This can be tough for guiders because many people think they have been transformed and may stop working at it (and therefore stop working with you). They then become disappointed and sometimes disillusioned when the effects dissipate over time. The dynamic seems fairly prevalent with smoking cessation, drug rehabilitation, anger management, and other such exceedingly difficult endeavors.

These three economic distinctions culminate in offering *time well invested*. As an effectual offering, all the time the aspirant spends under your tutelage, across the entire series of transformative experiences, pays off when the aspiration is achieved and the aspirant becomes an achiever. Each experience, progressing the person onward and upward, compounds the value of each one that came before. Inherently occurring inside each individual, the transformation offering is literally a self-investment in the aspirant's own being, whether transforming in degree or in kind. And that investment pays further dividends when it is sustained through time, ensuring that the aspirant truly is and will remain transformed.

In short, transformations are effectual outcomes that guide individuals to transform in a lasting way—and are achieved through the time they invest with you. You must therefore design that time to yield the effectual outcomes your customers desire, which means starting with their aspirations, with why they want to go on the transformation journey you will guide for them.

Achieving Aspirations through Transformation Offerings

Refinement, ambition, and cultivation aspirations—those that align with transformations in the middle segment of the Delta Model—are collectively much more common and straightforward to guide than those of metamorphosis. This type of aspiration is much less common and more difficult, but yields transformations

FIGURE 6-2

Types of transformations

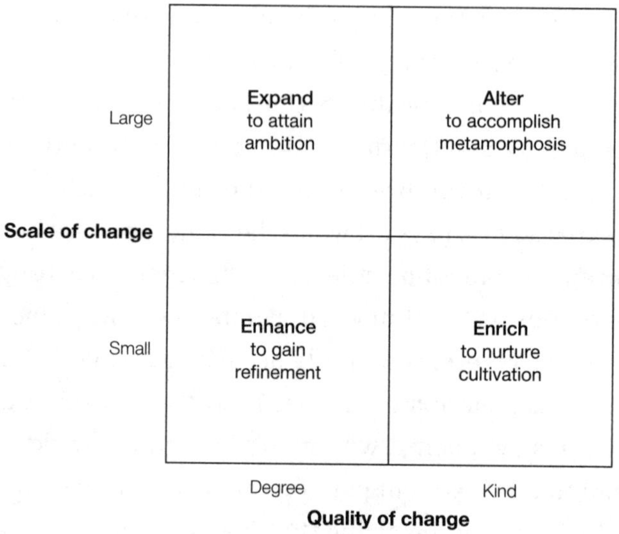

Scale of change	Degree	Kind
Large	**Expand** to attain ambition	**Alter** to accomplish metamorphosis
Small	**Enhance** to gain refinement	**Enrich** to nurture cultivation

Scale of change (vertical axis); Quality of change (horizontal axis)

of much greater impact and value, warranting its top position in the Delta Model.

How you design the time with your customers, then, depends on which type of aspiration they have. As shown in figure 6-2, for refinement aspirations, you need to *enhance* some aspect of identity that aspirants already have to gain a refinement in it. For ambition, you need to *expand* some capability they exemplify now in their identity to attain their ambition for what it could be in the future. You need to *enrich* aspirants in some new arena of identity to nurture its cultivation. You need to *alter* their identity in a major way to accomplish metamorphosis. I'll cover each in turn.

Refinement: Enhancing through expertise

Aspirations of refinement represent a small-scale change in degree. The desire here is not for wholesale change but for refining some aspect of self, something already there that you enjoy, relish, care for, delight in, or even love.

When you guide enhancing transformations to gain such refinements, think of your employees as experts. Customers come to you because they seek the knowledge necessary to refine an aspect of identity, looking for you to direct, instruct, lead, and interpret the process. As an expert, you must calibrate the level of help you provide to your customers to avoid thinking that they want to take full advantage of your expertise, such as treating it as an expanding transformation when they desire an enhancing one. On the other hand, you may also find that your work on the enhancing transformation *causes* the aspirant to desire more, to shift into the quadrant of ambition and aim to become an expert themselves. That can provide an opportunity to extend or offer a new transformation to do exactly that.

Being small in scale, enhancing transformations lend themselves to short-term sets of experiences. I think of the prototypical example as an academy or similar places, such as camps, institutes, online courses, certification classes, or workshops. I've attended a couple of three-day golf academies, for example, to improve my game. Others—adults and youths alike, recreationally and professionally—participate in a basketball camp, attend a coding institute, obtain a professional certification, boost their photographic skills with a community education course, enhance their leadership acumen via a virtual class, partake in a hobby workshop at a retail store, and so forth.

Sami Vesala, a friend of a friend in Finland, once excitedly told me about an enhancing transformation he had. He had long enjoyed whisky, so when on vacation in Scotland he visited many different distilleries. To Sami, though, the Springbank Distillery in Campbeltown felt different, and at the end of the tour, he heard it offered a program to expose guests to the art of distilling. Desiring to gain more knowledge, he paid to spend a week at the Springbank Whisky School, where he and a handful of others worked at the distillery for five days. They participated in the real labor of malting, peating, mashing, and distilling, as well as warehousing and bottling.[3]

Sami said that "the week itself was more than worth every penny," in no small measure because "the feeling of getting accepted as a part of the distillery 'family' was genuine"; he's even still in touch with some of the expert workers. The experience enhanced his appreciation and knowledge of whisky and how it's made, and moreover "really changed my view on the whisky business in general and highlighted the uniqueness of Springbank."

Springbank Distillery may not view itself as being in the transformation business, but it does aim to offer a very high-value experience that bonds guests to its brand and offerings. That's *its* aspiration, but nonetheless Springbank offers an invitational transformation—like the Johnnie Walker Princes Street experience and the Abraham Lincoln Presidential Library and Museum from chapter 3—an invitation many people gladly accept. Many guests of such marketing experiences, however, often have aspirations that go beyond having a great time. How much more value could experience stagers create if they intentionally catered to guest aspirations for refinement? And if they specifically designed the experience to spark aspirations, and guide transformations, for guests along the way?

Whether your enhancing transformation is invitational or intentional, the best way to effect it is through encapsulation. Provide resources for guests to prepare for the experience in advance, specifically encouraging them to think about the possibilities for change in viewpoints, understanding, capabilities, and/or appreciation. Offer opportunities for reflection at each stage in the experience, as the Springbank Whisky School does at the end of each day, with group reflection especially effective *during* the experience. Then afterward, provide resources for further reflection on the entire offering, plus ways for customers to integrate what they gained into their lives. This can be done via

Thesaurus of Enhancing Transformations

Each of the four types of transformations tends to have certain words that aspirants use to identify in which quadrant of the types of transformations 2×2 their aspirations lie—and therefore words you may want to use in promoting, selling, and guiding specific offerings. For enhancing aspirants to gain refinement, here are some typical words you might hear and use:

Adapting
Adjusting
Correcting
Decreasing
Developing
Diminishing
Distilling
Elevating
Enhancing
Filtering
Fine-tuning
Furthering
Honing
Improving
Increasing
Lessening
Polishing
Progressing
Purifying
Raising
Reducing
Refining
Sharpening
Shrinking
Touching up
Tweaking
Upgrading

Note that some of these words have negative, not positive, connotations—correcting, decreasing, diminishing—since remedial refinement aspirations have to do with eliminating aspects of identity that aspirants do not enjoy, relish, or delight in, but dislike and perhaps detest.

handouts, emails, website links, and even live one-on-one or group sessions, whether done in person or remotely. And in branded cases like Springbank Distillery or Johnnie Walker in particular, it also wouldn't hurt to provide some samples as memorabilia to both cement memories and stimulate integration.

Understand, too, that all this applies to remedial aspirations of refinement, as sometimes people desire small-scale changes that, for example, correct flaws, decrease unhelpful activities, or diminish bad patterns. Knowing which way the transformation goes proves crucial to designing the right set of transformative experiences for whatever type of academy you create (physical or virtual), what you do for encapsulation, and how you apply your expertise.

Ambition: Expanding through coaching

For both refinement and ambition aspirations, the task is more straightforward than those that involve a change in kind. In these cases the customer already *is* what they aspire to become—a physician, an accountant, a professor, a religious leader, a surfer, a quilter, or other professional or individual identities—and wants to be *more* of it, better at it, to deepen or broaden it in some sense. It's still important to differentiate between refinement and ambition aspirations, though, to understand the scale of what aspirants seek to attain. With ambitions, aspirants want to get significantly better at a dimension of self, obtain an elevated level of achievement, or reach a certain high standing in a field or endeavor. Your job is to greatly develop their skills and abilities, significantly increase their knowledge and competencies, and substantially magnify the possibilities of what they can do and be. Given both are changes of degree, not kind, it is the adverbs here that most clearly differentiate expanding transformations from enhancing ones: greatly, significantly, substantially.

With this type of transformation, you must act as a coach. Coaches of all stripes—fitness, sports, speaking, executive, organizational, life—are experts, certainly, but given the long-term nature of most ambitions, they must be so much more. They must know their aspirants on an individual level to deal with the personal ups and downs any ambition encounters. They must understand psychology (whether viscerally or learned) to inspire, encourage, cajole, persuade, coax, and sometimes even harass their charges to get them to continue and excel at the journey onward and upward. And they must know when to bring in other experts and coaches to deal with matters beyond their own abilities. Coaches must further recognize that at times they've done all the guiding they can do, and it's time for an aspirant to move to another coach, live with the level of attainment, or lower their aspiration.

Perhaps a personal trainer affords the prototypical example. While fitness centers can embrace any of the four types of transformations, depending on the aspirant and where they're at on their fitness journey, people tend to hire personal trainers only when (1) they already view themselves as having a certain level of fitness, however defined; (2) they have an ambition to attain (and maintain) a much higher level of fitness; and (3) they recognize that other ways of doing it (self-help books, a gym, a home weight room, apps, etc.) prove insufficient. (A lack of time but not of money tends to augur for going this route as well.) Personal trainers can help you benefit from the other offerings you're using, but most importantly they do everything they can to ensure you stay with the program and work at it, day in and day out, week by week, month after month, without letting up until you attain your goal. Then they help you maintain it over time or set a new goal.

There are equivalents in other arenas of life. While I had previously gone to golf academies and taken occasional instruction from PGA professionals, when I got serious about improving my game as I aged (actually, *re*improving it, trying to get back down to a single-digit handicap), I went to GOLFTEC. With over two hundred locations in the United States and around the world, the company has a particular point of view about how you can elevate your golf game. Better than the idiosyncrasies of any individual coach, GOLFTEC compares your swing with the pros' on video, and provides lessons on how to make changes that let you hit the ball more like they do, closing the gap over time—time very well invested. The company excels with at-home and on-range exercises that make the lessons pay off.

The key to both these examples and expanding transformations in general is having a program with a distinct *point of view* for how transformation happens within your field of know-how. The program is your way of guiding transformations, necessarily customized to the individual aspirant, that take them from where they are to the desired ambition over a series of experiences, usually over an extended period of time. As with all transformations, encapsulation proves important here so that each experience in the series progresses toward the goal. GOLFTEC, for example, records the key elements of lessons (I would recognize the voice of my coach, Oliver Darby, anywhere) overlaid on a video of your swing in comparison with a pro's, so you can reflect on what you learned. The exercises then enable students to integrate changes into their swings, which in turn prepares them for the next step in the methodical, programmatic transformation of their game.

There are several concerns to be mindful of with expanding transformations: aspirants not fully committing to achieving their goals, changing priorities over time, and decommitting or losing hope. A key to successfully getting them to achieve big goals is the obtaining and maintaining of commitment; without it, few ambitions ever get attained. Here the commitment should often be more to the *process* of transformation than to the specific *outcome*. The ambition can seem distant and foreboding in the early stages, but a commitment to the process can more consistently yield results over time. Consider weight-loss company Profile Plan, which merged in 2024 with HMR ("Health. Motivation. Results"). It guides people to improve their well-being through a customized health and nutrition program. Key to making it work

Thesaurus of Expanding Transformations

Here are some typical words associated with expanding aspirants to attain an ambition, including some for remedial transformations:

Advancing	Growing
Amplifying	Improving
Broadening	Increasing
Cutting	Lessening
Deepening	Losing
Elevating	Raising
Eliminating	Reducing
Enlarging	Strengthening
Extending	

You'll notice that some of these words are the same as with refinement, but here the aspiration is much larger in scale. Therefore, they may be accompanied by adverbs or adjectives, particularly comparative ones, such as:

Better	Less
Drastically	More
Extensively	Really
Extremely	Seriously
Faster	Significantly
Fewer	Smaller
Greater	Totally
Highly	Vastly
Importantly	Very
Largely	Substantially

Also note that with expanding transformations, aspirants tend to associate their ambition more with the term "goal" than "aspiration."

is obtaining a commitment from each participant—not to a specific weight-loss goal, but to how coach and consumer work together to change how the latter thinks about food and goes about eating. This involves talking together via phone, online chat, or in the company's face-to-face clinics for thirty minutes every week. And each discussion doesn't end without an appointment for the next one, extending the commitment each time.[4]

As with refinement, many ambition aspirations can be for remedial attributes, such as eliminating aggressive behavior, eradicating poor leadership conduct, or greatly lessening social media use. These are ambitions for *less,* not more, of some aspect of identity. They can thus slide over into metamorphic transformations if the aspect is core enough to the aspirant's identity, even if they don't recognize it at first. In either case, for the best possible outcome it's important to turn the negative description into a positive one: from eliminating aggressive behavior to gaining social management skills, from being a poor leader to becoming a great one, from lessening social media use to taking control of their time online.

Cultivation: Enriching through counseling

Enriching transformations—those that tackle the aspiration of cultivation—flip over to the right side of the types of transformations 2×2, entailing those that represent a change in kind, although of a small scale. Here people aspire to develop an unrealized attribute, to hone a fresh skill or capability, or to become something different, but not drastically so. The idea of *self-cultivation* has been around since the ancient Greek philosophers and remains prominent in Asian philosophies such as Confucianism and Taoism. But as with all manner of transformations, people and companies increasingly hire businesses to help them undergo enriching change to nurture cultivations.

Many professions exist for that purpose, including therapists, psychologists, and social workers. Thus, in serving as a guide, you should take on the role, generically, of a *counselor*. Customers hire you for the advice and counsel you provide in workshops, classes, events, and sessions of all stripes to nurture the cultivations they seek for themselves, for their organizations, for their businesses, and sometimes for their communities.

Yet they do it less to augment a capability, as with enhancing and expanding transformations (changes of degree), than to generate a new capability, make a lifestyle change, or stop a bad behavior (changes in kind). The prototypical example may be to build good habits. There are apps for that—a plethora of them, in fact. You can use Noom, Fooducate, or Lasta for healthy eating; Mint, Goodbudget, or EveryDollar for beneficial financial management; Quizlet, Memrise, or Wisdom Quotes for effective learning; Aura, Calm, or Headspace for focused mindfulness; and Hallow, PrayerMate, and Abide for virtuous praying. Many are used in combination with tracking devices, such as Fitbit, Apple Watch, or Oura, to cultivate sustainable fitness habits. And apps such as Habitica, Habitify, and Productive focus on nurturing habits in and of themselves.

It's not just about apps, of course. You can also enrich yourself in physical locations, such as at demonstrations in health food stores, financial literacy camps, all manner of courses in schools, and even religious education classes in places of worship. As one example, nonprofit Lemonade Stand Bootcamp offers a number of workshops, courses, and events "to help the underprivileged and under-served communities learn about self-actualization, financial literacy, and business development," using that classic way kids introduce themselves to finances: the lemonade stand. It also conducts a three-hour event for adults that doesn't "just teach financial literacy, it helps with investments, self-actualization, financial goal planning, and much more." And going beyond wealth & prosperity, some programs focus "on the betterment of oneself."[5]

As this example illustrates, enriching transformations aren't solely about habits but can nurture aspirations of cultivation for life skills, lifestyle changes, and various genres of practices. They also apply within businesses to instill new working habits, employee skills, process modifications, and organizational practices.

When guiding enriching transformations, recognize that any cultivation aspiration is a new direction, so customers may not yet be fully committed to it. (How many of us make New Year's resolutions, only to have them fade by February?) Obtaining commitment during the initial phases of the transformation is important here before getting too far, particularly if you charge for demonstrated outcomes. You also must worry about dilettantes, a word that originally meant "one who cultivates" the fine arts "for the love of them rather than professionally," but has come to be a mild pejorative.[6] Dilettantes flit from interest to interest and therefore may quit on any or all before achieving the outcomes they say they desire.

Notice, too, how aspirants may desire enriching transformations due to dissatisfaction with some part of their lives or businesses. People often focus on building good habits because they have bad ones, and counselors often must focus on remedial work to overcome issues before they can assist aspirants in nurturing new aspects of identity that will help them flourish.

As with the possibility of enhancing transformations sliding into expanding ones, so can enriching transformations shift into altering ones. When an aspirant gets into the journey and recognizes the greater potential, opportunities, and consequences of a much larger-scale transformation, you may need to shift as well into offering an altering transformation to accomplish such a metamorphosis. Therefore, you should be alert to such possibilities and be capable of the next type of transformation.

Thesaurus of Enriching Transformations

Here are some typical words associated with enriching aspirants to nurture a cultivation:

Becoming	Initiating
Beginning	Instituting
Creating	Launching
Developing	Making
Dropping	Nurturing
Ending	Obtaining
Establishing	Starting
Forming	Stopping
Fostering	Sustaining
Getting	Tracking

There are again a few negative words for remedial transformations. And given refinements are new, if small-scale, changes in kind, you will tend not to hear (or use) adjectives or adverbs that imply great change, as with expanding transformations.

Metamorphosis: Altering through alchemy

Metamorphic transformations change aspirants both in kind and on a large scale. In particular, such transformations take one or more elements of a person's core identity and alter who they are. Metamorphic transformations may be the most difficult and time-consuming to accomplish, but they prove by far the most rewarding—personally for aspirants, and economically for you.

I mentioned many examples of metamorphosis earlier in the book, but they're worth repeating here to fully understand the large-scale change in kind represented by altering transformations: getting married, getting divorced, having a religious conversion, starting the first job, graduating from college, permanently departing home, joining the military, becoming a professional athlete, being promoted to manager, going beyond a mom-and-pop shop to convert into a franchiser, becoming a homeowner, leaving a salaried job to become an entrepreneur, retiring, experiencing the death of a spouse, dealing with a serious illness (and recovering from a long battle with it).

For many such situations—and many more that could be cited—people attempt to accomplish transformations on their own. In other cases, they get some help from friends and family or seek assistance from goods & services—books, classes, apps, and more. But increasingly they hire companies to guide them through the journey, yielding much higher probabilities of success in a way that brings them greater flourishing, with reduced anxiety and greater ease, and in less time. There's also a sense in which some of the people undergoing metamorphosis do drastically change, but do not successfully achieve their aspiration: they get married, but later get divorced; they start that first job, but get fired in the first few months; they depart home, but stall on their way to adulthood; they become an entrepreneur, but that business, and the one after that, and the one after that, never catches on.

In all such situations, how much more likely would someone be to transform successfully if they sought and obtained the guidance of a company that truly was in the transformation business, that has the capabilities for the life-altering changes metamorphosis necessarily entails, and that created the offerings required?

Strange as it may sound, the particular role required to accomplish metamorphic transformations is *alchemist*. The term originally referred to one who "transmuted" elements, particularly metals into gold—a physical metamorphosis—and while it was often associated with nefarious schemes and "magic," alchemy was in fact a forerunner to modern chemistry. Today the word refers to the altering of one thing into another or to someone's reinvention, particularly when it appears magical because of the extent of change. So, while the term may seem strange at first, its modern-day meaning of "someone who transforms things for the better" perfectly fits the role required of any metamorphosis.[7]

And it is a role, not necessarily an individual person; a single guide may not be enough. This is true especially for metamorphic, life-altering transformations (plus those that significantly alter organizations, businesses, and communities), precisely because they are so vast, entail a journey deep into the unknown, more likely come with great trepidation (and hesitation), and greatly alter the self. For such journeys it's rare that one individual can offer everything needed; it will take many guides across the timeframe of the journey to meld together into the role of alchemist.

Consider recovering from cancer. If you or a loved one has been treated for cancer, you know it starts as a major disruption in your life. When you hear those words from a doctor, "You have cancer," it confirms your worst fears, and for most everyone, *immediately* changes their self-identity. You are now someone who has cancer. From what I have read and heard, it would be much better to think, *I am me experiencing cancer*, but that mindset jujitsu is tough to keep up over a long period and cannot mask the basic fact: you have cancer.

What does it take to recover? First, a great medical team: doctors, nurses, technicians, and others with the expertise to treat your cancer and handle any other curative issues. But as in all cases within the health & well-being sphere, treating your symptoms and disease is not enough; your whole person needs to be treated as well, including emotional, physical, psychological, and even spiritual issues that inevitably arise. You will need wise counsel, along with instruction and coaching, not only on your care path but on living your life with cancer, which the medical team cannot furnish on its own. You need the support of loved ones, family, friends, colleagues, clergy, and often therapists of differing types, combined across your journey to fulfill the role of alchemist as guide. With effective treatment, great support, and good fortune in place, your support system can take you through from crisis to recovery, where you can finally say you are cancer-free (or that you can live long and well with it).

Think of the alchemist as subsuming the care, support, and guidance of experts, coaches, and counselors all—the three guide roles for enhancing, expanding, and enriching transformations. Altering transformations then require the fourth role of guiding the overall metamorphosis: knowing when to use, take on, or bring in each of the other roles, keeping the aspirational outcome in mind, managing the inevitable ups and downs, and always keeping the individual, living, breathing human being (or beings, in the case of organizational or communal transformations) at the forefront of everything that happens.

The Modern Elder Academy (MEA) offers an example of using alchemy to guide metamorphic transformations. Boutique hotelier Chip Conley founded it after joining Airbnb as its chief hospitality officer—where, at twice the age of the typical employee, he became known as its Modern Elder. After a successful tenure at the company, Conley went through a midlife crisis, as detailed in his book *Learning to Love Midlife*. Coming out the other side triggered him to create MEA, which he describes as "the world's first midlife wisdom school," where "midlifers" can "reimagine and repurpose themselves: to create a life that's as deep and meaningful as it is long."[8] He calls midlife a "chrysalis" where "the transformational magic of metamorphosis occurs" so that you can become who you're meant to be—to flourish, in other words.[9]

MEA is itself a chrysalis, a place where people come to reflect on, think through, and transform their lives to "thrive in the second half of life."[10] Its science-based curricula at its campuses in Baja, Mexico, and Santa Fe—along with its online programs and events, videos, and *Wisdom Weekly* newsletter—all guide midlifers in making the leap from who they have been to who they will become. These are led not only by MEA's own set of guides but by a number of "superluminaries": "business leaders and entrepreneurs, artists and athletes, academics and spiritual seekers whose heart-inspired teachings are deeply aligned with our mission and values."[11] Among these are many experts, coaches, and counselors, all of whom together offer the alchemy that midlifers draw on. Moreover, participants become part of the alchemy team during and after their own transformations, for as Conley says, "We've learned that wisdom is not taught—it's shared."[12]

A chrysalis is a great metaphor for metamorphosis, that liminal place between what aspirants were and what they become where transformation happens. A hospital, the military, school, and apprenticeship are all chrysalises. So is the nondescript Vegas office building at which ChoiceCenter performs its magic. And so are whatever physical places or virtual spaces you create for your aspirants. In taking this perspective, what would you do differently in designing your location as well as determining what happens within it, particularly as aspirants who entered into the chrysalis of the transformation world exit back to the ordinary world?

Taking that perspective often involves remedial transformations. Think of how life-altering it is to stop drinking, quit smoking, halt drug use, end gambling, or discontinue other addictions. It's best, as with expanding transformations, to reframe the transformation as a positive rather than a remedial one, to aspire to live drink-free, to become a nonsmoker, or simply to go from "a person who experiences life on drugs" to "a person who experiences life naturally." As my friend and colleague Nathan Schock of consultancy FiveFour told me, "To quit smoking, identify with being a nonsmoker—then smoking is just something you don't do."

The Phoenix, a nonprofit movement that helps substance abusers become sober—hundreds of thousands since its founding in 2006—has its own point of view about transformations along these same lines. Here's how founder Scott Strode puts it:

> We're really focused on helping people with what's possible in their recovery. So it's very forward-looking. We start to dream

> of what's possible in our sober life. In the twelve-step community, people often identify as their disease. "I'm Scott, I'm an addict, I'm an alcoholic." But I always say, "I'm Scott, I'm in recovery, I'm an ice climber and so much more." We see everybody for their intrinsic strength, not a problem to be fixed.

He adds that "83 percent of Phoenix participants stay sober after three months, compared with an average of 40 percent to 60 percent from other programs."[13]

When facing remedial transformations such as addiction or disruptive catalysts such as trauma, you need to assure your customers that you can guide them by appropriately handling not only their emotional needs, but also their physical ones. As neuroscientist Stephen W. Porges and journalist Seth Porges write in their book on trauma and safety, "The impact of trauma is not isolated to our brains but stretches through our nervous system to virtually every part of our body, changing how our senses sense, how our organs operate, and just about every aspect of our physical and mental health."[14] Such effects can happen as much in businesses and their workers as in personal lives.

Organizations often need to accomplish deep, remedial transformations as well. Morgan Goodlander, a former professor of psychology and the founder of the GETI Institute, works with both individuals and organizations to address critical challenges such as stalled growth, internal conflict, and strategic misalignments. When engaged by a CEO or founder, Goodlander interviews each member of the leadership team to uncover their unique identity narratives—those facets of their personal heritage that influence their professional role. By identifying areas where beliefs, mindsets, or attitudes cause organizational stagnation, he helps people shift their narratives so their identities align with a cohesive organizational story. Goodlander calls his approach an experience organization practice (EOP), an ontological inquiry that involves reshaping perceptions of the past to create a renewed sense of meaning and purpose for the present and future. He often refers to his work as an "alchemical process of experiential transmutation."

Altering transformations require commitment even more than the other three types. Aspirants can't foresee what large-scale, core identity changes truly mean for them and how they alter their sense of self. Without commitment to see the transformation through, there is nary a chance of success; the disparity is just too great, too stark, too unknowable. Altering transformations may also require much more hand-holding, involve many twists and turns and backsliding, and take much longer to achieve. But your role as an alchemist is to ensure that customers do in fact accomplish these high-bar, high-value aspirations.

It's still true that aspirants always transform themselves—even in medical situations, where the disease may be eradicated but the person goes through the journey and comes out the other end forever changed. And the person is the one who *chooses* to go through a change that fundamentally alters who they are. Philosopher L. A. Paul notes about this journey:

> [It] teaches you something new, something that you could not have known before having the experience, while also changing you as a person. Such experiences are very important from a personal perspective, for transformative experiences can play a significant role in your life, involving options that, speaking metaphorically, function as crossroads in your path towards self-realization. The path you choose determines where you take your life, what you will become, and thus, by extension, your subjective future. Your own choices involving transformative experiences, that is, your *transformative choices,* allow you to causally form what it will be like to be you in your future. In this sense, you *own* your future, because it is *you* who made the choice to bring this future—your very own future self—into being.[15]

Thesaurus of Altering Transformations

Here are some typical words associated with altering transformations to accomplish metamorphosis:

- Altering
- Becoming
- Being
- Converting
- Joining
- Regenerating
- Reinventing
- Rejuvenating
- Renewing
- Revitalizing
- Reworking
- Transforming

There may be fewer words to associate with metamorphosis because it is less common and more impactful than the other types of transformations. A lot of them begin with "re-" not in the sense of returning to something from the past (although sometimes that may be the case), but rather in the sense of "anew," to "become again."

Note, too, that aspirants rarely use "transforming" and other such weighty terms—at least before the fact—but when they do, it is more likely to refer to metamorphic transformations. Likewise, in promoting, selling, and guiding your offering, you probably want to stay away from such potentially big and scary words, sticking to those that more specifically describe your offering and connect with your potential customers' aspirations. ChoiceCenter Leadership University, for example, doesn't say that participants will undergo a life-altering change and become someone completely new; instead, it uses such phrases as "elevate their life" and "accelerate their results."

Aspirants own their transformations. They create their very own "new you." *They* achieve their aspirations. And once a metamorphosis is accomplished, these achievers recognize that they can never go back; they are forever altered, just as material elements forever alter in alchemy. In guiding altering transformations, therefore, as the alchemist you have a high ethical bar in how you conduct yourself. You're affecting the innermost parts of people, forever. You have a fiduciary responsibility—a position of great trust—to ensure you do the right things for your aspirants, the designing and guiding of the right transformative experiences, as well as do right by them.

Harnessing the Delta Model

In thinking about these four types of transformations—the three within the middle segment of the Delta Model of enhancing refinement, expanding ambition, and enriching cultivation, as well as the fourth, residing within the top segment of altering metamorphosis—recognize that gray areas and overlaps exist between them, depending on the aspirant, their identity, their starting point, and their aspiration. Customers may also seek multiple, related aspirations at the same time.

These are all considerations you need to take into account as you design and guide your transformation offerings. You need not limit yourself to one type of transformation; enhancing and expanding—focused on changes in degree—go particularly well together, as do enriching and altering, focused on changes in kind. And if you can accomplish metamorphosis, you can likely easily guide the other types. Columbia Theological Seminary, for example, gives a metamorphic master's of divinity degree for those going into the ministry. Using largely the same capabilities and people, it also offers transformations for those not enrolled in their degree programs, such as enriching through certification programs for lay pastors, expanding through continuing education programs, and enhancing through lectures, workshops, and pilgrimages.

Metamorphosis can also explicitly include the other three types. That is, while guiding an altering transformation, subaspirations for refinement, ambition, and cultivation can be achieved as well, particularly since the guide role of alchemy likewise subsumes that of coach, expert, and counselor. For example, Symplany, the plan-driven investing company, facilitates advisers in helping their clients accumulate wealth during their work years to lead highly prosperous lives in retirement. This enables those clients to accomplish such a metamorphosis when they leave work and set their sights on entirely new pursuits that bring new meaning to their lives. While doing so, Symplany also helps end clients gain refinement aspirations by solidifying an existing peace of mind, giving permission to pursue pastimes more fully, or easing the financial burdens of their offspring sooner than they previously thought prudent. It aids them in attaining the ambition to achieve a greater impact with better-understood financial means, such as building a bigger financial legacy or providing greater support of a meaningful cause. And it supports cultivation aspirations such as nurturing newfound financial confidence that enables people to lead much richer lives.

Knowing which type of transformation you must guide for each aspirant enables you to customize it not only in the series of transformative experiences you design but in how you approach people with the appropriate guide role, whether expert, coach, counselor, or alchemist.

For those who stage experiences today, seek to shift up the successive levels of experiences from merely memorable to truly transformative. Remember that encapsulation is the key to progressing to that level, and for many guests it's all that is required to do so. This will allow you to create greater economic value from your current offerings, and then to unequivocally get into the transformation business through the middle or even top segment of the Delta Model as your guests turns into aspirants.

And for those with lower economic offerings, you still have the strategic choice of whether to shift up the Progression of Economic Value to determine and guide transformations. Recall that this fifth and final economic offering is built atop each genre of offering below it, so the possibility exists to embed your current offerings within those of experiences & transformations. If you opt to do so, then follow the guidance I've described to determine the higher-level offerings you can create. The key is to discover what ends your customers desire for which your current offerings are the means. *Why* are people buying your offerings? What aspirations do they have that you can aid them with? Incorporating the technique of asking five whys into your design process proves very useful here. Whatever transformational desires customers express, ask why they have them. Whatever the answer is, ask why again, and again, and again, however many times it takes to get down to the vital aspiration sought—*the* why—which so often remains unspoken and even unknown. Follow that course to its logical conclusion and then trace it back to see how you can subsume your current offerings into higher-level and higher-value ones. Even if you can't take them into the Delta Model, you can make your offerings more transformation*al* and partner with companies that can more fully do so. As mentioned in chapter 3, this is especially important for B2B companies, for businesses never buy your offerings in and of themselves; they are always a means to an end. Sell the end, rather than the means, and you will gain much more economic value.

And whatever the genre of offerings you have today, do not neglect the opportunities for guiding transformations for whatever communities you or your customers interact with—whether families, neighborhoods, locales, suppliers, investors, and even the general public and society at large. Recall how the Transformational Travel Council recognizes as part of its mission the communities to which people travel; recall too how Dignity Made explicitly went into business to help communities in the Philippines individual by individual, and then, based on the most prevalent local commodity, created physical goods (its coconut factory, and then its coconut oil), service activities (employment, distribution), and experiences (training, community events) to transform a local community from living in poverty to flourishing.

Finally, remember that is the goal of every transformation: to foster human flourishing.

REFLECTION

This chapter discussed turning experiences into transformations as illustrated in the Delta Model, matching the four types of aspirations learned in chapter 3 with the four types of transformations. Answer these questions:

- Did you find yourself gravitating toward certain words in the thesauri? If so, what might that say about your customers and your business?
- As you read about the four types of transformations, what ideas or exemplars most resonated with you? What can you learn from them?
- If you do not yet stage experiences or guide transformations, how might you make your offerings more transformational? In what ways could you subsume them in experience & transformation offerings, either your own or those of companies you might sell to or partner with?
- If you are in the experience or transformation business today, where do you fall on the Delta Model? Can you envision ways of guiding enhancing, expanding, enriching, and/or—reaching the top of the delta—altering transformations?

PREPARATION

The final chapter pulls together everything necessary to truly become a transformation guider, focusing on how to bring aspirants through three phases—diagnosis, encapsulated experiences, and follow-through. It further offers different ways of charging for the demonstrated outcomes customers achieve. To get the most out of reading it, think on these things:

- It's not always easy to draw out, decipher, and grasp customer aspirations, no matter the type. What ways do you have of communicating with customers that would lend themselves to such conversations? How can you build in more such opportunities?
- After reading chapters 4 and 5, do you have a good idea for how to encapsulate experiences and mass customize them to individual aspirants? If not, think a bit more about how these could be done.
- A transformation is not complete unless it is sustained through time. How might you ensure your aspirants' transformations last?
- How are you currently pricing your offerings? Do you see any missed opportunities for charging for outcomes?

7

GUIDING TRANSFORMATIONS

You began this book by understanding and, I trust, embracing the Progression of Economic Value, and now recognize the tremendous value—for you, for customers, for human flourishing—that can be created by getting into the business of guiding transformations. You've learned about aspirants and aspirations, about the experiences that underly every transformation, and about how to create offerings atop those experiences that address the different types of aspirations, up to and including those of metamorphosis.

In this final chapter, then, you will learn the final pieces of the puzzle for getting into the transformation business: how to guide transformations and how to charge for them. While I've discussed guiding throughout the first six chapters of the book, this one brings together those elements and places them within a final framework: the three phases of transformation, *diagnosis, encapsulated experiences,* and *follow-through.*[1]

Recall the example of ChoiceCenter Leadership University, which led off the last chapter. You can clearly see these three phases in its offering. The diagnosis phase begins when participants meet their coach virtually and finishes during the first weekend in Vegas, where they determine and commit to their individual answers to the question, "What do you want in your life, more than anything, that you haven't been able to figure out?" Then comes experience after encapsulated experience that pushes participants toward fulfilling their aspiration—no matter how outlandish, bold, or life-changing it may be. This phase begins that first weekend and then continues remotely, cohort by cohort, until participants come back for the second weekend, when they create their personal strategic plan. Many companies would consider that the end of their offering, but ChoiceCenter further guides follow-through with each participant across the one-hundred-day period during which they accomplish their plan and integrate the results into their lives, enabling them to sustain it over time.

With any aspiration and corresponding transformation, you must go through the three phases ChoiceCenter's example illustrates. Doing so allows you to (1) properly understand the aspiration—the individual from/to statement of each aspirant, (2) correctly design and stage the set of encapsulated experiences that enable each aspiration to be achieved, and (3) ensure that the transformation truly takes hold.

These three phases of guiding transformations (shown in figure 7-1) carry out encapsulation writ large. In addition to encapsulating each experience, you need to do so for the overarching offering, working with aspirants before, during, and after the bounds of what one might expect the offering to be until successful integration into their lives. You need to encapsulate the overarching offering, working with aspirants before, during, and after

FIGURE 7-1

The three phases of guiding transformations

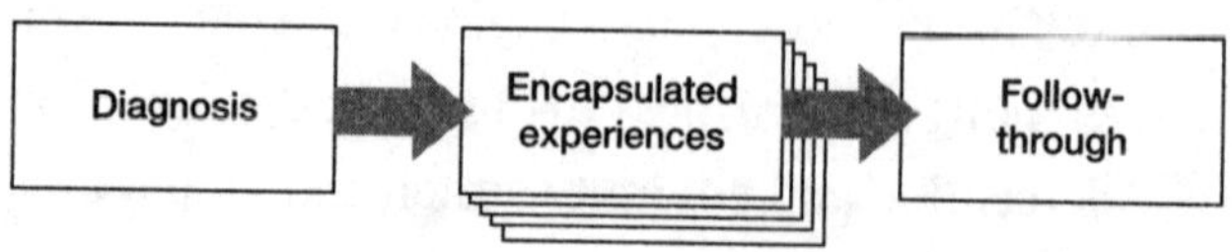

the bounds of the transformation until they accomplish that integration into their lives.

Also think of how the twelve-step Transformation Journey model overlays onto these three phases. First, the individual lives life within the ordinary world and then has an aspiration. After some period of hesitation, the aspirant meets the guide in step 4, who kicks off the first phase of diagnosis, which continues through the aspirant's commitment. The aspirant then enters the transformation world, initiated by preparation.

Encapsulated experiences involve starts and often fits that at times regress the transformation, eventually proceeding through the crucible—the most difficult of experiences and the climax of the offering—out of which comes the new creation, the new identity, the transformation.

Finally, the third phase of follow-through begins with reflection and, as the individual leaves the transformation world and returns to the ordinary world, integration. When follow-through is complete, the person emerges in the final step with greater flourishing and lives life anew at a higher level than before. The next aspiration, and the next transformation journey, awaits.

Let's look at the details of each phase.

Diagnosis

What do your customers hope to become? That's the first question of transformation guiding. Ahead of the transformation journey, you must take aspirants through a *diagnosis* phase, to borrow a health-care term. You get to know each customer (or beneficiary) as an individual person, organization, business, or community, and then ascertain each particular aspiration—their why—as well as where the aspirant is today relative to that desire. Such from/to statements, as we've learned, enable you to design, customize, and then guide the set of encapsulated experiences that first prepare the aspirant for the journey and then guide aspiration achievement. Because of the inherent value of the self-discovery that diagnosis entails, it can often be an offering unto itself.

Sometimes customers come with fairly general aspirations, such as becoming more fit, saving money, learning about a useful topic, or getting a job. Sometimes they are rather specific, such as running a marathon, saving for a first home, gaining a certification in web design, or getting a job as an AI data analyst. Sometimes they come with issues—health decline, lack of innovation or organizational agility, increasing crime—particularly when the catalyst is a disruption. Whatever the case, you need to understand the aspiration and its starting point well enough to get to a from/to statement usable to create the offering.

For example, many years ago doctors diagnosed my mother-in-law with stage 4 pancreatic cancer. There was no possibility of eliminating the disease, but they said through the proper oncology regime they could extend her life by months, maybe a year. After considerable thought, she told them that her oldest grandchild was getting married in a few months, and she wanted to be at the wedding, feel good, and look well. That was her aspiration. So the care team did an about-face, didn't poke and prod her, and did not order chemo, which would have made her feel awful and made her hair fall out. They wisely focused on what would give her a high quality of life in her final months. She made it to the wedding, looked absolutely beautiful—and died two weeks later.

Sometimes people have aspirations that are deleterious to themselves and restrict their own flourishing—in which case, you have a fiduciary responsibility to set them straight. Sometimes they delude themselves in where (and who) they are today or in their ability to achieve their aspirations. It can often be of benefit, then, to preface the diagnosis phase with *triage* to determine whether a transformation opportunity actually exists for this particular aspirant at this time.

If not, you can guide them to a proper understanding of the situation and work with them on an interim transformation to get them to the point where they can realistically achieve their initial desire. For example, in 2022 the US Army created the Future Soldier Preparatory Course for recruits who could not meet its academic or fitness standards. Those who still want to join the army can head to Fort Jackson, South Carolina, for special instruction and training, with standard exams every week that mark would-be recruits' progress. Every three weeks (up to ninety days), the army retests the participants, who have failed, and when they meet the same standards as everyone else, they can then join. As of fall 2024, with a 95 percent graduation rate for the course, the US Army has added almost twenty-five thousand soldiers it would not have otherwise.[2]

Ascertaining aspirations

You need to ascertain aspirations at two different levels: generically, to determine the nature of the transformation offerings you must provide; and specifically, to determine what particular transformations you will guide. In your business, you may start with a generic from/to statement, such as from stressed to relaxed, from wage earner to lifelong saver, from neophyte to expert, or from recruit to soldier. This can be informed by what customers seek from your current goods, services, experiences, and even existing transformations, as well as from what you've learned in earlier chapters, in particular about the spheres of transformation and the types of aspirations and transformations.

For some businesses that may be enough, especially when aspirants are at the beginning of a continuing journey. But for most, you need to get down to that second level: the specific aspirations for this particular aspirant. Even when a generic aspiration suffices—such as with joining the army—keep in mind that you still guide individuals, who vary individually. The more you know about them, design to them, and work with them, the more likely they will be transformed.

Perhaps the best way to think about your transformation offerings, as with all economic offerings, is to analyze customers' *jobs to be done* (JTBD), what they desire to accomplish. Popularized by late Harvard Business School professor Clayton Christensen, the jobs customers want to complete "are never simply about function—they have powerful social and emotional dimensions."[3] While Christensen focused primarily on goods and services and how people "hire" them, functional, emotional, and social JTBD also apply to transformations.[4] A *functional* job represents a task customers want to complete (such as hiring a smart watch to track fitness) or a problem they want to resolve (hiring a treadmill to get more steps in the winter). *Emotional* jobs address the feelings people want to heighten or diminish in any given moment or future circumstance (such as enabling that smart watch to notify you of daily accomplishments you can celebrate). Emotional JTBD prove incredibly important for transformations, since emotions go up and down with progress and regress, and if an aspirant's emotions are at odds with the transformative experience, then the process is unlikely to be done well. Finally, *social* jobs concern how people want to be perceived by others (healthy, fit) or relate to others (encouraged, supporting others' own fitness journeys).

These three JTBD support the aspirations customers have, which are best defined by what Stone Mantel founder Dave Norton and I call *aspirational* jobs.[5] These always involve the sentiments behind from/to statements, but it helps to focus on how aspirants hire you and your offerings to achieve them. As Dave likes to point out, through their branding, advertising, and selling, many companies say they create transformations, but don't actually effect them. They may deliver on emotional or social jobs, but so often cannot produce the effect that people expect when hiring a business.

The process to gain insights into the full JTBD for aspirants can include interviews, observation, and ethnography. But the method is less critical than the focus on what customers desire to become, including what motivates them, what goals they have, and what problems they want resolved. What is critical is talking with them to gain the insight needed to create offerings that meet their needs.

For aspirational JTBD, diagnosis is a place where you can, for example, probe for the measuring stick by which the aspirant assesses progress and establish milestones along the way, putting a number on it if possible (such as a specific financial gain or spending reduction). This makes the aspiration more meaningful and achievable. In some cases goals tend to be more discrete—on or off, yes or no, without measuring sticks—especially when the transformation is *from* something the person is not, *to* what the person wants to be (or, remedially, *from* something they do not want to be, such as having bad habits).

Especially with large-scale change—think back to expanding transformations to gain ambition and altering transformations to accomplish metamorphoses—the length of the journey means you may need to reassess aspirational jobs multiple times. Diagnosis then becomes a regular activity, something to be done over and over as a part of your reflection/preparation cycle within encapsulation. At each step on the journey, you must get aspirants to internalize the knowledge and capabilities gained, so hitting interim achievements becomes second nature, something to be celebrated.

While in every situation understanding the aspirational job remains paramount, functional, emotional, and social jobs prove important in diagnosing aspirations as well. Functionally, diagnosis can be a place to show off your expertise while simultaneously assuring customers that because of that expertise, achieving their aspirations will be doable. It is also a time when your guides can emotionally connect with customers to help resolve the inevitable ups and downs that will happen in the future transformation journey. There's great emotional resonance, too, with the final determination of and commitment to the aspiration, as you help customers understand themselves well enough to form a very personal from/to statement. And since many people today like to share their progress, you might want to help them do so here, a social job to be done, when the transformation begins.

Designing transformations

As with all economic offerings, customers often don't know what they want, and even when they do, they can't always articulate it. You need to draw it out of them, helping to uncover vaguely known desires or discover previously unknown aspirations. That requires a design tool that guides people in figuring out what they truly want—preferably visually, and ideally viscerally—and guides you in determining what specific, customized transformation offering will enable them to achieve their aspirations.[6]

While artificial intelligence promises to revolutionize them, design tools don't have to be rocket science. Travel design company Explorer X, the company that does so very well with encapsulation, uses a simple, three-minute "Your Journey Begins Now" form and then schedules a video call to discuss potential explorers' travel dreams.[7] Craig Towle, executive partner at broker-dealer J.W. Cole Financial, teaches the company's independent financial professionals to use readily available software for creating estate plans and bringing together all financial information into one place for families, but also designed a custom card game to make a timeline for families to see if they are investing their time as wisely as their finances. He told me that time is "one of the secrets to a life transformation, where personal, deep, and hopefully fun tools can be used to push people toward a genuinely better life."

There are many technology-based tools for physical goods that enable customers to visualize what they want. Think of any mass-customized good you've designed on the web or in a store, such as shoes, travel bags, or cosmetics. Precious few tools exist for experiences, however, much less transformations.

Experience and transformation platforms, though, naturally incorporate design tools, such as Symplany's visualization tools for financial discovery. And remember Princess Cruises' MedallionClass platform? Now imagine something like it in a hospital or health system. This platform would have access to all your records, remember every interaction you have with the system, know all your appointments, and guide you through them in real time. In concert with doctors and other caregivers, it would learn your desires, needs, and aspirations with every encounter, and make suggestions on how to proceed. Operationally, it would also know the whereabouts and status of not only you but caregivers, equipment, rooms, and everything else in the hospital, and so could ensure that everything necessary for an appointment is ready, eliminating wasted time on both sides and ensuring that the time invested pays off for your health & well-being transformation journey.

As previously discussed, modularity is the key to efficiently customizing all these components. A modular architecture lets you design a mass-customized transformation with every interaction, encounter, and step along the journey, each module mass customized to the individual. While the scale of a transformation offering does not always afford the creation of a platform, there are many out there today, with many more to come in the future. For smaller companies, the modules may in fact be more crafted than mass customized, yielding a more personal touch even without the lowest costs.

Starizon Studio, a very different consulting company in which I partnered, exemplifies how to diagnose aspirations and design transformations, specifically to turn companies into premier experience stagers. From 2002 to 2017 (before founders Gary and Leigh Adamson could no longer be persuaded not to retire),

Starizon's potential clients—or "explorers"—came to our experience design center in Keystone, Colorado, for a twenty-four-hour diagnosis. They got to see what it was like to work, eat, and stay in the very place where their design work would happen, with us Starizon guides drawing out of them their current circumstances and future aspirations while giving them a peek at what their future could be. At the end of the diagnosis, we presented our proposal of designed transformative experiences to them. How many visitors went on to a full engagement? Over 90 percent. How many gained value from the diagnosis in and of itself? Every last one.

It didn't hurt that Starizon was its own first client, using its meaningful purpose of "Explore. Discover. Transform." to design its place and methodology. Gary envisioned such results, despite all the naysaying he heard from his former consulting colleagues, for an integral part of the methodology was designing back from the future. We would guide explorers in first picturing their outcomes from the engagement, and then design the steps—all the modular experiences—it would take to get from that future state backward to the present to where they were today. Though the aspirations were from/to statements, the experience plan was really a *to/from* design! Every transformation guider should consider this technique, for research shows that when people envision their future selves, they make better decisions in the present.[8]

Starizon also excelled at *partnering* with its aspirants.[9] It was never a normal consulting company that asked clients for all their data, pumped it into a black box, and spit out a plan. Rather, Starizon elicited the intentions, ideas, and initiatives of the experience design plan—beginning with clients determining their own theme/meaningful purpose—by working directly with each explorer team at the Keystone studio, and then massaging them into the best versions possible, ensuring that they fit together into one cohesive plan. When presented back to a team—first verbally, then in written form—explorers saw their own concepts, heard their own words, and, most importantly, owned each element of the plan. They would not allow it to fail, for it was fully *their* experience design plan.

Similarly, you should partner with your customers in ascertaining their aspirations and designing and preparing for their journeys—and in guiding their transformations through encapsulated experiences.

Encapsulated Experiences

Transformative experiences form the nucleus of transformation guiding, the middle phase where you stage the right experiences at the right time in the right order for each aspirant. As discussed in chapter 4, you should properly encapsulate these experiences, preparing aspirants beforehand and then guiding them afterward in reflecting and integrating them into their lives. This should be done in concert with each successive experience, each one building on top of the previous one to move aspirants onward and upward toward, and eventually to, their aspiration.

Few transformations follow a nice, simple path, however (which is why "journey" really is the right term). There are ups and downs, advances and retreats, progression and regression. As the old military saying has it, no plan survives contact with the enemy, and when it comes to transformations for individuals—metamorphic ones in particular—there are enemies within and without, and even more so for the collective aspirants of organizations, businesses, and communities.

Sensing and responding

You must therefore be prepared to adapt your transformation offering, no matter how well designed, in different ways for different aspirants. A modular architecture enables not only efficient design but effective adaptability through sensing how well or not the transformation journey is going and triggering different modules on demand, in real time, at point of need.

Think of every transformative experience as one of many steps along the journey. Some are short, while some are long; some go smoothly, while some cover difficult terrain; some move forward in a straight shot, while others meander. There are milestones along the way, steps that should be recognized and celebrated, even when you are not sure exactly when each aspirant will reach them or what precise modules will precede them.[10]

Recall how street theatre presents a model for experience guiding. Both disciplines sense and respond in real time to new, unforeseen circumstances and figure out what to do about it, how best to intervene to keep the offering on track. Street performers encounter heckles they've never heard before and outside interruptions of their routines, while transformation guiders occasionally encounter unfamiliar issues that arise with particular aspirants and the experiences they undergo, as well as disruptions outside of their control. In such cases, you must improvise to handle the situation as best you can, figure it out as you go along, and invent some new intervention that can get the transformation back on track.[11] Don't stop there, though, for similar circumstances may arise for other aspirants down the road. Work to turn what you did here into a module that can be added to your architecture, available to be called on whenever circumstances require, and thereby renew your capabilities.

Street artists always perform several milestone bits and end with the finale, the high point with the most engaging and amazing routines, such as juggling lit torches on a unicycle or blowing a fireball out of one's mouth. This climatic closing segment is akin to the achievement of the aspiration, the capstone experience of the offering.

Rituals and ceremonies can be especially appropriate at such a time. Think of graduations, weddings, bar and bat mitzvahs, baptisms, even retirement parties. ChoiceCenter Leadership University has a graduation ceremony for every program. Starizon orchestrated opening and closing rituals for every visit to its experience design place, holding a signing ceremony where explorer teams accepted the declaration of their theme or meaningful purpose; additionally, we didn't just give reports to clients but staged unveiling ceremonies at the client's own place.

At the capstone celebration, consider presenting emblems of transformations, such as diplomas, certificates, physical or digital badges, rings, insignias, trophies, medals, or other meaningful items. Emblems are to transformations as memorabilia are to experiences, tangible signifiers of achievement of an aspiration—to others but more importantly to achievers. United Kingdom–based coach Karrin Simpson refers to them as "transformational objects that hold deep personal significance and meaning. They often serve as more than just reminders of the past; they can inspire and guide us in our present and future. These objects can be imbued with memories, emotions, and symbolism, making them powerful tools for personal growth and self-discovery."[12]

Avoiding failure

Of course, not all transformations succeed. I once saw a performance in Dam Square, Amsterdam, where the street performer gave up after five or six minutes; everything he tried just could not get the audience going. (I'm not saying it was the audience's fault; sometimes performers have bad days.) Similarly, many transformations stall and even flat-out fail, with the blame sometimes on the aspirant, occasionally the guider, and at times both.[13]

While no means a complete list, here are particular issues to keep an eye on to lessen the possibility of failure:

- *Too little support.* As emphasized throughout this book, transformations are just plain hard. Many don't even get off the ground because aspirants don't have enough support to achieve them on their own. Kyle Coolbroth, founder of strategic advisory and coaching firm Cothink'r, likes to say, "The biggest impediment to coaching is inaction"—a statement that applies to transformation overall. Which is one reason transformation offerings prove to be such a great opportunity! But it also means that one of your first tasks in guiding is to offer aspirants the support they need *right now,* in whatever state they sit, and show them that you will be alongside them throughout the journey.

- *Poor preparation.* This happens on both sides of the transformation offering and can include lack of clarity on aspirations, competing goals, and insufficient time on the aspirant side, as well as inadequate diagnosis, weak design, and meager customization on the guider side. On both sides, sometimes the aspiration aims too high—and sometimes too low. Sande Golgart, founder of SEG Way Growth Consulting, told me, "It is often said that your 'why' needs to be stronger than the obstacles you will face along the way. Otherwise, you will give in too easily." For your part, focus on your up-front offering design to best ensure success, including identifying when aspirants are not sufficiently prepared to achieve the aspirations they seek and then planning what to do about it.
- *Lack of commitment.* Does every transformation need commitment? No, particularly not enhancing transformations (including invitational ones), which have neither great scale nor a change in kind, only in degree. But in all other cases, even with well-supported and prepared aspirants, sometimes people just aren't committed to their own cause. This can be detrimental to success, so consider how to ensure your aspirants stay the course by folding commitment into the transformation journey. It may be the strongest form of preparation; should it be part of your diagnosis? Or the first

Transformations must be sustained through time. Aspirants who purportedly have transformed may still encounter all the issues of achieving the aspiration in the first place. As life and business goes on, their progress—great though it may be—may regress, their focus deteriorate, their behavior backslide, their identity de-align, and so forth. In which case the aspirant wasn't truly transformed.

To help your aspirants keep all this at bay, you must conduct the third phase of transformation guiding, *follow-through*. Not to be confused with follow-up, which is akin to asking, "Hi, how ya' doin'?," follow-through means ensuring the transformation takes hold so that it is sustained through time without relapse, reversion, or decline. This phase continues to guide the aspirant, but in keeping the transformation as an integrated part of the person, organization, business, or community. That's what leads to higher levels of flourishing.

Sustaining transformations

This is where companies ostensibly in the transformation industry often fail their aspirants, guiding them in hitting not just a major milestone but *the* highly anticipated capstone—and then thinking they are done. Health-care providers diagnose and heal patients and then prescribe medicine, but do little when up to a third of the patients do not even take their meds as directed.[16] Financial advisers manage their clients to retirement (or hitting "the number" that enables it), but rarely shift to helping them with what to do with their time or how to create an identity away from work. Educational institutions hand out diplomas and certifications but fail to help students apply what they learned in the real world. Many religious advisers focus on a baptism, bar or bat mitzvah, commission, or other such ceremony of spiritual significance, but don't extend the relationship into discipling.

Follow-through is essential. Frances Turner, a longtime friend and one of Strategic Horizons' certified Experience Economy experts, has had a lifetime struggle with weight, reaching over three hundred pounds as an adult. An assistant professor of marketing at Ithaca College, she was always trying diets, fitness programs, and the like, but never managed to lose or keep significant weight off. Almost twenty years ago bariatric surgery enabled her to lose 140 pounds, but the health-care system didn't provide any follow-through—no tracking of how things went afterward, no weight maintenance advice, no counseling—and her weight crept back up ever so slowly, but persistently, until she had gained half of it back. Frances told me:

> During Covid-19 I started seeing ads for a company called Calibrate. It emphasized "metabolic health" combined with weight-loss drugs. I talked with my doctor, and then joined, spending the first three months focused on tracking my eating, drinking water, sleeping properly, monitoring my emotions, working with a nutritionist, all those sorts of things. I lost ten pounds. The next month they introduced Wegovy into the regime.

In concert with the healthy habits, the GLP-1 drug Wegovy enabled Frances to get down to around 150 pounds. Most importantly, she's kept her weight there thanks specifically to how Calibrate excels at the follow-through phase.

The company knows how difficult it is to keep a large weight loss off over time and works to "maintain your progress no matter what life throws your way."[17] It therefore offers each member a personal coach who, through biweekly one-on-one meetings, works with them on their personal why and discusses and adjusts individual goals across a number of elements (food, sleep, emotions, exercise) to support the aspiration, a process that continues even after the weight goal is met. Calibrate's app also offers interactions that spark enduring inspiration and commitment. Membership starts with a virtual session with a clinician, who meets with you again as the follow-through phase begins, usually after nine to twelve months. The coach, clinician, and medical team (those responsible for the Wegovy treatments) continue the focus on being healthy through this phase, which Calibrate very appropriately calls "Sustaining."

Sustaining transformations is so crucial that many people seek guidance for changes they've already made, for the follow-through other companies neglected to do. It's actually a huge business opportunity; as Tara-Nicholle Nelson writes in *The Transformational Consumer,* "Most of the transformational spending people will do in their lifetime will go toward buying supplies that help them maintain baselines."[18] And not just supplies but follow-through experiences as well. Othership, for example, calls itself "a space for transformation" that offers "social self-care" through its ice baths and saunas in Toronto and New York. Cofounder and CEO Robbie Bent told me that many customers have, say, an ayahuasca experience to get off drugs, but start up again in a month or two. Othership's expert guides work with them to take that transformative experience back to where they live, helping them through its "healthy, fun, good-for-you space" via classes (many of them intensely psychological and highly emotional), night socials, sound immersions, and other activities—but with no alcohol, no drugs, and no phones.

One way or the other, a true transformation must take hold and be sustained through time. How much time is enough? It depends on the aspirant, aspiration, and transformation. But if you or an aspirant isn't sure, it hasn't been long enough.

Encapsulating transformations

Recall how transformation guiding is encapsulation writ large. After whatever experience aspirants view as the one at which they achieve their aspirations, it's critical to have them reflect on and integrate that particular experience. But even more so, reflect on and integrate the entire *series* of experiences that effected the transformation. This means ensuring the transformation takes hold by integrating it into the person's life from that capstone point onward. At this level, reflection and integration aren't about closing the gap between aspiration and becoming; rather, they seek to sustain what the person has become at or above the level achieved so that behaving matches being. Work on the transformation thereby shifts from liminal to lasting.

Commitment and accountability are key. Marshall Goldsmith, the epitome of executive coaching, believes that accountability is crucial to change and growth and insists that "my coaching clients fully advertise their plans to change their behavior to the people they work with: Disclosure makes the effort to change visible; visibility elevates accountability."[19] This concept applies to sustaining the change as well. How can you provide that accountability as follow-through to your transformation offerings?

Thus there is a fifth kind of job to be done, as Dave Norton discovered through ethnographic research. He calls it *systemic* jobs, those that help people manage their lives, including their transformations. In family dynamics, for example, systemic JTBD include managing all of the individual goals and activities of a household of both young and older groups of aspirants. Parents and children use tools, patterns, and dialogue to help them keep their family systems in balance so that they can grow and develop individually and as a group. Systemic jobs prove most important in the integration stage of encapsulation and the follow-through phase of guiding.[20]

Consider how integration and follow-through can work for each of the four types of aspirations and transformations:

- *Refinement aspirations.* As the expert, you must ensure aspirants retain their level of enhancement. Consider turning the offering into an ongoing membership or at least a relationship that continues long after the initial encounter. Sami Vesala, who attended the Springbank Whisky School, is still in contact with its permanent workers, saying that "the feeling of getting accepted as a part of the distillery 'family' was genuine," which helps him retain his affection for whisky and continue to learn more about it. Given the typical academy or workshop model for enhancing transformations, companies can add on continuing ed or boost programs specifically for those who've graduated from earlier ones.

- *Ambition aspirations.* As the coach, you must ensure aspirants maintain their expansive gains. Coaches naturally continue their work once the aspiration is met, although often on a less frequent basis for maintenance. Memberships work here too, as with GOLFTEC, which keeps aspirants coming back periodically. For the duration of their membership, people can look at any and all video-capture lessons to revisit particular points. B2B coaching company BetterUp added a B2C option so people whose company once paid for their coaching can continue on their own. All such ongoing integrations can lead to the ambition beyond the current one on the appropriate measuring stick.
- *Cultivation aspirations.* As the counselor, you must ensure aspirants nourish their enrichment (and not be mere dilettantes). Apps help people cultivate good and healthy habits, and prove highly effective at sustaining them. Often in concert with devices, they excel at tracking against baselines, showing progress during enhancing or expanding transformations, but also against the new baseline of an enriching transformation to help ensure aspirants stay at or exceed it. They also provide access to all manner of know-how, lessons, physical coaches, and mental health

counselors, and even to other aspirants that bring accountability, during the transformation and the follow-through.

- *Metamorphosis aspirations.* As the alchemist, you must do something very different. Why? Because with metamorphic transformations *you can't go back*. If you can, it wasn't a metamorphosis.

  Nonetheless, the integration of follow-through is still crucial, but of a different kind. It's a matter of helping aspirants get comfortable in their new skin. You must aid them in dealing with the ramifications of the transformation across all aspects of their identity, including in letting go of facets now misaligned with the new self. In handling how others now view them—or how friends, acquaintances, and colleagues incorrectly view them. And, as the case may be, in smoothing the way to overcoming impostor syndrome.

Just as an alchemist subsumes the other three forms of guiding, so too can follow-through incorporate each of the methods given above. For example, ChoiceCenter offers a number of programs, workshops, and retreats, while its coaches provide ongoing support. Participants often become coaches themselves, further cementing the lessons they learned and sustaining the transformations they underwent. Modern Elder Academy (MEA) has an alumni department that Chip Conley says is like "a learning concierge helping our alums to explore affinity groups, group travel options, and other programs that might support them." MEA also supports its participants after they emerge from their "midlife chrysalis" with monthly video calls that have accountability baked in, more than fifty regional chapters around the world that stage their own events, and an annual membership offering, called Corazón, that lets alums go deeper into content, connection, and community, each one enabling further integration into their now purposeful, thriving lives.

Following through on metamorphosis is not just a onetime experience but deservedly an entire phase of transformation offerings. In *The Map to Wholeness,* Suzy Ross views integration to be more crucial to identity change than the initial transformation. At the end of the latter, so often "the shock and mystique of the life-changing event slowly wear thin," while integration yields "an unmistakable sense of peace and fulfillment that comes not from what you created or did but from who you have become. You are intact, whole, and complete."[21]

Iterating transformation offerings

Effective follow-through also sets the stage for the next offering, aiding aspirants in setting their sights on some new aspiration—one you may be perfectly equipped to guide. Fully recovered patients may want to shift their energy to having greater well-being. The recently retired may decide on a primary activity that fills their days, whether it be an enriching part-time job or volunteer opportunity, a travel or gardening hobby, or time with grandchildren. Graduates may want to take the next step in their education or need guidance in taking their careers to the next level. And finding one's purpose in life can lead to needing help in actualizing that purpose.

So why should someone shift to another guide when they can stay with the one that proved so useful in the last transformation? The follow-through phase not only cements their change in identity; it can cement the relationship between aspirant and guider. You can use it to cycle back to diagnosis, helping customers develop new aspirations.

It's therefore good to find ways to keep in touch with aspirants, such as through intermittent check-ins, app reminders, or cohort reunions. Each of the activities ChoiceCenter and MEA employ for follow-through also proves useful in creating opportunities for returning to diagnosis.

Many situations make it easy to create an ongoing relationship that involves transformation after transformation and can last for a lifetime, such as working with financial advisers, lawyers, and counselors. Membership offerings can also foster such ongoing relationships. Think about how you can go from counselor to consigliere, coach to confidant, or management adviser to house consultant.

Charging for Outcomes

While guiding transformations themselves may feel good (after all, you're contributing to human flourishing), we must remember the economic aspect. Recall from chapter 1: you are what you charge for! With transformations, that means aligning what customers pay with what they value by charging for the demonstrated outcomes they achieve.

Most enterprises that are or should be in the transformation business, however, charge at the service level—fixed prices, hourly billing, time and materials, or cost-plus. Economically, they've always been service providers, charging for the activities they do, for *inputs* even while guiding customers in achieving *outcomes.* As experience businesses increasingly move into transformations, they too tend to keep charging admission or other time-based fees rather than charging for the aspirational achievements that time effects.

Certainly, such companies learn to secure premium pricing for the increased value they create and beef up their profits, but they're still charging at the service or experience level and are nowhere close to capturing the full value generated. The simple fact of the matter is that if you don't implement outcome-based pricing, you are less likely to guide your customers in achieving their aspirations. It's when you make your income dependent on your customers' outcomes that you fully understand everything it requires—and do whatever it takes—to guide them toward achievement and ensure they sustain it through time.

Many companies do the exact opposite, paying people instead of charging them, usually as an element of encouragement or gamification. The Future Soldier Preparatory Course, for example, pays bonuses to those who pass and join the US Army because of the benefits to Uncle Sam. Insurer YuLife, based in London, offers employees of its clients rewards to exercise, meditate, even help clean the ocean, all to enhance employee fitness and well-being so they cost their employers less money in benefits.

That's not a bad thing, and gamification can work here, at least in the short term. But what the individual aspires to become rarely matters, other than in great generalities such as exercising more, eating less, or volunteering. The incentives and progress tend to peter out over time since they offer only extrinsic motivation, when what it takes to achieve true aspirations is intrinsic to the aspirant.[22]

Ways to charge for change

In researching over a hundred companies that charge for change, I found four distinct ways they do it:

TRANSFORMATION GUARANTEES. First, the aspirant agrees to a specific fee, but with some or all of it subject to the value of the outcome achieved. This is often employed when a company primarily charges at the service or experience level but puts some of those fees at risk, subject to if (or how much) the aspirant transforms.

Calibrate, for instance, has a "Results Money Back Promise" that offers a 50 percent refund of its membership fees whenever members do not lose at least 10 percent of their weight over twelve consecutive months. And recall how Texas State Technical College puts it all at risk, guaranteeing that graduates in certain majors get a job within six months or it refunds their entire tuition. Scores of other colleges, certification programs, and assorted educational institutions do the same, whether for all or some of the up-front fees.

Consider, too, Service & Co., founded by Palle Højsholt in Skanderborg, Denmark, which has been transforming young Danish people into tourist guides for over twenty-five years. In a five-week program, they learn the ins and outs of being "onstage" on buses and boats, in museums, and at historical sites. "Our vision is to inspire all students," Højsholt told me. "They have to give it their all for five weeks and be the best version of themselves, especially working with all the things they are good at." His school has a job guarantee—if students graduate and are not employed as a guide within four months, they get their money back. It has never had to pay out that guarantee, although a few people do not graduate for various reasons (two out of 143 students across all 2024 classes). As Højsholt made clear to me, that guarantee encourages him and his instructors to do whatever it takes to ensure students learn the vocation, and they work directly with potential employers throughout the process.

Starizon Studio also made its income dependent on the outcomes of our aspirants. Twenty-five percent of its fees were paid *completely at the explorer team's discretion*, based on whether explorers received the outcomes committed to in the engagement. In fifteen years of business before the founders retired, only two customers did not pay the entire fee (and in one case, additional work yielded the full payment), precisely because we viewed the arrangement as a catalytic mechanism for ensuring we did what we said we would do and aspirants got out of it what they desired.

SUCCESS FEES. Second, companies get paid not a predetermined amount but one established after the fact or on an ongoing basis, based on outcomes. Success fees are not an all-or-nothing proposition with a set fee; the end amount charged varies based on a sliding scale of how much value was realized.

Management consultants have long charged based on success for at least some engagements, using such parameters as efficiency gained, revenue increased, and market cap valuation improved. But such charging mechanisms have never become endemic in consulting, even though the industry has always been a transformation one. Some accounting, legal, and other professional firms use "TIP" clauses—for "to improve (or insure) performance," also known as retrospective or success prices—where customers decide on the value of the work afterward and pay accordingly.[23]

A number of US state governments now recognize the power of paying for outcomes in social services. Massachusetts, for example, authorized its agencies to switch to "pay-for-success contracts." One social service agency stopped paying for the time employees spent in English fluency classes—whether or not they learned anything—and instead paid vendors for demonstrated fluency that resulted in steady employment.[24] Connecticut uses "outcome rate cards" that set the rates at which state agencies pay providers for specific outcomes, such as finding employment for the jobless or housing for the homeless.[25]

INCOME SHARE AGREEMENTS. Third, companies charge nothing up front but instead invest in the transformation journey, recouping the investment afterward to the degree of success aspirants have. Similar to success fees, income share agreements pertain to situations where aspirants' incomes provide recognition of a transformation achieved, with the amount of income a proxy for the level of achievement.

For example, the San Diego Workforce Partnership focuses on economic mobility, working with both employers and individuals to succeed. In 2019 it created a fund to help disadvantaged low-wage workers gain the necessary capabilities—and, importantly, have the right support systems (systemic jobs to be done)—to find better employment, and in some cases to be employed at all. It raised private and public funds to institute income share agreements that financed education and support systems, where recipients would repay 8 percent of their income above the $40,000 threshold with a total payment cap, usually $11,700 over five to seven years.[26]

Over fifty institutions work with or supply these investment vehicles, and it would be possible for them to be used for a portion rather than all of tuition, fees, and support services required by students.[27] While I've seen them only in educational situations, there are other contexts for which they could work. By laying people off, for example, rather than providing a straight severance package, companies could use that money to invest in those former employees' future income streams, whether they join another company or start their own.[28] Startup boot camps could do the same, proclaiming that their programs are so effective that they're willing to invest in each participant's entrepreneurial endeavor.

OUTCOME FUNDS. Finally, companies can receive financing based on the outcomes they produce. This is appropriate for situations where enterprises secure funding, such as from governments, to guide transformation offerings for beneficiaries, such as their residents. This is exactly how the state of Texas now funds Texas State Technical College, as discussed in chapter 1. It used to pay for student credit-hours regardless of actual accomplishments, but now the state pays TSTC based on how much their graduates contribute to state tax revenue. At least thirty state governments in the United States now apportion their funding to public universities in part based on overall student outcomes.[29]

ADTC (originally known as American Diesel Training Centers) lets students—mostly unemployed or underemployed—join its diesel mechanics and other programs with no up-front fees, using a "career impact bond." This concept, which also funds support services such as career coaching and financial literacy instruction, was developed by Social Finance, a nonprofit and investment adviser. The bonds provide up-front funding to learners, with many employers repaying program costs while learners are employed with them.[30] As ADTC says in the mission statement on its website, "Our success is measured by the transformative impact we have on the lives of our candidates and the positive contributions they make to the organizations they join."[31]

How to implement outcome-based pricing

Transformative impact—that's exactly how all transformation guiders should be measured. None of the methods we've explored are mutually exclusive. Recognize, too, that when the payoff comes largely once aspirations are achieved, performing triage within the diagnosis phase becomes very important. If you accept aspirants who cannot in fact achieve their aspirations, you'll never recoup your investment in them.

No matter the method used, the first step you want to take in charging for outcomes is measuring them, and ideally not just at the end of the offering but on an ongoing basis. This means ascertaining that from/to gap between "I am X" and "I aspire to be Y" and how it closes over time. Then you can make course corrections via the right encapsulated experience(s) within your modular architecture. Rhode Island, for example, uses "active contract management" to monitor the performance of its contracts for employment and training in real time, specifically on "meeting their intake, retention, and employment goals."[32] It hasn't taken the step to fund decisions based on the outcomes delivered to date, but an interim move could be charging at the experience level rather than the service level, again charging for time rather than activities. Starizon Studio, in addition to working with "explorers," had "members" and charged membership fees to get the experiential aspect of our offerings across, and it is those fees to which the transformation guarantee applied.

In health care, many primary physician groups now employ "concierge medicine," also known as the direct primary care model, where they charge subscription or membership fees. Plum Health is a practice that does so, but it goes beyond most by measuring (if not yet charging for) outcomes such as hospitalizations prevented, urgent care and emergency department visits, weight goals achieved, patient anxiety and depression levels, and morbidity and mortality in communities served.[33] Paul Dunn and Ronald Baker, whose book *Time's Up!* has many examples of such subscription models and even many companies that charge for outcomes, wrote that Plum Health measures success "the same way the customer does," which has "a predictive correlation with the success and profits of the practice."[34] The follow-through phase of transformations could also be charged via membership fees, although sustaining the transformations may warrant its own outcome-based charging.

Of course, in many situations it's difficult to quantitatively measure outcomes and their value to aspirants. Qualitative charging, such as that of Starizon Studio and TIP clauses, requires qualitative measurements. The Old Fire Station, a "centre for creativity" in Oxford, England, decided not to use "outcomes to measure against" but "to let those we work with identify outcomes for themselves by telling us a story. What changed for them? How did it happen? Why is it important?"[35] The organization developed a storytelling evaluation methodology to evaluate the impact of its work, which is now used by more than a dozen other transformational organizations.

Certainly, qualitative measuring and charging can be opaque and challenging. When charging this way for outcomes, guides should incorporate such activities as check-ins, monitoring the aspirant's "pulse," discussing the value gained thus far, and using milestone celebrations and other mechanisms for ensuring aspirants and guides remain aligned on the journey. Focusing on emotional jobs to be done can also help endear aspirant and guide in ways that can subjectively help with the aspirant's view of the transformation. That was part of the "secret sauce" with Starizon Studio, as explorer teams became so emotionally invested in their transformation that they would take any setbacks or shortfalls personally, and then redouble their own efforts to make it succeed.

Is charging for outcomes mandatory? No. As with charging for time with experiences, it will take quite a while for not just companies but customers themselves to realize how both sides are better off if companies charge for outcomes. And have no doubt, such actions could benefit both sides of the offering equation.

Mindset matters. You could say that when wealth management and financial advisory firms charge for assets under management (as opposed to commissions on trades), it's an outcome-based fee, for when they make decisions that cause assets to increase in value, the result is greater wealth. But that's not how they *view* such charges; the industry mindset thinks of it as a fee for the activities done, which reinforces a service mentality. Symplany, interestingly, believes that total assets are *not* the outcomes people desire, or should desire. Rather, the outcomes lie in each individual's life and legacy. This cannot be so easily measured, and Symplany decided it would be wrong to "financialize" what is a very personal relationship between its advisers and their clients. It therefore finds charging for assets under management the most practical approach. It does so, however, with the proper mindset, shared with its advisers, that customers should feel free to spend whatever reasonably available assets they have to live life more fully and leave a more impactful legacy.

Whatever your situation, ask yourself: *What would we do differently if we charged for outcomes?* Then you will have the proper mindset to create transformation offerings and work with customers to yield the best outcomes on their behalf, even if today you feel it unwise, infeasible, or too early to do so. Eventually, that mindset will pave the way for outcome-based pricing down the road.

For that is where the Transformation Economy is headed—a destination where, ultimately, what you charge for must align with what customers value: the achievement of their aspirations.

Individualization

In closing, the one word that most fully captures the impact of the Progression of Economic Value is *individualization*. It incorporates the customization dynamic that enables enterprises to counteract commoditization and successively shift up the Progression to create more value. It also treats customers as the individuals they truly are. For customers are not a market, nor a segment, nor a niche, nor a generation, nor a persona, nor any other agglomeration of anonymous buying units of indeterminate size. A customer is a living, breathing individual person—or, if you sell to other businesses, an active, adaptive individual enterprise. All customers are unique—undeniably, unremittingly, unalterably unique.

But individualization means so much more than that for businesses. Each successive economic offering going up the Progression gets you closer and closer to the desires, needs, and aspirations of each individual customer (and not just people and businesses, but organizations and communities as well). Commodities supply merely the raw materials for manufacturing goods. Goods furnish merely the means for delivering service activities. Together, these three lower-order offerings lead to time well saved. Services provide merely the means underlying the staging of memorable experiences, which offer time well spent. And experiences present the means by which you can guide customers to achieve their aspirations, to transform their identity from "I was X" to "now I am Y," to go from aspirant to achiever. Transformations yield the greatest economic value, time well invested, as customers become who they want to become.

Moreover, commodities, goods, and services exist outside of us, while experiences happen inside of us and transformations change our very identity. Commodities are arms-length stuff we hardly ever touch and feel anymore. Goods are tangible objects that we own, such as our cars and clothes. Services are activities performed on those objects, such as changing the oil in our car or cleaning our clothes, or on ourselves, such as cutting our hair or measuring our blood pressure. Experiences reach inside, engaging us in reaction to events staged in front of us. And transformations change us from the inside out based on the experiences we undergo. With transformations, the customer *is* the product—it is a changed *being* that individuals seek from transformation guiders.

With every step of further individualization, you generate more and more economic value for your enterprise precisely because you create more and more value within your customers, helping them become who they want to become and be who they are meant to be. Individualization is the route to human flourishing.

REFLECTION

After reading this last chapter in the book, reflect on these things:

- Can you imagine how you might interact with your customers to diagnose their aspirations? What processes already exist in your organization on which you can build?
- How might you sense and respond with each customer to make corrections and avoid failure? What signals should you look out for that might indicate backsliding or a forthcoming obstacle?

- How might you ensure that customers sustain their transformations over time and lead into the next transformation they might want to undergo?
- Do you see how you might charge for the demonstrated outcomes your customers achieve? Were there any ways or examples in the chapter that you could best relate to your business?

PREPARATION

Even though this was the last chapter, don't stop reading! Go to the afterword, aptly called "reflection," so you can contemplate the ideas, principles, and frameworks from the entire book—and begin to integrate them into your business, and your life.

REFLECTION

In the opening preparation, I noted that the purpose of each chapter's closing questions was to push you along on your own journey of understanding transformations and thereby increase the chances this book will have an impact on you and your business. And that is my intention for this closing reflection, that you would change what you do and offer through the ideas, principles, and frameworks you have learned.

Now is the time to shift from learning to acting, from absorbing to applying, from being to becoming. From selling whatever offerings you have today to using those offerings to help your current and future customers achieve their aspirations through the transformations you guide. That, of course, requires your own transformation, starting with ascending to the proposition that *you* are in the transformation business, and then using what you've learned here on behalf of not only your customers but yourself.

To that end, consider these reflection questions as you think about how you can apply what you've read in the forthcoming Transformation Economy:

- Now that you fully understand transformations, what business are you really in?
- What really hit home with you in this book and changed your thinking—whether an idea, principle, or framework; a

story of a person or company; or your personal response to some reflection or preparation question?

- How might you contribute to human flourishing personally, professionally, and corporately?
- What aspirations, and which aspirants, are you best equipped to guide?
- How might you use memorable, meaningful, and transporting experiences to stage transformative ones? How can you encapsulate them?
- How could you use the Transformation Journey model as a framework for guiding your aspirants?
- How might you use the Delta Model as a template for your own economic offerings, incorporating whichever of the four types of transformations you guide?
- What do you need to do to have all three phases of transformation fully realized in your offerings?

And one final, overarching question:

- What do you intend to do about it?

Intention is an underlying concept weaved throughout the book. What business you decide to be in is your intention for how you create value. As the raison d'être of business, fostering human flourishing is the central intention of any transaction between buyer and seller as both seek to better themselves. Aspirations are individuals' intentions for becoming what they want to become and being who they are meant to be. The theme you define for each of your experiences functions as the intention for every element of design, creation, and staging—including the acting intentions of every employee. And the meaningful purpose of your business defines its intention, the change it wants to be in customers' lives, just as your personal purpose defines your intention for your life.

Intention declares the reason you do anything. You can express it through this simple statement:[1]

Perform ________ in order to ________.

You've read this book in order to . . . what? Was it just an informative and (I trust) enjoyable romp through what's going on in the world of business? Or will it make a real difference in your life, your work, and your company?

And if the latter, again: What do you intend to do about it?

Completing Your Transformation Journey

If my intention has been realized in you, then one lesson you'll remember is that you need to *integrate* what you have learned, who you intend to be, and the transformation your business undergoes and then put it all into action.

To that end, let this book be your guide. You can come back to it again and again, using it as a reference in your own transformation journey, finding nuggets in the ideas, profits in the principles, valuable archetypes in the frameworks, real-world benefits in the examples, and meaning in your personal responses throughout your reading.

You will also find that there are many people and companies that have been there before, that have undergone their own transformations or helped other companies do it. They can serve as your experts, coaches, counselors, and even alchemists on your journey.

I have also created a suite of offerings at Strategic Horizons that can help guide you and integrate what you've learned. Go to www.StrategicHorizons.com/integration to learn more about them.

Don't just let what you've learned sit on the shelf; now is the time to act. Now is the time for your enterprise to become what it was meant to be—a transformation guider.

I look forward to seeing the measurable increase in human flourishing because of the work you do.

NOTES

Preparation

1. James H. Gilmore and B. Joseph Pine II, "Beyond Goods and Services," *Strategy and Leadership* 25, no. 3 (1997): 10–18, https://www.emerald.com/insight/content/doi/10.1108/eb054585/full/html.

2. Gilmore and Pine, "Beyond Goods and Services," and B. Joseph Pine II and James H. Gilmore, *The Experience Economy: Work Is Theatre & Every Business a Stage* (Boston: Harvard Business School Press, 1999). For details on the discovery and its initial promulgation, see Joe Pine, "The History of the Experience Economy," Strategic Horizons, August 4, 2017, https://strategichorizons.com/the-history-of-the-experience-economy/.

3. Lance A. Bettencourt et al., "The 'New You' Business," *Harvard Business Review*, January–February 2022, 70–81, https://hbr.org/2022/01/the-new-you-business.

Chapter 1

1. Lance A. Bettencourt et al., "The 'New You' Business," *Harvard Business Review*, January–February 2022, 70-81, https://hbr.org/2022/01/the-new-you-business.

2. Joseph A. Schumpeter, *Capitalism, Socialism, and Democracy* (New York: Harper Perennial, 1942).

3. I discovered experiences and transformations through the concepts in my first book, *Mass Customization: The New Frontier in Business Competition* (Boston: Harvard Business School Press, 1992).

4. The key principle of the system of mass customization is modularity, and this type is mix modularity. You'll read about more types in chapter 5, but for the complete list, see Joe Pine, "The Power of Modularity," Strategic Horizons, October 5, 2018, https://strategichorizons.com/the-power-of-modularity/.

5. Extract, make, deliver, stage: these terms represent the economic function required to create each economic offering. It is the core dynamic in the Progression of Economic Value: commodification, the turning of something into an economic offering. Commoditization and customization present the other two dynamics, all represented in figure 1-1 by arrows.

6. For more, see B. Joseph Pine II and James H. Gilmore, *The Experience Economy: Competing for Customer Time, Attention, and Money* (Boston: Harvard Business Review Press, 2019), 7–19.

7. For more, see B. Joseph Pine II and Louis-Étienne Dubois, "How Starbucks Devalued Its Own Brand," hbr.org, June 26, 2024, https://hbr.org/2024/06/how-starbucks-devalued-its-own-brand.

8. Lucy McCauley, "Measure What Matters," *Fast Company*, April 30, 1999, https://www.fastcompany.com/37017/measure-what-matters.

9. For more on these economic distinctions, see Pine and Gilmore, *The Experience Economy*, 223–230.

10. In *The Experience Economy*, Jim and I refer to companies that guide transformations as transformation *elicitors*, a somewhat obscure term. *Guider* now seems the more fitting word.

11. Friend and colleague Dave Norton first referred to experiences as "time well spent," and many years ago impressed on me the usefulness of the term. We together wrote an article on it: David W. Norton and B. Joseph Pine II, "Unique Experiences: Disruptive Innovations Offer Customers More 'Time Well Spent,'" *Strategy and Leadership* 37, no. 6 (2009): 4–9. But it wasn't until 2015, when I spoke at the announcement of the Ford Vignale automobile in Spain, that the impression finally took hold. Paul Cowan of Imagination Ltd., the experience designer of the event, used the term "time well saved," and I was immediately struck by how wonderful was the juxtaposition of time well spent and time well saved.

12. This focus on time was published in B. Joseph Pine II and James H. Gilmore, "Competing for Customer Time," *Dialogue*, Duke Corporate Education, September 2021, https://www.dukece.com/insights/competing-for-customer-time/. The first publication of it was actually focused on employees, not customers, in a white paper issued by experience consultancy Rightpoint. See B. Joseph Pine II, "Embracing the Employee Experience," Rightpoint, 2020, https://www.rightpoint.com/landing-pages/embracing-the-employee-experience.

13. I owe this example to Lance Bettencourt, professor of professional practice at Texas Christian University's Neeley School of Business and lead author of Bettencourt et al., "The 'New You' Business."

14. "About Us," Noom, https://www.noom.com/about-us/, accessed July 21, 2025.

15. "What types of questions can my coaching team answer?" Noom, https://www.noom.com/support/faqs/premium-features/my-program/2024/03/what-types-of-questions-can-my-coaching-team-answer/, accessed July 21, 2025. For research on the efficacy of Noom's approach, see https://www.noom.com/research/.

16. The idea of integrating solutions was impressed on me by Lance Bettencourt. See the section "Designing the Offering" in Bettencourt et al., "The 'New You' Business."

17. "The Hogeweyk," Be the Care Concept, https://www.bethecareconcept.com/en/hogeweyk-dementia-village-hogeweyk-netherlands/, accessed July 21, 2025.

18. See Pine and Gilmore, *The Experience Economy,* 80–91.

19. Peter Loftus, "Medtronic Moves to a New Health-Care Model: Pay Only If It Works," *Wall Street Journal,* February 19, 2018, https://wsj.com/articles/medtronic-moves-to-a-new-health-care-model-pay-only-if-it-works-1519096141.

20. Loftus, "Medtronic Moves."

21. Glenn D. Steele Jr. and David T. Feinberg, *ProvenCare: How to Deliver Value-Based Healthcare the Geisinger Way* (New York: McGraw Hill, 2017), 188.

22. *Workforce Realigned, Vol. 1: How New Partnerships Are Advancing Economic Mobility,* Social Finance, Federal Reserve Bank of Atlanta and Federal Reserve Bank of Philadelphia, 2021, 113, https://socialfinance.org/work/workforce-realigned/.

23. *Workforce Realigned, Vol. 2: New Incentives for Improving Workforce Outcomes,* Social Finance, Federal Reserve Bank of Atlanta, Federal Reserve Bank of Chicago, Federal Reserve Bank of Philadelphia, and Federal Reserve Bank of Richmond, 2025, 191, https://workforcerealigned.org/.

24. *Workforce Realigned,* Social Finance, 119.

Chapter 2

1. Aristotle, *Nicomachean Ethics,* 1.4 1095a14-20. Before Aristotle, a psalmist recognized flourishing as a reward of the righteous in Psalm 92:12–14 (ESV) with imagery that offers a good sense of what it means: "The righteous flourish like the palm tree and grow like a cedar in Lebanon. They are planted in the house of the Lord; they flourish in the courts of our God. They still bear fruit in old age; they are ever full of sap and green."

2. Martin E. P. Seligman, *Flourish: A Visionary New Understanding of Happiness and Well-Being* (New York: Atria, 2011), 26.

3. Seligman, *Flourish,* 26–27. He's citing Felicia A. Huppert and Timothy T. C. So, "What Percentage of People in Europe Are Flourishing and What Characterises Them?" prepared for the OECD/ISQOLS meeting "Measuring Subjective Well-Being: An Opportunity for NSOs?" in Florence, July 23–24, 2009, https://citeseerx.ist.psu.edu/document?repid=rep1&type=pdf&doi=1cbb72d9b0da0c61f59035a39737cae02b80827b.

4. "Program Overview," Human Flourishing Program at Harvard's Institute for Quantitative Social Science, https://hfh.fas.harvard.edu/about, accessed July 21, 2025, emphasis added. This definition cites the program's director, Tyler J. VanderWeele, in "On the Promotion of Human Flourishing," *PNAS* 114, no. 31, August 1, 2017, https://www.pnas.org/doi/pdf/10.1073/pnas.1702996114 and "Our Flourishing Measure," Human Flourishing Program at Harvard's Institute for Quantitative Social Science, https://hfh.fas.harvard

.edu/measuring-flourishing, accessed July 21, 2025. It eventually added a sixth element of financial and material stability because, it seems, it is to a large degree an enabler of the others.

5. This definition was in part inspired by Dianela Perdomo of Johns Hopkins Medicine, who summed up Aristotle's thinking on *eudaimonia* as "the way we are supposed to be as human beings" in "Human Flourishing: Could a Philosophical Concept Impact Health?" *Biomedical Odyssey* (blog), Johns Hopkins Medicine, October 28, 2021, https://biomedicalodyssey.blogs.hopkinsmedicine.org/2021/10/human-flourishing-could-a-philosophical-concept-impact-health/.

6. Mark Drewell and Björn Larsson, *The Rise of the Meaningful Economy* (London: Foresight, 2017), 35.

7. As John Kay writes in *The Corporation in the 21st Century: Why (Almost) Everything We Are Told about Business Is Wrong* (New Haven, CT: Yale University Press, 2024), 347: "I believe it is appropriate—indeed necessary—to view the business organization in the same way. The proper goal of corporate activity is the flourishing of the multiple stakeholders of the corporation: employees, investors, suppliers and customers, the communities in which it operates, and the corporation itself. For the corporation to flourish, it must contribute to the flourishing of the society in which it operates."

8. "'A Family Company at Work for a Better World' Highlights SC Johnson's Global Impact," S.C. Johnson, April 23, 2018, https://www.scjohnson.com/en/press-releases/2018/april/a-family-company-at-work-for-a-better-world-highlights-sc-johnsons-global-impact.

9. "This We Believe: Our Company Values Have Guided SC Johnson for Five Generations," S.C. Johnson, https://www.scjohnson.com/en/about-us/this-we-believe, accessed July 21, 2025.

10. See "Regenerative Managing," Regenerative Managing, www. regenerativemanaging.com/managing/overview, accessed July 21, 2025.

11. Jeff Bezos, "2020 Letter to Shareholders," April 12, 2020, https://www.amazon.com/p/feature/z6o9g6sysxur57t, accessed August 8, 2025.

12. Arjun Kharpal, "Amazon CEO Jeff Bezos Has a Pretty Good Idea of Quarterly Earnings 3 Years in Advance," CNBC, May 8, 2017, https://www.cnbc.com/2017/05/08/amazon-ceo-jeff-bezos-long-term-thinking.html.

13. "Purpose," Truist, https://www.truist.com/purpose, accessed July 21, 2025.

14. Wildwood Ventures, https://wildwood.vc/, accessed July 21, 2025.

15. Eventide Asset Management, https://www.eventideinvestments.com/, accessed July 21, 2025.

16. Commonwealth Impact Investing, https://cwimpact.org/, accessed July 21, 2025.

17. Tara-Nicholle Nelson calls them "the Three Aspirations" in *The Transformational Consumer: Fuel a Lifelong Love Affair with Your Customers by Helping Them Get Healthier, Wealthier, and Wiser* (San Francisco: Berrett-Koehler, 2017), 16.

18. Chipotle, "A Bowl for Every Lifestyle," https://www.chipotle.com/lifestyle-bowls, accessed July 21, 2025.

19. Remedy, https://www.remedyplace.com/, accessed July 21, 2025.

20. Submersive, https://www.submersive.com/about, accessed July 21, 2025.

21. Matthew Hennessey, "From the Western Canon to West Point," *Wall Street Journal*, May 15, 2024, https://www.wsj.com/articles/from-the-western-canon-to-west-point-cardinal-kung-military-academy-630e9b4e.

22. Paul Dunn and Ronald J. Baker, *Time's Up! The Subscription Business Model for Professional Firms* (Hoboken, NJ: Wiley, 2022), 105.

23. There is a direct correspondence between the hierarchy of intelligence and the progression of economic value, where transformations ≈ wisdom; experiences ≈ knowledge; services ≈ information; goods ≈ data; and commodities ≈ noise. See Pine and Gilmore, *The Experience Economy*, 244–248.

24. Viktor Frankl, *Man's Search for Meaning* (Boston: Beacon Press, 2006).

25. William J. Winslade, afterword to Frankl, *Man's Search for Meaning*. Before actually reading the book but knowing its premise, I assumed Frankl had basically performed ethnography during his time in concentration camps and determined that those Jews with meaning in their lives tended to survive, while those without rarely did. In fact, before the Holocaust he developed a school of psychotherapy he called "logotherapy," which focused on helping patients find meaning in their lives, and his experience then validated it.

26. A. H. Maslow, "A Theory of Human Motivation," *Psychological Review*, vol. 50, no. 4 (1943): 370–396, https://doi.org/10.1037/h0054346.

27. Modern-day research demonstrates how very much religion contributes to human flourishing. Decades of study at the Center for Spirituality, Theology and Health at Duke University Medical Center, led by Dr. Harold Koenig, suggests links between religious involvement and, among other outcomes, "lower rates of depression . . . lower anxiety, greater well-being, improved coping with stress, positive personality changes, [and] greater social support." See "Center for Spirituality, Theology and Health: Vision, Mission, Accomplishments and Future Plans," Center for Spirituality, Theology and Health, 2023, https://spiritualityandhealth.duke.edu/files/2023/05/CSTH-Vision-Mission-Accomplishments-and-Future-5-10-23-updated.pdf.

28. David Foster Wallace, *This Is Water: Some Thoughts, Delivered on a Significant Occasion, about Living a Compassionate Life* (New York: Little, Brown and Company, 2009), 98–101.

29. "Educating the Whole Student," *Spectrum*, Massachusetts Institute of Technology, 2024, https://betterworld.mit.edu/spectrum/issues/2024-fall/educating-the-whole-student/.

30. *Spectrum*, "Educating the Whole Student."

31. *Spectrum*, "Educating the Whole Student."

Chapter 3

1. *The Oxford English Dictionary*'s first definition is "absolute or essential sameness," with the second as "the sameness of a person or thing at all times or in all circumstances." See *The Oxford English Dictionary,* "identity," 2nd ed., vol. 7 (Oxford: Clarendon Press, 1989), 620. The word applied to people was influenced by its use in philosophy, logic, and mathematics. Even when the second definition relates itself to "personal identity (in Psychology)," it defines identity as "the condition or fact of remaining the same person throughout the various phases of existence."

2. French philosopher Paul Ricoeur wrote of "a key distinction between two kinds of identity in relation to selfhood. *Idem* identity is the identity of something that is always the same which never changes, *ipse* identity is sameness across and through change. Self-identity involves both dimensions: I am and am not the person I was ten years ago." See *Stanford Encyclopedia of Philosophy,* "Paul Ricoeur," updated February 16, 2025, https://plato.stanford.edu/entries/ricoeur/. Transformation, therefore, only applies to our *ipse* identity, not our *idem* identity (which, recall, is the Latin word meaning "same").

3. "Identity," *Psychology Today,* https://www.psychologytoday.com/us/basics/identity, accessed July 22, 2025.

4. Suzy Ross, *The Map to Wholeness: Real-Life Stories of Crisis, Change, and Reinvention* (Berkeley, CA: North Atlantic Books, 2020), 10.

5. "Flavorman Celebrates 30 Years," Flavorman, January 14, 2022, https://www.flavorman.com/media/flavorman-celebrates-30-years.

6. A word of warning about so-called digital transformation, as least as it is commonly practiced: it rarely leads to flourishing. Digital transformation is often played up by consultants, pundits, and media as a way of increasing economic value, and perhaps for some it is. But far more often it is a route to commoditization, focusing on automating people—replacing them with digital technology—rather than augmenting their skills, abilities, and experiences to truly create new economic value through offerings that provide more customer value. For one approach playing off some of the ideas in this book, see David W. Norton and B. Joseph Pine II, "Are Your Digital Platforms Wasting Your Customers' Time?" hbr.org, March 27, 2023, https://hbr.org/2023/03/are-your-digital-platforms-wasting-your-customers-time.

7. The late Stan Davis highlighted this in his classic book *Future Perfect* (Reading, MA: Addison-Wesley, 1987), writing on page 197 that "organizations exist to carry out business; businesses do not exist to carry out an organization." Reading his book was a key landmark in my intellectual journey, setting me on the path that eventually led to this book.

8. See "Learning to Doing to Being: The Science Behind Lasting Transformation," BetterUp, https://grow.betterup.com/resources/learn-about-our-scientific-approach-to-transformation, accessed July 22, 2025. A few years ago, BetterUp started offering its app to employees to coach them as individuals, not as part of an organizational initiative.

9. For how companies should view employees in today's Experience Economy, see James H. Gilmore and B. Joseph Pine II, "Employment as Transformation," *Dialogue,* Duke Corporate Education, February 15, 2022, https://dialoguereview.com/employment-as-transformation/.

10. See B. Joseph Pine II, "Embracing the Employee Experience," Rightpoint, June 2020, https://www.rightpoint.com/landing-pages/embracing-the-employee-experience. Businesses should also consider potential beneficiary transformations not just for employees but for all contributors to the enterprise, as Kim Korn likes to call them, whether contractors, suppliers, volunteers, or even customers themselves; see "Regenerative Managing," Regenerative Managing, https://regenerativemanaging.com/managing/overview/, accessed July 22, 2025.

11. This framework was inspired by Ross, *The Map to Wholeness,* 13–23 in particular, where she discusses "three types of transformations." She in turn credits Joseph Campbell, in *The Hero with a Thousand Faces,* 2nd ed. (Princeton, NJ: Princeton University Press, 1981), 13, as concluding "that people transform as a result of three major causes: trauma, unexpected powerful experiences, and consciously intended journeys."

12. Suzy Ross further helped me understand how trauma is such a major catalyst for transformations. See *The Map to Wholeness,* 13–16, which includes a long list of such transformation-inducing disruptions.

13. See Agnes Callard, *Aspiration: The Agency of Becoming* (Oxford: Oxford University Press, 2018), 3–8 in particular.

14. *The Oxford English Dictionary,* "metamorphosis," 2nd ed., vol. 9 (Oxford: Clarendon Press, 1989), 675.

15. L. A. Paul, *Transformative Experience* (Oxford: Oxford University Press, 2014), 16.

16. Paul, *Transformative Experience,* 17.

17. See Paul, *Transformative Experience,* 71–94. In a thought experiment extended throughout the book, she likens the decision of becoming a vampire to that of having a child, arguing the two are similarly epistemically unknowable.

18. Laura Pritschet et al., "Neuroanatomical Changes Observed over the Course of a Human Pregnancy," *Nature Neuroscience* 27 (2024), https://www.nature.com/articles/s41593-024-01741-0. For less academic discussions, see Jo Craven McGinty, "Pregnancy Shrinks Your Brain. But It Strengthens It Too," *Wall Street Journal,* May 10, 2024, https://www.wsj.com/science/pregnancy-brain-0aa642c5, and Pam Belluck, "How Does Pregnancy Change the Brain? Clues Are Emerging," *New York Times,* updated September 17, 2024, https://www.nytimes.com/2024/09/16/health/pregnancy-brain-changes.html.

19. Darby Saxbe, "Dad Brain Is Real, and It's a Good Thing," *New York Times,* June 16, 2024, https://www.nytimes.com/2024/06/16/opinion/dad-brain-fatherhood-parenting.html. See Belluck, "How Does Pregnancy Change the Brain?" as well.

20. Saxbe, "Dad Brain Is Real."

21. When I discovered in 1994 that experiences and transformations were distinct economic offerings, I originally called the fifth offering "becomings." I eventually changed the term, as it didn't seem "business-y" enough. My original Economies of Man table is reproduced in B. Joseph Pine II and James H. Gilmore, "The Experience Economy: Past, Present and Future," in *Handbook on the Experience Economy*, eds. Jon Sundbo and Flemming Sørensen (Cheltenham, UK: Edward Elgar, 2013), 21–44, https://www.researchgate.net/publication/260917972_The_experience_economy_past_present_and_future.

22. There seems to be a correlation between major catalyst instigations and large-scale aspirations, as well as between minor instigations and small-scale aspirations, but it is not absolute.

23. For a great discussion of impostor syndrome and other such issues, see William Ian Miller, *Faking It* (Cambridge: Cambridge University Press, 2003).

24. While Callard, in *Aspiration*, never wrote that her thinking on aspirations formed a 2×2 matrix, in my Frameworks "R" Us mind the possibility practically leaped off the page with her use of cultivation and ambition. On page 74 she writes, "I have labeled the class of pursuits that involve a small-scale change in what one cares about 'self-cultivation.'" She would, however, have labeled the upper-right quadrant simply "aspiration" or "self-transformation," since she reserves such terms solely for the longing for deep changes in values, being, identity; everything else—cultivation, ambition, and refinement—is, to her, shallow and "mere."

25. On page 74 of *Aspiration*, Callard writes, "When a pursuit is large in scale without being transformative [meaning, in her parlance, without encompassing a change in core identity], I will describe the agent as ambitious."

26. At the twenty-fifth anniversary event for the publication of our book *The Experience Economy*, one person asked how quickly someone could be legitimately transformed. Another participant shouted out, "Say 'I do!'"

Chapter 4

1. According to the World Travel & Tourism Council, travel and tourism in 2025 will account for 10.5 percent of global GDP ($11.7 trillion) and 10.9 percent of global employment (371 million jobs), with both growing faster than the rest of the global economy. See "Travel & Tourism Economic Impact Research," World Travel & Tourism Council, https://wttc.org/research/economic-impact, accessed June 1, 2025. Psychologist Jeffrey Kottler has a simple but profound premise in *Travel That Can Change Your Life: How to Create a Transformative Experience* (San Francisco: Jossey-Bass, 1997): we are most open to change when we travel. He further writes that travel is "by its very nature a transformative experience."

2. "Quick Facts about Medical Tourism," Patients Beyond Borders, https://www.patientsbeyondborders.com/media, accessed July 28, 2025.

3. "REVĪVŌ," World Travel Marketing Bali, https://www.wtmbali.com/revivo, accessed July 22, 2025.

4. "The Traveler's Manifesto," Transformational Travel Council, https://www.transformational.travel/manifesto, accessed July 22, 2025.

5. Of course, in the English language the word "experience" covers an expansive set of meanings. There is a sense that if we are awake and conscious, we are experiencing, but such mere "sensing" is not an economic offering. In *Designing Experiences* (New York: Columbia Business School, 2019), J. Robert Rossman and Mathew D. Duerden provide a similar progression of experiences to the one presented here, starting with what they call, after John Dewey, "prosaic experiences"—those for which our brains are on autopilot. They point out that such "experiences are a necessary part of an experience journey but not ones you design for participants to remember" (33). They also discuss "mindful experiences"—also below the level of experiences as a distinct economic offering—where "something catches our attention and cues our brain to shift out of autopilot to figure out what's going on" (34). Their five-stage progression then finishes with memorable, meaningful, and transformational experiences (35–39), and does not include transporting.

6. Of course, meaningful experiences are not a new phenomenon; they've always been around, always a part of the Experience Economy. Albert Boswijk, with whom I cofounded the European Centre for the Experience and Transformation Economy in the Netherlands, impressed on me the importance of meaningful experiences. See *Economy of Meaningful Experiences: Humanising Business*, 5th ed. (European Centre for the Experience and Transformation Economy, 2021), by Albert and his coauthors Ed Peelen and Steven Olthof. They note on pages 139–140 that the Dutch language has two words for "experience": *belevenis* relates to the word for "life" and implies things experienced in the moment, while *ervaring* is about those experiences that have significance, stimulate reflection, and matter more over time—that are meaningful. For a more detailed discussion of how the two types can work together to be transformative, see Hans Gelter, "Total Experience Management—A Conceptual Model for Transformational Experiences within Tourism," in *Conference Proceedings: The Nordic Conference on Experience 2008,* eds. Sol-Britt Arnolds-Granlund and Peter Björk (Vaasa, Finland: Tritonia, 2010), 46–78.

7. In a related but different take, Rossman and Duerden say, in *Designing Experiences,* "The key characteristic that differentiates a meaningful experience from a memorable one is discovery. Meaningful experiences teach us something about ourselves or expand our knowledge about the world" (37).

8. Michael F. Steger, "Meaning in Life," in *The Oxford Handbook of Positive Psychology,* 2nd ed., eds. Shane J. Lopez and C. R. Snyder (Oxford: Oxford University Press, 2009), 685.

9. Or, rather, *cocreated* by the individual, where both parties—aspirant and guide—contribute substantially to what occurs during and within the experience. See Boswijk et al., *Economy of Meaningful Experiences,* 196–197 in particular, as well as Rossman and Duerden, *Designing Experiences,* 37–38 and

109–111. Albert Boswijk was also the first person to impress on me the importance of cocreation with experiences, although of course all experiences are cocreated (with both experiencer and experience stager needed to create the experience within the guest)—even the merely memorable—because of their inherently personal nature. But as they progress from memorable to meaningful to transporting and finally to transformative, the level of cocreation necessarily goes up significantly. At the level of transformation, aspirants do most of the work, with guidance from the company, as it changes them from the inside out.

10. Liminality is an important concept to understand in designing both transporting and transformative experiences. A great place to start is Johan Liedgren, Pieter M. A. Desmet, and Andrea Gaggioli, "Liminal Design: A Conceptual Framework and Three-Step Approach for Developing Technology That Delivers Transcendence and Deeper Experiences," *Frontiers in Psychology* 14 (2023), https://doi.org/10.3389/fpsyg.2023.1043170.

11. Abraham H. Maslow, *Religions, Values, and Peak-Experiences* (London: Penguin Books, 1964).

12. Joseph Pine and Wendy Heimann-Nunes, "Peak Experiences," *Attractions Management* 2, 2024, https://www.attractionsmanagement.com/attractions-management-magazine/Talking-point-Peak-experiences/37103. Some of the introduction to this section is based on this article. The other three articles in this issue also give examples and design principles for designing attractions to be peak experiences.

13. Mihaly Csikszentmihalyi, *Flow: The Psychology of Optimal Experience* (New York: Harper Perennial, 1990), 3.

14. Csikszentmihalyi, *Flow*, 74. He goes on to say that a flow experience "transformed the self by making it more complex," but generally not in the way I'm defining transformations here.

15. Csikszentmihalyi, *Flow*, 66. Getting into flow is an example of what I call playing with time, which means staging transporting experiences as they take you, again, out of the present space or time and move you metaphorically to another realm. I write much more about playing with time (keying off that great phrase "freedom from the tyranny of time") in B. Joseph Pine II and Kim C. Korn, *Infinite Possibility: Creating Customer Value on the Digital Frontier* (San Francisco: Berrett-Koehler, 2011), 63–78. The writing on flow here borrows from there.

16. *The Oxford English Dictionary*, "awe," 2nd ed., vol. 1 (Oxford: Clarendon Press, 1989), 831.

17. Dacher Keltner, *Awe: The New Science of Everyday Wonder and How It Can Transform Your Life* (New York: Penguin Press, 2023), 11. As with earlier such statements, the promise of the subtitle certainly can happen, but transporting experiences by themselves do not tend to yield transformation. The next section of this chapter shows what you as a transformation guider need to do to make it happen.

18. Keltner, *Awe*, 3–18. There's also an "other" category found in 5 percent of the responses that includes "incredible flavors, video games, overwhelming sensations, and first experiences of sex."

19. Keltner, *Awe*, 18–19.

20. Keltner, *Awe*, 13.

21. Keltner, *Awe*, 11.

22. See Heather Gallagher, "From Party to Paradigm Shift: A Burning Man Masterclass on Transformative Experiences," video, April 12, 2024, by Futurespace, YouTube, https://www.youtube.com/watch?v=tDB5ZvsEPs8&t=5s, and "WXS 2024 Reflection: Part 1 of 5: The Art of Experience," World Experience Organization, 2024, https://worldxo.org/wp-content/uploads/2024/07/WXS24-Reflection-Part-1-Art.pdf.

23. "WXS 2024 Reflection," World Experience Organization.

24. One academic study of large-scale gatherings, specifically including Burning Man, concluded that they "may be associated with lasting changes in moral orientation" and that "self-reported transformative experiences at mass gatherings were common, increased over time, and were characterized by feelings of universal connectedness and new perceptions of others." See Daniel A. Yudkin et al., "Prosocial Correlates of Transformative Experiences at Secular Multi-Day Mass Gatherings," *Nature Communications* 13, no. 2600 (2022), https://doi.org/10.1038/s41467-022-29600-1.

25. See Gallagher, "From Party to Paradigm Shift" at the 44:47 mark for a slide listing these payoffs.

26. Other than the term "encapsulation," these three activities are not original with me. Many people writing and talking about experiences, transformative experiences in particular, refer especially to post-experience reflection and integration, sometimes by other labels. In *Designing Experiences*, Rossman and Duerden talk of three stages of any kind of experience—anticipation, participation, and reflection (9–12). The Structured Experience framework shown there on page 10 is sourced back to Mat D. Duerden, Peter J. Ward, and Patti A. Freeman, "Conceptualizing Structured Experiences: Seeking Interdisciplinary Integration," *Journal of Leisure Research* 47, no. 5 (2015): 601–620. This model interestingly includes integration as part of the third stage, even for experiences that fall short of being transformative. And it in turn refers back to the Interaction Ritual model in J. Robert Rossman and Barbara Elwood Schlatter, *Recreation Programming: Designing, Staging, and Managing the Delivery of Leisure Experiences*, 8th ed. (Urbana, IL: Sagamore-Venture, 2019), which has three stages: (1) intake, (2) thinking-processing-planning (i.e., reflection), and (3) action (i.e., integration). In a personal email on August 8, 2024, Rossman told me that "the three basic stages of intake, processing, and acting are discussed in much sociological literature with many different terms that mean the same thing." All roads seem to lead back to David A. Kolb, whose book *Experiential Learning: Experience as the Source of Learning and Development* (Englewood Cliffs, NJ: Prentice Hall, 1984) introduced the Kolb Experiential Cycle of

experiencing, reflecting, thinking, and acting, where reflecting and thinking combine to form what I'm calling reflection here, and acting is integration.

27. Academics often use "preflection" here. Mat Duerden introduced this term to me, and used it in Marcel Bastiaansen and Mat D. Duerden, "Conceptualizing Meaningful Experiences," *Journal of Hospitality & Tourism Research* 49, no. 5 (2025): 877–890, https://journals.sagepub.com/doi/10.1177/10963480241308344. The term comes out of the teaching field; see, for example, George M. Slavich and Philip G. Zimbardo, "Transformational Teaching: Theoretical Underpinnings, Basic Principles, and Core Methods," *Educational Psychology Review* 24 (2012): 569–608, https://doi.org/10.1007/s10648-012-9199-6. The earliest citation I could find on preflection is Diana Falk, "Preflection: A Strategy for Enhancing Reflection," *Evaluation/Reflection* 22 (1995), https://digitalcommons.unomaha.edu/slceeval/22.

28. Interestingly, Bastiaansen and Duerden, in "Conceptualizing Meaningful Experiences," say that the process of remembering turns an episode into a memorable experience, reflection then turns that into a meaningful one, and integration turns that into a transformative one.

29. Suzy Ross, *The Map to Wholeness: Real-Life Stories of Crisis, Change, and Reinvention* (Berkeley, CA: North Atlantic Books, 2020), 29–30.

30. Eric Rupp, *The Transformational Travel Journal: Your Guide to Creating a Life-Changing Journey* (Seattle: Transformational Travel Council, 2020), 13.

31. Rupp, *The Transformational Travel Journal*, 18–19.

32. Explorer X, https://www.explorer-x.com/, accessed July 22, 2025.

33. Michael Bennett, "The Inner Journey: 5 Before You Travel Questions," Explorer X, https://www.explorer-x.com/journal/2023/5/31/the-inner-journey-5-before-you-travel-questions, accessed July 22, 2025.

34. The Journey Reflection Guide is available at https://www.explorer-x.com/toolkit, accessed July 22, 2025.

35. "The Explorer X Process," Explorer X, https://www.explorer-x.com/how, accessed July 22, 2025.

Chapter 5

1. In the preview to the 2020 rerelease of our book *The Experience Economy*, Jim Gilmore and I introduced these four elements plus one more—*transformative*, naturally—to summarize the experience design principles. Note that while in all three editions we placed the chapter on robust experiences before the chapter on cohesive ones, it's better to start with the organizing principle before tackling the four realms of experience.

2. Sociologist Mark Gottdiener makes this point in *The Theming of America: Dreams, Visions, and Commercial Spaces* (Boulder, CO: Westview Press, 1996).

3. To do this properly, in *The Experience Economy* (xv–xvi and 57–80) Jim and I delineated five design principles that enable you to design, create, and stage cohesive experiences. It begins with the theme and proceeds with the

most appropriate mnemonic: **T**heme the experience; **H**armonize impressions with positive cues; **E**liminate negative cues; **M**ix in memorabilia + media; and **E**ngage or evoke the five senses.

4. James H. Gilmore and B. Joseph Pine II, *Authenticity: What Consumers* Really *Want* (Boston: Harvard Business School Press, 2007), 123.

5. This is based on work I have been doing with Kim Korn of Create Advantage to further develop his ideas on how companies can thrive forever, rather than fall into mediocrity and eventually fail. He's developed the concept of *regenerative managing* to guide enterprises in what they need to do differently to sustain and build on their competitive advantages by innovating faster than their ecosystems. Core to regenerative managing are seven requirements, one of which is to *pursue purpose,* which entails an enterprise infusing meaning within all its contributors. See "Regenerative Managing," Regenerative Managing, https://regenerativemanaging.com/managing/overview/, accessed July 23, 2025.

6. For more, see Mark Scott and Leland Kaiser, *Courage to Be First* (Bozeman, MT: Second River HealthCare Press, 2009).

7. For more on this, see Pine and Gilmore, *The Experience Economy,* xiv–xv and 35–56.

8. To be clear: we do not use the term "esthetic" over "aesthetic" merely to begin all terms in the model with "e" just so we can call it our 4E model. *Aesthetic* refers to beauty and its appreciation, while *esthetic* refers to the place in which people are immersed, as it is more of an architectural term describing the built environment. Our use of it comes from the wonderful tome *For an Architecture of Reality* (New York: Lumen Books, 1987) by University of Texas at Austin architecture professor Michael Benedikt. On page 4 he writes that "in our media-saturated times it falls to architecture to have the direct esthetic experience of the real at the center of its concerns," something that applies to all experience stagers.

9. You can find a fuller description related directly to authenticity in Gilmore and Pine, *Authenticity,* 51.

10. See Todd Adkins and Jeremiah J. Castle, "*Moving* Pictures? Experimental Evidence of Cinematic Influence on Political Attitudes," *Social Science Quarterly* 95, no. 5 (2014), https://onlinelibrary.wiley.com/doi/abs/10.1111/ssqu.12070. The authors studied the possibilities for viewpoint transformation through films, concluding that "popular movies possess the ability to change political attitudes, especially on issues that are unframed by the media."

11. Entertainment experiences with their own point of view can only *invite* people to change their viewpoints, akin to the invitational transformations discussed in chapter 4.

12. Susan Magsamen and Ivy Ross, *Your Brain on Art: How the Arts Transform Us* (New York: Random House, 2023), ix. While much of the examples and research given are of experiences that fall short of being transformative—changes in state, not in identity—they are all informative. The book also has an entire chapter on human flourishing.

13. Magsamen and Ross, *Your Brain on Art*, 114.

14. Magsamen and Ross, *Your Brain on Art*, 114.

15. Magsamen and Ross, *Your Brain on Art*, 157.

16. Brad McLain discusses customizing to individual aspects of aspirant identity in *Designing Transformative Experiences: A Toolkit for Leaders, Trainers, Teachers, and Other Experience Designers* (Oakland, CA: Berrett-Koehler, 2023).

17. For more on this, see Pine and Gilmore, *The Experience Economy*, 93–126, and B. Joseph Pine II, *Mass Customization: The New Frontier in Business Competition* (Boston: Harvard Business School Press, 1993), 196–212.

18. For more on all seven types of modularity and their applicability, see Joe Pine, "The Power of Modularity," Strategic Horizons, October 5, 2018, https://strategichorizons.com/the-power-of-modularity/. This post extends the six types of modularity given in Pine, *Mass Customization*, 196–211, which in turn extend the original five types of modularity from Karl Thatcher Ulrich and Karen Tung, "Fundamentals of Product Modularity," working paper 3335-91-MSA, MIT Sloan School of Management, Cambridge, 1991.

19. Jim Gilmore and I call this "customering," a term he coined. See B. Joseph Pine II, "Customering: The Mindset of a Revolutionary Model," *Strategy & Leadership* 47, no. 6 (2019): 2–8, https://doi.org/10.1108/SL-08-2019-0124.

20. Joe Pine, "Introducing Experience Platforms," Strategic Horizons, February 3, 2022, https://strategichorizons.com/introducing-experience-platforms/.

21. Blake Taylor, "Creator of Disney's MagicBand Evolves Vision for Princess Cruises," *Attractions Magazine*, February 27, 2024, https://attractionsmagazine.com/disney-magicband-evolves-princess-cruises/.

22. For more on understanding how powerful it is to learn about individual customers' desires, needs, and aspirations over time, see B. Joseph Pine II, Don Peppers, and Martha Rogers, "Do You Want to Keep Your Customers Forever?" *Harvard Business Review*, March–April 1995, https://hbr.org/1995/03/do-you-want-to-keep-your-customers-forever.

23. See Pine and Gilmore, *The Experience Economy*, 175–185. For street theatre we leaned heavily on Sally Harrison-Pepper's wonderful ethnography and analysis *Drawing a Circle in the Square: Street Performing in New York's Washington Square Park* (Jackson, MS: University Press of Mississippi, 1990). On page 117 she offers a figure of the typical "street performance text," which beautifully shows the modularity described here. We reprinted it in *The Experience Economy* on page 177, a figure that also (excepting the time frame in minutes) well represents modular transformation journeys.

24. See Pine and Gilmore, *The Experience Economy*, 8, table 1-1.

25. See Jon Adams Jerde's introduction to *The Jerde Partnership International: Visceral Reality* (Milan: l'Arca Edizioni spa, 1998).

26. See Pine and Gilmore, *The Experience Economy*, xviii–xx and 141–143, where we offer various dramatic structure frameworks with seven, five, three, and even one stage.

27. Joseph Campbell, *The Hero with a Thousand Faces*, 2nd ed. (Novato, CA: New World Library, 2008). Campbell borrows the term "monomyth" from James Joyce to describe what everyone now calls the hero's journey, but this reader came away from the book thinking the collected stories exhibited anything but a single story type. The journey becomes a template only by piecing together many different parts of the examined stories.

28. What helped make Campbell's hero's journey so well-known was director George Lucas talking about how he used it in writing the *Star Wars* movies. While there's no indication J. R. R. Tolkien used Campbell's work, it's surprising that Campbell didn't cite Tolkien's. The hero's journey is right there in the subtitle to *The Hobbit*, his first foray into Middle-earth: *or There and Back Again*.

29. A way of thinking about and executing on this can be found in our Here-and-Now Space model given in Gilmore and Pine, *Authenticity*, 179–218.

30. Gamification is almost always used for transformative experiences where another party, usually an employer, gains a benefit from—and is willing to pay for—people striving for the rewards. Without the transformation focus, the experiences would be actual games.

31. I discuss alternate reality as one way to fuse the real and the virtual in B. Joseph Pine II and Kim C. Korn, *Infinite Possibility: Creating Customer Value on the Digital Frontier* (San Francisco: Berrett-Koehler, 2011), 49–61.

32. Eddie Yoon, *Superconsumers: A Simple, Speedy, and Sustainable Path to Superior Growth* (Boston: Harvard Business Review Press, 2017), 9–10, emphasis added.

33. See also Yoon, *Superconsumers*, 78–83.

Chapter 6

1. In the 1997 movie *The Game*, Conrad Van Orton, played by Sean Penn, gives his brother, Nicholas, played by Michael Douglas, a life-altering transformation as a birthday present. I highly recommend the film, not just for the entertainment value but because it demonstrates many principles of transformation guiding.

2. In 2024 immersive art experience stager Meow Wolf added an education unit with a curriculum of "learning guides for field trips, schools, and curious minds." See Erin Barnes, "Learning in Technicolor: New Meow Wolf Education," Meow Wolf, October 1, 2024, https://meowwolf.com/blob/education-lesson-plans-field-trips.

3. This is what Jim Gilmore and I have long called "paying labor," a work experience so distinctive and interesting that people gladly pay for it! See James H. Gilmore and B. Joseph Pine II, "Experience-ing Your Event," *Corporate Magazine*, March 2005, 19–22.

4. This is based on the research done for Lance A. Bettencourt et al., "The 'New You' Business," *Harvard Business Review*, January–February 2022, https://hbr.org/2022/01/the-new-you-business, which highlights this exemplar.

5. All quotes are from Lemonade Stand Bootcamp, "Our Programs," https://lemonadestandbootcamp.com/our-programs/, accessed July 28, 2025.

6. *The Oxford English Dictionary*, "dilettante," 2nd ed., vol. 7 (Oxford: Clarendon Press, 1989), 665, emphasis added.

7. *Merriam-Webster Dictionary*, "alchemist," https://www.merriam-webster.com/dictionary/alchemist, accessed July 28, 2025. Before discovering "alchemist," I could not find any synonym of "guide" that fit metamorphic transformations. I thought about using the neologism "metamagos," the Greek *magos* meaning "wise man" or "priest" (you'll likely recognize the plural *magi*). But no. Particularly in looking at the hero's journey, which was derived from stories that always entailed a metamorphosis, the only term that seemed even close was "wizard," which is not without issues itself. However, when I realized that metamorphic transformations require a combination of the other three roles of expert, coach, and counselor (and then some), alchemist seemed appropriate.

8. Chip Conley, *Learning to Love Midlife: 12 Reasons Why Life Gets Better with Age* (New York: Little, Brown Spark, 2024), 15.

9. Conley, *Learning to Love Midlife*, 7. Chip—a longtime friend and winner of Strategic Horizons' 2001 Experience Stager of the Year award for his THEMEing of Joie de Vivre Hospitality hotels—quotes David Bowie as saying, "Aging is an extraordinary process whereby you become the person you always should have been." On page 65 he begins a story of one of his midlifers with the heading "Becoming Who You're Meant to Be," my definition of flourishing.

10. Modern Elder Academy, https://www.meawisdom.com/, accessed July 28, 2025.

11. Modern Elder Academy, accessed July 28, 2025.

12. Conley, *Learning to Love Midlife*, 15.

13. Andy Kessler, "A New Approach to Addiction," *Wall Street Journal*, March 23, 2025, https://www.wsj.com/opinion/a-new-approach-to-addiction-phoenix-fitness-community-mental-health-a3591f99.

14. Stephen W. Porges and Seth Porges, *Our Polyvagal World: How Safety and Trauma Change Us* (New York: W. W. Norton & Company, 2023), xv.

15. L. A. Paul, *Transformative Experience* (Oxford: Oxford University Press, 2014), 17–18.

Chapter 7

1. Jim Gilmore and I introduced these three phases and the figure, with one modification here, in *The Experience Economy: Work Is Theatre & Every Business a Stage* (Boston: Harvard Business School Press, 1999), 176–180, and included them in the subsequent editions.

2. Doug G. Ware, "Army Prep Course Has Seen 95% Grad Rate, $15M in Bonuses in 1st Year," *Stars and Stripes*, August 7, 2023, https://www.stripes.com/branches/army/2023-08-07/army-recruiting-prep-course-enlistment-10975470.html; Todd South, "The Army Has Graduated 25,000 Soldiers

through Pre-basic Prep Course," *Army Times*, September 10, 2024, https://www.armytimes.com/news/your-army/2024/09/10/the-army-has-graduated-25000-soldiers-through-pre-basic-prep-course/.

3. Clayton M. Christensen et al., "Know Your Customers' 'Jobs to Be Done,'" *Harvard Business Review*, September 2016, https://hbr.org/2016/09/know-your-customers-jobs-to-be-done.

4. This discussion on jobs to be done is based in part on Lance A. Bettencourt et al., "The 'New You' Business," *Harvard Business Review*, January–February 2022, https://hbr.org/2022/01/the-new-you-business. Dave Norton, the founder of insights consultancy Stone Mantel and a longtime expert on jobs to be done, and I discovered aspirational jobs when thinking of these jobs in context with the Progression of Economic Value.

5. For more on aspirational jobs and the other three jobs to be done, see Dave Norton, "What Exactly Do Customers Mean by a Functional, Emotional, Social, or Aspirational JTBD?" Experience Strategist, August 20, 2024, https://theexperiencestrategist.substack.com/p/what-exactly-do-customers-mean-by. He further notes that when companies choose to get aspirational jobs done for their customers, their resources, capabilities, and solutions must support the following requirements: a transformational goal/objective (from/to), a diagnostic that explains the current state, guidance toward the goal, new knowledge along the way, and a sense of flow throughout the process.

6. For more on design tools and designed interactions that turn them into experiences, see Pine and Gilmore, *The Experience Economy*, 99–101, and B. Joseph Pine II, "Customering: The Next Stage in the Shift to Mass Customization," in *Mass Customization and Design Democratization*, eds. Branko Kolarevic and José Pinto Duarte (London: Routledge, 2019), 13–28. Frank Piller, professor of technology management at RWTH Aachen University, has also written extensively on design tools, calling them tool kits. See, for example, Frank T. Piller and Fabrizio Salvador, "Design Toolkits, Organizational Capabilities, and Firm Performance," in *Revolutionizing Innovation: Users, Communities, and Open Innovation*, eds. Dietmar Harhoff and Karim R. Lakhani (Cambridge, MA: MIT Press, 2016), 483–510, https://www.researchgate.net/publication/371078899_Design_Toolkits_Organizational_Capabilities_and_Firm_Performance.

7. Explorer X, "Your Journey Begins Now," https://sgv2timqetb.typeform.com/to/D0RP942j, accessed July 28, 2025.

8. See, for example, Hal Hershfield, "You Make Better Decisions If You 'See' Your Senior Self," *Harvard Business Review*, June 2013, https://hbr.org/2013/06/you-make-better-decisions-if-you-see-your-senior-self.

9. The idea of partnering with customers was impressed on me by Lance Bettencourt. See the section "Designing the Offering" in Bettencourt et al., "The 'New You' Business."

10. Catharsis can be one such milestone. Brad McLain discusses this, issuing the "catharsis challenge" for designers: "an experience element that powerfully challenges an experiencer's initial identity narrative, initiating a

change process that includes letting go of their prior sense-of-self in some way, and inviting new self-perceptions" (emphasis removed). See Brad McLain, *Designing Transformative Experiences: A Toolkit for Leaders, Trainers, Teachers, and Other Experience Designers* (Oakland, CA: Berrett-Koehler, 2023), 209.

11. This means employing improv, one of the three forms of theatre beyond street. It is the model not just for innovation on the fly but for innovation, craft customization, job shops, and other such business models that constantly come up with new offerings via dynamically changing processes. See endnote 7-24 in Pine and Gilmore, *The Experience Economy*, 284–285, for the core framework behind this, which is also a regeneration matrix that shows how individuals transform.

12. Karrin Simpson, "The Magic of Transformational Objects: How They Shape Our Lives," on Karrin Simpson's website, November 28, 2023, https://karrinsimpsonartist.co.uk/2023/11/28/the-magic-of-transformational-objects-how-they-shape-our-lives/.

13. Regarding organizational transformation, research by Andrew White, Adam Canwell, and Michael Smets shows that "96% of all transformations face significant challenges that can derail the whole program, with executives forced to step in." They recommend interventions at such "turning points," focused in particular on the organization's "emotional energy." See Andrew White, Adam Canwell, and Michael Smets, "Is Your Organizational Transformation Veering Off Course?" hbr.org, August 28, 2024, https://hbr.org/2024/08/is-your-organizational-transformation-veering-off-course.

14. On organizational transformation, see a precursor article to the one cited in the previous note: Andrew White, Michael Smets, and Adam Canwell, "Organizational Transformation Is an Emotional Journey," hbr.org, July 18, 2022, https://hbr.org/2022/07/organizational-transformation-is-an-emotional-journey.

15. Even though with follow-through aspirants have achieved their aspirations, it still makes sense to continue calling them aspirants, but I have also used "achievers" in this book.

16. Richard Mark Kirkner, "Almost a Third of Patients Don't Take Drugs as Directed," Medscape, August 8, 2022, https://www.medscape.com/viewarticle/978837.

17. "How Calibrate Works: Getting Started," Calibrate, https://www.joincalibrate.com/how-it-works, accessed July 28, 2025. Much of the information in this paragraph was found and then verified with Frances Turner.

18. Tara-Nicholle Nelson, *The Transformational Consumer: Fuel a Lifelong Love Affair with Your Customers by Helping Them Get Healthier, Wealthier, and Wiser* (San Francisco: Berrett-Koehler, 2017), 18.

19. Cited in Bill Sommers, "The Earned Life Learning Omnivores," https://learningomnivores.com/what-were-reading/the-earned-life/, accessed July 28, 2025.

20. See Dave Norton, "Your Solution Should Fit within a Customer's Life System," Stone Mantel, https://www.stonemantel.co/blog/your-solution-should-fit-within-a-customers-life-system, accessed July 28, 2025.

21. Suzy Ross, *The Map to Wholeness: Real-Life Stories of Crisis, Change, and Reinvention* (Berkeley, CA: North Atlantic Books, 2020), 31 and 32, respectively. Ross divides transformations into two cycles, integrative and transformative, that form a figure eight. It's not unlike the Transformation Journey model, but with the transformative cycle having four steps and the integrative nine, reflecting the importance she places on the latter.

22. Much more could be said on intrinsic versus extrinsic motivation, and for a seminal article on this point see E. L. Deci, R. Koestner, and R. M. Ryan, "A Meta-analytic Review of Experiments Examining the Effects of Extrinsic Rewards on Intrinsic Motivation," *Psychological Bulletin* 125, no. 6 (1999); 627–668, https://doi.org/10.1037/0033-2909.125.6.627.

23. See Paul Dunn and Ronald J. Baker, *Time's Up! The Subscription Business Model for Professional Firms* (Hoboken, NJ: Wiley, 2022), 228–232. The book has many examples of charging for outcomes, as well as many great ideas for professional firms that want to shift from services to transformations.

24. *Workforce Realigned, Vol. 1: How New Partnerships Are Advancing Economic Mobility,* Social Finance, Federal Reserve Bank of Atlanta, and Federal Reserve Bank of Philadelphia, 2021, 46–63, https://socialfinance.org/work/workforce-realigned/.

25. *Workforce Realigned,* Social Finance, 64–84.

26. *Workforce Realigned,* Social Finance, 252–271.

27. See, for example, "Top Income Sharing Agreement Programs Startups," Tracxn, updated April 5, 2025, https://tracxn.com/d/trending-business-models/startups-in-income-sharing-agreement-programs/__fVNiRR-1BvGUOzOESQQU5-wztU7Oh8fDZ5psdjRW3HY/companies.

28. This thought first occurred to me after IBM paid my wife and me six months' salary to leave the firm in 1993. I thought of how stupid that was, as instead the company could have made an investment in me and thousands of others in starting our own firms based on everything we learned through its prior investment in our education, training, and work experience over the years.

29. Melissa Korn, "States Challenge Public Universities to Prove They Are Worth Their Funding," *Wall Street Journal,* March 11, 2017, https://www.wsj.com/articles/states-challenge-public-universities-to-prove-they-are-worth-their-funding-1489233600.

30. "Empowering Economic Mobility: How Social Finance US and American Diesel Training Centers' (ADTC) Workforce Investment Is Transforming Lives," World Economic Forum, December 2024, https://initiatives.weforum.org/reskilling-revolution/adtc.

31. "Get to Know ADTC," ADTC, https://www.adtc.co/about, accessed July 28, 2025.

32. *Workforce Realigned,* Social Finance, 89–90.

33. Paul Thomas, *Startup DPC: How to Start and Grow Your Direct Primary Care Practice* (Detroit: Plum Health DPC, 2020).

34. Dunn and Baker, *Time's Up!*, 270.

35. "Storytelling Evaluation Method," Old Fire Station, https://oldfirestation.org.uk/our-work/storytelling-evaluation-methodology/, accessed July 28, 2025.

Reflection

1. This formulation is inspired by actor and teacher Michael Kearns's wonderful tome *Acting = Life: An Actor's Life Lessons* (Portsmouth, NH: Heinemann, 1996), 45. See also B. Joseph Pine II and James H. Gilmore, *The Experience Economy: Work Is Theatre & Every Business a Stage* (Boston: Harvard Business School Press, 1999), 155–158.

INDEX

ACKNOWLEDGMENTS

As you can imagine, this book is the product of many experiences—encounters, conversations, and crucibles. While I can't name or even remember all of those involved, many deserve special mention and my gratitude.

First, thank you to the unknown IBM consultant who (in early 1994, I think it was) asked what customization turned a service into. Due to Providence, no doubt, I responded, "Customization turns services into experiences." And thus was born the idea that experiences were a distinct economic offering, which in turn led me to ask myself what customization turned experiences into. The answer: transformations.

Second, thank you to my partners at Strategic Horizons LLP, Jim Gilmore and Doug Parker. I told Jim about the Progression of Economic Value when he was my biggest client at CSC Consulting, and he soon joined me to form our company, flesh out the ideas, and write *The Experience Economy.* Its last two chapters are on transformations, concepts that Jim and I jointly developed and wrote about, and many ideas from that book are present in this one. I greatly appreciate your contributions over the years, Jim. Doug originally worked for Jim in marketing at CSC, and he helped us create a firm around the idea of "two gurus and a marketer." In addition to doing everything to run the business so I could write and work with companies around the world, Doug was especially helpful with this book, acting as my agent, providing an oft-used sounding board, facilitating our desire to use Substack to write the book, and often serving as my first reader. As I write this, we are creating a suite of offerings that help individuals and enterprises embrace and apply the ideas, principles, and frameworks of *The Transformation Economy*. Thank you, Doug! Your contributions have been immense.

For ten years now, Kevin Dulle, owner and chief experience guide (what a great title!) at Wonder Mint, has illustrated my ideas in his inimitable style, which has made my speeches and workshops not only unique but so much more effective. He also created all the original figures you see in this book. I don't tell Kevin what to draw; I explain what I am trying to get across and how I think it might look, and then through our discussions he improves the ideas and sparks new ones—and for that I am very grateful. Thank you, Kevin, for becoming my consigliere.

Dave Norton and I have been working together for more than twenty-five years, even before he founded insights consultancy Stone Mantel, in which he invited me to partner. Thank you for all your contributions to my work, Dave, especially your expertise in jobs to be done—and I would not have the time progression without you impressing "time well spent" on me many years ago. The Stone Mantel Collaboratives have also proven to be a font of ideas, particularly with their focus on transformations over the past five years. That was one of the things that made me confident I could finally write this book and the world was ready for it.

Thank you, too, to James Wallman for founding the World Experience Organization. I so wanted something like it to be created, and you were just the guy to do it. Thank you for all the opportunities you gave me to share my ideas on transformations. Another milestone in convincing me the business world was prepared to understand the Transformation Economy was discovering—across numerous campfires, several summits, and many, many conversations with WXO members—almost every experience designer that belonged to it was already thinking about or creating transformative experiences.

Kim Korn of Create Advantage has been a longtime friend and colleague, coauthor of *Infinite Possibility: Creating Customer Value on the Digital Frontier*, and a terrific sounding board for, contributor to, and promotor of the concepts in this book. He helped with many big ideas in the Transformation Economy particularly around meaningful purpose, which is an integral part of his thinking on regenerative managing. (Please tell me, Kim, that by the time you read these words that book is finally in progress!) Two of the frameworks for which Kim provided help and original thinking did not make it into this book: the seven aspects of identity and the regeneration matrix. (You'll find a bit about them on my Substack.) Nonetheless, I greatly appreciate your thinking, Kim; those frameworks will be used with clients and hopefully written up someday. Thank you, too, for proselytizing the ideas in this book and some of the previous ones through your chairmanship of Symplany. Thanks to you, no company has embraced the ideas in here more—even before publication!

I also owe a debt of thanks to Gary Adamson, the founder of Starizon Studio, the company that embraced the ideas in *The Experience Economy* more than any other (and made me a partner). Gary and our fellow Starizon guides took to heart THEMEing, customization, theatre, and so many other experience-staging principles to create transformative B2B experiences. We even charged for outcomes via a transformation guarantee! Thank you for taking me along with you on that amazing fifteen-year journey in guiding companies to become premier experience stagers and being an exemplar in this book.

I owe much gratitude to Eddie Yoon, founder of think tank EddieWouldGrow as well as partner in the boutique strategy and private equity services firm Greyspace. It is because of Eddie that I wrote this book on Substack. He and his fellow category pirates Christopher Lochhead and Katrina Kirsch showed the way through their ideas, example, and encouragement.

My Substack subscribers caused me to stay in writing mode—and made the book better through their feedback and interactions. I really appreciate every one of them, but especially those who offered me responses through posts and video calls. The biggest impact came in the development of the Delta Model. I had posted about two different models for understanding transformations, but neither of them lit a fire under my readers. So I sought another avenue, and after discussions with Kevin Dulle, out came the Delta Model. (I chalk that one up to Providence as well, since it popped into my head during a sermon at church.)

I can't name every Substack subscriber who provided feedback, and while I'm sure I'm forgetting someone significant, these folks made the biggest difference: Dart Lindsley, David Rowe, Doug Wilson, Dwight Gibson, Gary Ellis, John Gusiff, Kenny Lauer, Linda Watkins, Mark Hatch, Matthew Waller, Meghan Gardner, Morgan Goodlander, Ric Mora, Ron Baker, Sahara Rose De Vore, Sande Golgart, Sarah Huibregtse, Stan Hustad, Suzy Ross, and Wouter Blokdijk. I appreciate you all! Thank you.

I'll single out Stan Hustad from that list as someone who has had a profound impact on my life, beginning in high school. (If you meet either one of us, ask for that story and how we reconnected.) A performance coach and podcaster, Stan has collected a number of stories of people and businesses that have transformed, some of which made it into this book (such as Frances Turner's story in chapter 7). And I can still remember one particular Zoom session with Substack subscribers where Stan exclaimed, "If a business doesn't help people flourish, it's a racket." That statement was so good I had to put it in here!

There were a great number of people who contributed to my thinking through their writing and/or conversations. I'm sure I'm leaving some out, but my gratitude goes to (with a few repeat Substackers): Agnes Callard, Alain Thys, Albert Boswijk, Ben Hunnicutt, Bob Rogers, Bob Rossman, Brad McLain, Chip Conley, Christopher Vogler, Dacher Keltner, David Kolb, David Phelps,

Deirdre McCloskey, Dianela Perdomo, Frank Piller, George Gilder, Grant McCracken, Jake Haupert, Jake Segal, Jeffrey Kottler, Kyle Coolbroth, L. A. Paul, Lance Bettencourt, Mat Duerden, Morgan Goodlander, Nathan Schock, Paul Dunn, Ron Baker, Sally Harrison-Pepper, Sande Golgart, the late Stan Davis, Suzy Ross, and Wendy Heimann-Nunes.

Thanks to Steve Prokesch, my longtime editor (since 1993 and counting!) at *Harvard Business Review,* who's always made my ideas better and whose championing and editing of "The 'New You' Business," my 2022 article with Lance Bettencourt, Jim Gilmore, and Dave Norton, was one final milestone in convincing me the world was ready for transformations as a distinct economic offering. Please don't ever retire, Steve!

And a strong, heartfelt thank-you to Courtney Cashman, my editor at Harvard Business Review Press. We've discussed book possibilities for at least five years, and I appreciate your thinking in coming up with the proposal for this one, advocating for it within the company, and then marshaling it through multiple drafts, reviews, and finally to completion. We had a lot of discussions and many disagreements over ideas, frameworks, and wording, but I can't say as I ever "lost" an argument. If I did what you recommended, it's because you convinced me it was, in the end, the right thing to do. The book is much better because of our collaboration; thank you.

Finally, thanks be to God, who has providentially given me many ideas, big and small, and led me to write books and help companies around the world create greater economic value. My personal, God-given purpose is to understand what's going on in the world of business and to develop frameworks that first *de*scribe what's happening and then *pre*scribe what companies can do about it. My fervent hope is that this book will continue in that tradition and make a difference across the globe.

ABOUT THE AUTHOR

B. JOSEPH PINE II is an internationally acclaimed author, speaker, and management adviser to *Fortune* 500 companies and entrepreneurial startups alike. He is cofounder of Strategic Horizons LLP, a thinking studio dedicated to helping businesses conceive and design new ways of adding value to their economic offerings.

In 2020 Pine and his partner James H. Gilmore rereleased in hardcover *The Experience Economy: Competing for Customer Time, Attention, and Money*, featuring an all-new introduction/preview of their bestselling 1999 book, *The Experience Economy: Work Is Theatre & Every Business a Stage*. Across three editions, *The Experience Economy* has been published in fifteen languages and was twice named one of the 100 best business books of all time.

Pine has also cowritten *Infinite Possibility: Creating Customer Value on the Digital Frontier* and *Authenticity: What Consumers* Really *Want*. His first book was the award-winning *Mass Customization: The New Frontier in Business Competition*.

In his speaking and teaching activities, Pine has addressed the World Economic Forum in Davos, Switzerland; TED in Monterey, California; CES in Las Vegas; and South by Southwest in Austin, Texas. Currently he is a lecturer at Northeastern University's D'Amore-McKim School of Business.

To help readers embrace the ideas, principles, and frameworks of *The Transformation Economy* and apply them to their companies, Pine has created a suite of offerings available at www.StrategicHorizons.com.